THE MARINE CORPS WAY

★ ★ ★ ★ ★ ★ ★ ★ ★

USING MANEUVER WARFARE TO LEAD A WINNING ORGANIZATION

★ ★ ★ ★ ★ ★ ★ ★ ★

JASON A. SANTAMARIA

VINCENT MARTINO

ERIC K. CLEMONS, Ph.D.

McGraw·Hill

New York Chicago San Francisco Lisbon London Madrid Mexico City
Milan New Delhi San Juan Seoul Singapore Sydney Toronto

1 2 3 4 5 6 7 8 9 0   AGM/AGM   2 1 0 9 8 7 6 5 4 3

ISBN 0-07-142377-X

McGraw-Hill books are available at special quantity discounts to use as premiums and sales promotions, or for use in corporate training programs. For more information, please write to the Director of Special Sales, Professional Publishing, McGraw-Hill, Two Penn Plaza, New York, NY 10121-2298. Or contact your local bookstore.

This book is printed on acid-free paper.

To the United States Marine Corps,
its sister services, and corporate America,
which, together, safeguard our society
and provide for our prosperity

CONTENTS

ACKNOWLEDGMENTS

First and foremost, we would like to thank the following people, without whom this book would not have been possible:

Our families and loved ones. Jason would like to thank his mother, Nancy Santamaria, our most impatient "in-house" editor; his father, Joe Santamaria, whose grasp of military history and command of the English language made him one of our most valuable "in-house" editors—when he wanted to be; and Kim Seidel, who endured daily progress updates for almost a year and provided us with unique insights based on her experiences as a Wall Street equity research analyst. Vincent would like to thank his wife, Stacy, who, pregnant with their first child for the majority of the book-writing process, endured his routine absence due to many late nights and long weekends, read every word of this book (over and over again), and helped him through countless bouts of writer's block. Eric would like to acknowledge the support and love of his wife, Jean, and daughter, Julia, throughout a demanding academic career and, more recently, during the doubly demanding process of pursuing that career *and* writing a book "the Marine Corps way."

Fellow Marines, both former and current. Frederick Smith, who, embodying the Marines' motto, *Semper Fidelis*, took time out of an extremely busy schedule to talk to a couple of young "pups." Guy Wyser-Pratte, who similarly showed the true meaning of *Semper Fidelis* and who made sure that the junior Marines ate first when he treated Jason and Vincent to his version of the Wall Street power lunch—New York's best hot dogs. Michael Buckingham, who provided us with insights for Chapters 10 and 12 that only a former recon officer could. Howard Zonder, a former communications officer, who offered us several examples from his experiences in the business world, provided ongoing feedback, and was an indispensable source for chapter-leading quotes. Sean Brosnihan, a former company commander, who offered his combined business-Marine perspective.

Lieutenant Colonel Charles Tulaney, formerly Vincent's commanding officer and mentor, who introduced us to Guy Wyser-Pratte and provided us invaluable "field-grade" perspective on our ideas. Lieutenant Colonel Mitch McCarthy, formerly Jason's commanding officer and mentor, who was a member of 5/11 in Operation Desert Storm and provided a firsthand account of the raids we describe in Chapter 10. Captain Chris Rogers, former artillery officer and instructor at The Basic School, who provided us with unique, cutting-edge insights into how the Marine Corps has been training its new officers since Jason and Vincent were students there back in 1995.

Our business associates and professional colleagues. Jon Katzenbach, who gave Jason his "first big break" in writing in 1999 and who provided us with the sage advice that only a five-time author could in the early stages of our effort. Mike Useem, who teamed with Jason and Vincent to introduce to the Wharton School intense, hands-on Marine Corps leadership training in 2001 and who also provided invaluable advice in the early stages of our efforts. Donna Conover, who took time out from her never-ending duty of safeguarding Southwest Airlines' tradition of "outrageous customer service" to help us with Chapter 13. John Gatlin, who managed to give us thorough, insightful feedback and find all of our split infinitives, even while making a cross-country move and starting a new job. Robert Howard, a Desert Storm veteran who offered an "Army perspective." Matt Lazaro, who helped tremendously with Chapter 6. Sean Cohan, an "in-house" editor whose creativity and insights as a nonmilitary business reader helped us refine our first four chapters. Kevin Barry, who has argued passionately about strategy with Eric over the past decade. And Tom Grace, who was indispensable in our research efforts.

Jason and Vincent would like to thank Eric, their professor and adviser at the Wharton School, for letting them into his classroom as alumni guest speakers in the fall of 2002.

ACKNOWLEDGMENTS

Warfighting. Throughout this book, we repeatedly reference the Marine Corps's doctrinal publication, *Warfighting.* Like all lieutenants at The Basic School, Jason and Vincent read this masterfully written pocket-sized manual from front to back many times over, which no doubt planted the seeds that cultivated this book.

Our editor. Last, but certainly not least, we would like to thank Barry Neville, a consummate professional, tough negotiator, keen editor, and savvy marketer—all rolled into one.

INTRODUCTION

FROM THE BATTLEFIELD TO THE BUSINESS WORLD

"I never could have done what I did at FedEx had I not served in the Marines."

—FREDRICK W. SMITH, CEO, FEDEX[1]

This book aims to show you how you can use *maneuver warfare*, the modern-day combat philosophy of the United States Marine Corps, to lead a winning organization in the business world.

In the simplest of terms, maneuver warfare is the use of speed, surprise, and concentrated force against an opponent's weakness to achieve a *maximum impact with a minimum expenditure of resources* in the presence of strategic uncertainty and hostile intent. In warfare this outcome implies shattering the enemy's will to resist with minimum friendly losses of combat equipment and human life. In business this outcome implies maximizing profits by employing information, capital, physical equipment, and personnel in the most efficient manner.

HOW MANEUVER WARFARE IS RELEVANT TO BUSINESS

We are not advocating a facile and superficial comparison between business and warfare, nor are we advocating the "brutalization" of business. Furthermore, it is not our intent in this book to glorify warfare and the associated loss of life. But we firmly believe that the concept of maneuver warfare is directly relevant to leadership in business, precisely because it has been developed to address conditions that in many ways mirror those faced by modern executives.

First and foremost, leaders in war face the harshest of trade-offs—knowingly placing their men and women in harm's way to seize an objective. While lives are not at stake in the marketplace, we believe that decisions made in war give insight into the deployment and conservation of resources in business because those resources being expended—human lives—are so precious. Second, in much the same manner that commanders position men and matériel on the battlefield, business leaders deploy information, capital, personnel, and physical assets to capitalize on market opportunities. Third, as in armed conflict, altering the conditions that govern competitive encounters in the business environment enables companies to approach market opportunities along a path of least resistance from a position of relative strength. Finally, business, while not as extreme as warfare, is a dynamic interplay between opposing wills, where human and environmental attributes mediate resource-based conflict. Companies compete aggressively—even viciously—for strategic advantage in a chaotic arena that is increasingly similar to the modern theater of war.

Accordingly, we believe maneuver warfare to be a useful guide for business thinking, particularly in the fast-paced, complex, fluid, and uncertain business environment of the twenty-first century. Companies that can effectively shape the conditions that govern competitive encounters will flourish; those that cannot will fail. Perhaps more significant, companies that "win" using outdated strategies—for example, through lengthy wars of attrition, such as protracted price wars—may find themselves so exhausted that their executives, their shareholders, and their market valuations may not recover for an extended period of time.

WHY THE MARINES?

This book features the U.S. Marines because they are arguably the world's most advanced practitioners of maneuver warfare and because they place an unparalleled emphasis on *leadership*, which we believe to be the backbone of maneuver warfare. The practices they employ to ensure battlefield success should, therefore, be the most logical point of departure for the employment of maneuver warfare in an environment other than warfare, such as business.

Facing budget cuts and an increasingly difficult madate to meet mission requirements in the late 1980s, the perennially underfunded Marines adopted maneuver warfare as doctrine in an effort to "do more with less." Owing to the leadership of General Alfred M. Gray, 29th commandant of the Marine Corps, and to the publication of the field manual *Warfighting* in 1989, the maneuver warfare philosophy spread rapidly throughout the organization. After fourteen years of innovation and refinement, the Marines have honed their practice of maneuver warfare to a sharp edge, and today it pervades every aspect of their strategic and tactical thought.

While maneuver warfare is a relatively new initiative, superior leadership has been a hallmark of the Marine Corps since its inception in 1775. As we characterize it, Marine Corps leadership comprises three pillars— *leadership by example, taking care of those in your charge,* and *leadership development.* These pillars, in turn, inspire and reinforce *trust, integrity, initiative,* and *unselfishness,* without which maneuver warfare would fail.

WHAT YOU ARE ABOUT TO READ

In this book we will use historical examples to present the intuitive, integrated approaches of master practitioners of maneuver warfare as a systematic set of problem-solving techniques that an aspiring practitioner can clearly understand. We will also draw on the modern-day practices of the Marine Corps to offer an accompanying set of enabling leadership prescriptions that an aspiring practitioner can easily apply.

We will begin by defining maneuver warfare, providing the context into which it fits and distilling it into seven *guiding principles.* We will follow with in-depth treatments of each of the principles that include numerous supporting examples and prescriptions from the Marines. We will also use selected "counterexamples" to illustrate the disastrous effects of the failure to employ certain principles. And we will include a handful of examples that illustrate the application of the principles in subsets or as an integrated whole. Collectively, the military history lessons and business case studies we offer are designed to mirror and complement one another, with numerous anecdotes added that will hopefully make this book not only engaging but also an enjoyable read.

The warfare examples we have selected come from all militaries and all countries, irrespective of political motivation. As students of military history, we recognize that strategic and tactical genius is not confined to the winning side or to the politically virtuous. We also realize our own limitations; as much as we would have liked to include accounts from Operation Iraqi Freedom, a pending print deadline and our deference to more qualified military historians kept us from attempting to interpret these most recent events ourselves.

The business examples we have selected come from a changing continuum where companies that succeed in one encounter find themselves thwarted in another. As students of business we recognize that few companies stay on top forever and that truly great organizations show resilience and adapt to constantly changing markets.

Finally, given the indispensable role that leadership plays in maneuver warfare, this book is not solely about strategy and tactics; it is about bridging the gap between grand strategy and operational implementation in your organization. We will, therefore, conclude with perhaps our most important message—a thorough discussion of Marine Corps leadership as it pertains to the business environment.

Many of you may have worked for a company where trust is the exception rather than the rule, where ethics are a secondary consideration, where control is suffocating, where individuals "look out for number one," and where overall performance is correspondingly uninspired. Alternatively, some of you may be fortunate enough to have been part of an organization where positive intent is assumed at all levels, integrity is both beyond reproach and infectious, self-starters are afforded the latitude they need to pursue emerging opportunities, co-workers look out for one another, and overall performance is correspondingly inspired. Applied in the business environment, the Marine Corps's three-pillared leadership philosophy promises to be a solution to the former and a catalyst for the latter.

OUR MISSION

The Marines' experience and the examples we are about to offer suggest that maneuver warfare has the potential to transcend environments—just as it has transcended time—to deliver breakout results in the business world. In the ensuing chapters, our mission is to convince you that this is, indeed, the case.

CHAPTER 1

MANEUVER WARFARE

"Battles are won by slaughter and maneuver; the greater the general, the more he contributes in maneuver."

—WINSTON CHURCHILL[1]

Reality is chaotic; events in business never proceed exactly as planned. Environmental factors such as unforeseeable contingencies, fleeting opportunities, rapid and disruptive change, and market-altering technological innovations all contribute to a natural tendency toward disorder that frustrates business leaders and military leaders alike. Opponents' actions, designed to alter or even destroy order, limit the successful implementation of well-laid plans.

A heightened threat of global terrorism and the recent slew of corporate scandals have only aggravated this tendency toward disorder. The events of September 11, 2001, have altered our personal and professional sense of safety, security, and certainty—perhaps for many years to come. And the blatant lapses in integrity by executives at companies such as Enron, HealthSouth, Tyco, and WorldCom have eroded investors' faith in corporate America and underscored the need for trust and integrity in the character of our business leaders.

Business leaders thus need a novel approach that takes these realities into account and even enables organizations to thrive in their midst. Such an approach exists, but outside the business world—on the battlefield.

Maneuver warfare aims to outflank the enemy through a sequence of rapid, focused, and unpredictable moves that target his weaknesses and render him unable to analyze or respond effectively. Equally compelling should be the emphasis that maneuver warfare places on *trust, integrity, initiative,* and *unselfishness,* four intangibles that we could use a little more of in today's business environment. Finally, the approach that we are advocating is a prescription that recognizes the ethical implications of actions taken. In business, as in war, the line between "fighting smart" and "fighting dirty" should never be crossed.

MANEUVER WARFARE DEFINED

Maneuver warfare represents—in the words of *Warfighting*:

> A state of mind bent on shattering the enemy morally and physically by paralyzing and confounding him, by avoiding his strength, by quickly and aggressively exploiting his vulnerabilities, and by striking him in a way that will hurt him most.[2]

Its ultimate objective is not to destroy the adversary's forces but simply to render them unable to fight as an effective, coordinated whole. For example, instead of attacking well-established enemy defensive positions, maneuver warfare prescribes bypassing those positions, capturing the enemy's command-and-control center in the rear, and cutting off supply lines. Moreover, it embraces the uncontrollable factors that inevitably shape competitive encounters as keys to vanquishing the foe. This approach stands in stark contrast to more simplistic and brutish forms of combat, so-called wars of attrition, where combatants lined up in fixed positions and endeavored to overwhelm one another with superior firepower, as wars were generally fought through the First World War.

THE NATURE OF WARFARE

To understand maneuver warfare, you must first understand warfare—the larger context into which maneuver fits. A resource-based conflict mediated by human and environmental factors, warfare is a continuous process of move and countermove where opposing forces are constantly trying to impose their respective wills on one another.

This ultimate test of will takes place on multiple levels. On the physical level it is a test of firepower, weapons technology, troop strength, and logistics. At the psychological level it involves intangibles such as morale, leadership, and courage. At the analytical level it challenges the ability of commanders to assess complex battlefield situations, make effective decisions, communicate their decisions through highly distributed information systems to widely dispersed forces, and formulate tactically superior plans to implement those decisions. If these dimensions seem familiar to most business leaders, so will the four human and environmental factors that, according to *Warfighting*, shape military conflict: friction, uncertainty, fluidity, and disorder:

1. **Friction** is the phenomenon that "makes the simple difficult and the difficult seemingly impossible."[3] The most obvious source of friction is the enemy, but it can also result from natural forces such as terrain or weather, internal forces such as a lack of planning or coordination, the independent nature of human will, or even mere chance.

2. **Uncertainty** is the atmosphere in which "all actions in war take place—the so-called fog of war."[4] Uncertainty about the opponent's intentions and capabilities and about environmental factors cloud decision makers' judgment and prohibit the optimal deployment of resources.

3. **Fluidity** describes the battlefield situation in which each event "merges with those that precede and follow it—shaped by the former and shaping the conditions of the latter—creating a continuous, fluctuating flow of activity replete with fleeting opportunities and unforeseen events."[5] Combatants must constantly adapt to these changing conditions and actively seek to shape emerging events.

4. Combined, these three factors constitute the final key attribute of military conflict, the state toward which warfare naturally gravitates: **disorder**. "In an environment of friction, uncertainty, and fluidity," according to the Marines' manual, "plans will go awry, instructions and information will be unclear and misinterpreted, communications will fail, and mistakes and unforeseen events will be commonplace."[6] Quite simply, disorder implies a competitive situation that deteriorates as time progresses.

Functioning—or even surviving—in a disordered environment is a major challenge. But the military commander, as well as the business leader, must be sure that his troops do more than survive; they must prevail. Because the four human and environmental factors that shape competitive encounters can rarely be controlled, the successful commander will opt for the only viable alternative: using them to his advantage. This notion serves as the core of maneuver warfare: instead of succumbing to disorder, the military commander turns friction, uncertainty, and fluidity against the enemy to generate disorder in *his* ranks, ideally creating a situation in which the opposition simply cannot cope.

THE EVOLUTION OF MANEUVER WARFARE

With a better understanding of the larger context into which maneuver warfare fits, we now turn to history. You will, no doubt, recognize many of the names that follow; what may be less readily apparent is *why* they have stood the test of time. But understanding why and seeing how maneuver warfare has evolved over time are, in our estimation, crucial to the process of distilling it into a set of problem-solving techniques and leadership lessons that can be applied in business.

Armed conflict between opposing groups is as old as humanity itself, and as long as war has existed, military leaders have endeavored to develop innovative tactics and methods to defeat their adversaries. Maneuver warfare's emergence is a direct result of this process. Only after many centuries did it develop into a fully articulated doctrine, but in the past sixty-five years its evolution has accelerated so dramatically that it now occupies a preeminent place in military thought.

Elements of maneuver warfare first appeared in the tactics employed by the ancient Greeks, who pioneered the use of unbalanced formations to attack opponents' weaknesses, and in the writings of Chinese General Sun Tzu. In the *Art of War*, written around 500 B.C., Sun Tzu prescribed a series of distracting tactics—the cheng—and rapid, calculated moves, the ch'i, that pitted strength against weakness to achieve a decisive outcome. Indeed Sun Tzu epitomized maneuver warfare when he suggested that the best victories were achieved when the enemy realized he was defeated and simply did not offer battle.

Sixteen centuries later, Genghis Khan led his Mongol hordes halfway around the globe and nearly conquered the known world. No army could match the blistering speed of his highly skilled, entirely horse-mounted forces, and no commander could match his use of communications—a sophisticated system of swift messengers and signal flags—to react to and shape events as they unfolded. Genghis Khan repeatedly used these advantages to seize the initiative from opponents and dictate the terms of battle. Equally effective was his masterful use of arrows, javelins, and even Chinese firecrackers and his employment of diversionary tactics to disrupt opponents' cohesion.

The next major wave of innovation in maneuver warfare hit eighteenth- and nineteenth-century Europe. In the eighteenth century, the Prussians pioneered the use of *mission orders*, which maximized flexibility and speed by stating broadly what needed to be accomplished and leaving completion of the task at hand to the ingenuity and resourcefulness of subordinate leaders. At the dawn of the nineteenth century, the legendary French general Napoléon Bonaparte repeatedly achieved decisive victories by splitting his forces in the face of a larger enemy and unexpectedly bringing overwhelming might to bear on his opponent's weakest point at the most opportune moment.

In World War I, the Germans pioneered a new type of attack—infiltration—to break the stalemate created by the conventional tactics of trench warfare: once highly skilled scout units had identified weak points in enemy lines and had penetrated far behind enemy strong points, large reinforcements immediately followed. Complementing this unique decentralized approach was the use of mission orders, a Prussian legacy, to preserve maximum flexibility during the attack. The initial successes of these innovative tactics, coupled with the sting of eventual defeat at the hands of the Allies, prompted the Germans to develop an entirely new, sophisticated approach to combat after the war.

The first broadly disseminated articulations of this new approach—widely regarded as maneuver warfare's modern conceptual foundation—appeared in 1937 with the publication of *Attacks* by German military officer Erwin Rommel, later known as "the Desert Fox," and with the publication of *Achtung-Panzer!* by Heinz Guderian, another well-known German military officer. These two master tacticians advocated a radically new approach to combat: fast-moving, decentralized forces that deeply penetrated an enemy's rear area at breakneck speed, disrupted his balance, and prevented him from using his reserve forces.

This last point is critically important: in World War I the time needed for an attacker to exploit an initial advantage was so long, and consolidation of gains so slow, that the enemy nearly always had time to bring up reserves from behind the lines and plug any gap created by the attacker. Thus, even if the attacker achieved *breakthrough*, an initial tactical advantage, he seldom converted it into *breakout*, a momentum-shifting strategic advantage. Achieving breakout by exploiting gains before the enemy had time to respond was the aim of this new approach to warfare.

The second half of the twentieth century witnessed a major contribution to modern maneuver warfare theory and several landmark victories that validated the viability of maneuver warfare as a modern combat philosophy. U.S. Air Force colonel John Boyd's contention that conflict could be understood in terms of "OODA loops"—time-competitive cycles of observing, orienting, deciding, and acting—brought considerable focus on *relative* decision-making speed as a key determinant of success in combat. And resounding victories by modern practitioners of maneuver warfare—notably the Germans during the invasion of France in 1940, MacArthur at Inchon in 1950, the Israelis in the 1967 War, and the Coalition Forces in Operation Desert Storm in 1991—all proved that maneuver warfare theory was devastatingly effective when applied in practice.

The latest in this long line of practitioners of what we now know as maneuver warfare is the United States Marine Corps, which has long prided itself on being at the leading edge of tactical innovation. Ever since its first landing on the beach at Nassau, Bahamas, during the Revolutionary War in 1776, the Marine Corps has continuously refined the doctrine of amphibious ship-to-shore attacks. In the 1930s and 1940s the Marines were among the first Allied aviators to provide close air support to troops on the ground by dropping bombs or strafing with machine guns at low altitudes. In the 1950s the Marines pioneered the use of the helicopter to support and transport ground forces, thereby revolutionizing mobility and operations on the battlefield.

But not until the late 1980s, under the guidance of General Gray, did senior Marine leaders come to the realization that their organization needed to rethink how it approached armed conflict. A perennially underfunded and undermanned organization, the Marine Corps would once again have to do more with less. Defense drawdowns in the wake of the cold war threatened to further erode its budget and manpower levels. But as "America's 9-1-1 Force in Readiness," Marines would continue to be called on to face more heavily equipped foes in unfamiliar and distant locales. With the publication of *Warfighting* in 1989, the Marines—once a devil-be-damned, charge-up-the-middle outfit—formally adopted maneuver warfare as doctrinal philosophy.

MANEUVER WARFARE TODAY

The maneuver warfare philosophy, tailor-made for a smaller, lighter force with limited resources, is particularly well suited to today's combat environment. Traditional battle lines have blurred. Weapons have become incredibly accurate and, therefore, extremely lethal. Communications advances have increased the flow of information on the battlefield, often to the point of overload, and have created a new dimension in armed conflict—electronic warfare. Speed and distance in engagements have increased. Multinational coalition warfare has become common practice. Entirely new types of "low-intensity" conflicts have emerged—in countries such as Somalia, Bosnia, and Afghanistan—where the identities of amorphous enemies are increasingly difficult to distinguish, rules of engagement restrict available alternatives, media scrutiny is intense, and the liability of collateral damage has heightened. Accompanying all of this change are the enduring constants of human fear, exhaustion, and confusion, as well as exogenous factors such as unforeseeable contingencies and unpredictable weather. Indeed the pressure to make sound and timely decisions in armed conflict has never been greater.

As you can surely attest, the pressure to make sound and timely decisions in business is also greater than it has ever been. To guide and improve your decision making amid friction, uncertainty, fluidity, and disorder and to show you how you can use maneuver warfare to lead your organization in the modern business environment, we dedicate the remainder of this book to examining, in great detail, maneuver warfare's seven guiding principles and enabling leadership prescriptions.

But first, to set the stage, we offer in the coming chapter the Arab-Israeli War of 1967. In this textbook example of maneuver warfare, an undermanned, resource-constrained force achieved an overwhelmingly decisive victory against a numerically superior opponent in a minimal amount of time and with a minimal loss of human life. This is not a story about the U.S. Marines, but you can bet that the Marines have studied it extensively and have emulated many of the practices that made the Israelis successful in this war. We hope you will find it—and the detailed review of the Israelis' actions in Chapter 2—equally enlightening.

CHAPTER 2

AN INTEGRATED ATTACK

The Arab-Israeli War of 1967

"All of Sinai is in our hands."
—GENERAL YESHAYAHU GAVISH, FIFTY-TWO HOURS INTO THE WAR[1]

At 8:15 A.M. on June 5, 1967, under a bright sun and clear skies, the unsuspecting Egyptian Air Force was conducting a changeover of patrols, as it always did at that hour. Suddenly, 250 aircraft—almost the entire Israeli Air Force (IAF)—appeared out of nowhere and unleashed a preemptive air strike against eleven Egyptian air bases that gave the IAF total air supremacy.

As the bombs landed on Egyptian airfields, Israeli Defense Force (IDF) commanders cried, "*Kadimah!* Head for the enemy," and launched a three-pronged ground attack across the Sinai Peninsula.[2] The IDF ripped through the Egyptians' defensive lines, wreaked havoc in their ranks, and shattered their command infrastructure. A mere four days later, on the verge of total collapse, the numerically superior and more heavily equipped Egyptians agreed to a cease-fire.

BACKGROUND

By the spring of 1967, Middle Eastern tensions had reached a flash point, and the third war between Israel and its Arab neighbors in less than twenty years was imminent. The first theater of the war would be the Sinai Peninsula: the barren, rugged landmass separating Israel and the Red Sea from more than one hundred thousand troops and a thousand tanks along Israel's relatively expansive southern border. Egypt had also built air bases on the Sinai, positioning its bombers within minutes of the Israeli capital.

Israel feared that its very existence as a nation was in jeopardy. Even after a nationwide activation of all available reservists, it could muster only 200,000 ground troops, 800 tanks, and 262 airplanes. The combined Arab coalition force, which comprised Egypt, Syria, and Jordan with support from Saudi Arabia, Lebanon, Iraq, Kuwait, Algeria, and Sudan and threatened Israeli borders on three fronts, totaled approximately 465,000 soldiers, 2,880 tanks, and 810 aircraft.[3] The linchpin of the Arabs' air power, Egypt, alone possessed more than 400 planes.

Rather than wait to be attacked, Israel devised a plan to launch an all-out preemptive strike against the Egyptians in an attempt to secure the safety of its homeland and dictate the course of events of the engagement. Israeli leaders surmised that if Egypt, the leader of the Arab coalition, were defeated, the other members would follow suit.

General Yeshayahu Gavish led the Israeli ground forces in the Sinai. Gavish split his army into three divisions, which were led by Generals Yisrael Tal, Ariel Sharon (who would later become prime minister of Israel), and Avraham Yoffe. All four men were veterans of the Arab-Israeli War of 1956 and knew the Sinai well. Tal's division would attack through the North. Sharon's division would attack and eliminate the multilayered Egyptian defensive positions in the central Sinai. And Yoffe would secure the axis between Sharon and Tal, thereby protecting their flanks from the vast enemy reinforcements that were staged in defensive rings throughout the Sinai.

AIR ATTACK AND THE ONSET OF WAR

By identifying its own greatest weakness first—susceptibility to Egyptian air attack—Israel concluded that it must first remove the Egyptian air threat. Israel reasoned that air superiority was absolutely essential not only to protect its homeland but also to preserve its ability to wage a successful ground campaign. The smaller IDF ground force would need to conduct its lightning-strike-style attack across the Sinai without fear of enemy air attack. Unbeknownst to the Arab coalition, Israel would hurl all but twelve of its planes at Egypt.[4] This *bold* move, which left the Israeli homeland

Figure 2.1 ISRAELI AIR ATTACK, 1967[5]

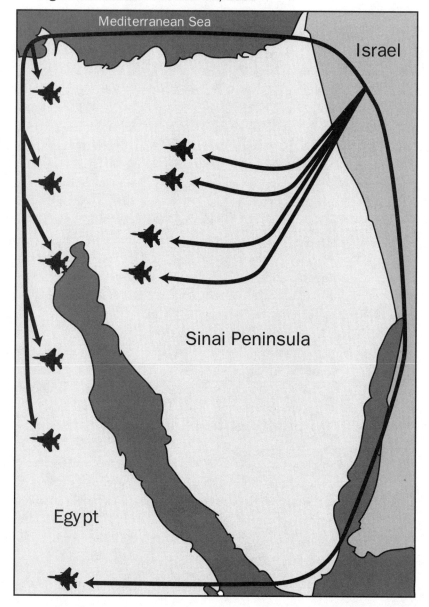

almost completely vulnerable to attack from the air, created the risk of catastrophic loss, but the potential reward of destroying the Egyptian air force on the ground was adequate justification.

The Israeli attack relied heavily on the element of *surprise*. Israel carefully planned the time of attack not at dawn, as the Egyptians expected, but at 8:00 A.M., during the Egyptians' regularly scheduled breakfast and rest period. Israeli pilots stealthily approached at dangerously low altitudes and maintained strict radio silence to ensure that they were not detected by Egyptian radar or communication systems. And, by launching at carefully calculated intervals, the Israeli aircraft arrived at their targets at exactly the same time and delivered a simultaneous strike. Egyptian air bases could not warn each other of attack, because they were all under attack at the same time. Moreover, during the previous two years, the Israelis had staged some sort of flight exercise every morning at the same time. This repetition created *ambiguity* for the Egyptians in their interpretation of radar signals. When Egyptian radar spotted an unusually large number of Israeli planes taking off on June 5, air defense commanders dismissed the blips as simply a larger number of routine training flights.

The Israelis knew of the Egyptian practice of sending pilots to their planes as soon as enemy aircraft appeared on radar and exploited it accordingly. As they neared their target, the IAF pilots suddenly increased altitude and "appeared" on the Egyptians' radar screens. This deliberate forewarning set a trap: as the Egyptian pilots scrambled to man their planes, the IAF was in prime position to eliminate both the aircraft and their crews.

The results were devastating. The Egyptians were not fully aware of the attack until some three hundred of their aircraft, over half of their Air Force, had been eliminated and one-third of their pilots had been killed. By 10:30 that morning, a top Egyptian general noted, "The Egyptian Air Force ceased to exist."[5] The IAF had eliminated what it deemed the principal threat to the Israeli homeland and paved the way for the IDF ground forces to attack the Sinai with little threat of air attack.

GROUND ATTACK

The Egyptians had positioned their ground forces in three heavily fortified lines covered by massive interlocking firepower. This configuration,

Figure 2.2 ISRAELI GROUND ATTACK, 1967

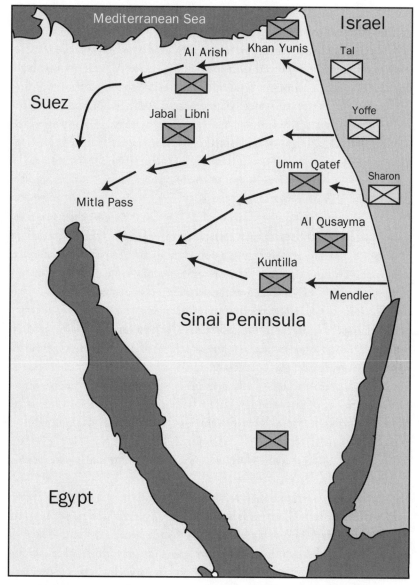

Practitioner of Maneuver Warfare   Adversary

modeled after the Soviet doctrine of "defense in depth," was formidable. But Israeli senior leaders, owing to their experiences in previous wars and to years of exhaustive intelligence gathering (the Israelis' version of due diligence), had identified Egypt's Achilles' heel, or *critical vulnerability*: a slow and cumbersome centralized decision-making process, far removed from the action on the ground and the information needed to control it.

Under the Egyptian system of command and control, rigid, detailed orders were given from central locations, thereby leaving scant opportunity for frontline commanders to make decisions or react to changing situations. Egyptian frontline units were not free to open fire or make decisions without approval from higher command, and frontline soldiers were removed from officers with decision-making authority by many layers. These shortcomings, coupled with an understanding of the paralyzing fear associated with isolation in desert warfare, led the Israelis to believe that they could cause their enemy's collapse by rapidly bypassing frontline units, penetrating deep into rear areas, and systematically dividing forces— all before the Egyptians could organize an effective counterattack.

General Tal moved first and, though assigned the least ground to cover, had perhaps the most daunting task: ahead of him lay four Egyptian divisions, each heavily armed and densely compressed along the northernmost route between the Israeli border and the Suez Canal. Rather than match his strength against that of his much larger opponent, Tal opted to selectively attack key points in the Egyptian defenses with overwhelming force. In several instances he ordered the three brigades under his command to *focus* all of their tanks into fists of armor,[6] which were sufficiently powerful to punch through the Egyptians' lines and then fan out to attack several key objectives.

Tal's tactics were so effective that, by the end of Day One, his forces had moved beyond Khan Yunis and penetrated all the way to the town of Al Arish, well ahead of where he planned to attack on Day Two. When his forces reached Al Arish, Egyptian frontline units, isolated from their supporting units and cut off from communications with their higher commands, were flailing in disorder and beginning to flee their positions.

Meanwhile, to the south, Sharon's objective was to crack through the first defensive line, anchored at Umm Qatef, and then join Yoffe to assault the second line at Jabal Libni. To increase his chances of success, Sharon dispatched armor units to the south in a diversionary move intended to *deceive* his opponent into believing that the attack was coming from that direction and distract the Egyptian forces at Al Qusayma and Kuntilla.

Colonel Avraham Mendler was responsible for conducting the deceptive effort to the south at Kuntilla but received no explicit orders to attack enemy troops. Nevertheless, as he saw events unfold before him, he realized that Egyptian forces were being sent north to reinforce Umm Qatef. Rather than wait for specific guidance from Sharon, Mendler made a *decentralized decision* to attack and routed the Egyptian forces at Kuntilla. This apparently minor tactical victory would later be recognized as a significant contribution to Sharon's overall efforts at Umm Qatef.

Through a heavy dust storm and constant enemy shelling, Sharon's forces, breaking through the perimeter defense, converged on the confused Egyptians from all directions and prepared for an all-out assault. Not all of the Israeli troops would arrive in time for the battle, and dense minefields would slow other attacking units. But Sharon's units pressed through the night and, by dawn, had penetrated deep into the Egyptians' labyrinthine defenses. Before daybreak the Israelis' tanks breached the heavily mined route toward Umm Qatef and fought a vicious, close-range duel with the Egyptian tankers. By daybreak on Day Two, Sharon's forces secured Umm Qatef.

Twenty-four hours into the war, the Egyptian army was already crumbling, as a result of the confusion and chaos created by the fast-moving Israelis.

As Sharon's forces advanced, Yoffe penetrated deep into the western Sinai and cut off the vital road junctions. To accomplish his daunting mission, Yoffe decided to attempt a crossing of the Wadi Haridin, a treacherous sandy area previously deemed "only fit for camels."[7] He boldly ordered one of his brigades to strip its tanks of all "excess weight"—almost all food, water, and spare parts—and make the passage through the Wadi Haridin.

On the morning of Day Two, Tal dispatched his brigades on multiple axes to secure the northern part of the Sinai and the Gaza Strip. Sharon's forces proceeded toward Al Qusayma after squelching the remaining resistance at Umm Qatef. Meanwhile, Yoffe's forces had already sent the Egyptians reeling after a tank battle near Bir Lahfan. Massive confusion and chaos reigned within the Egyptian command, and most of the frontline units had fled their initial positions. Communications effectively ceased to exist. By the middle of the second day, Supreme Headquarters apparently lost the will to continue fighting—even though half of its fighting force remained fresh and intact—and ordered a full retreat from the Sinai.

Tal, Sharon, and Yoffe had advanced so far ahead of their initial battle plans that they had no specific guidance for continuing the war. But they did not allow a lack of guidance to slow the momentum of their offensive. Throughout the war these three generals repeatedly analyzed the rapidly evolving situations they faced, made sound and timely decisions, and seamlessly transitioned to the exploitation of subsequent battlefield opportunities—all in real time. The Egyptians could not match this blistering decision-making *tempo*. Their responses came increasingly late, and they were eventually overcome by events; that is, their responses were no longer appropriate to the situation on the ground by the time their orders were issued.

The next day, Gavish issued new orders to his commanders. Tal was to move westward toward the Suez Canal to remove any remaining pockets of resistance. Sharon was dispatched south with the goal of circling the Egyptians and driving them to the north. Yoffe was to split his forces and head for the Mitla and Giddi Passes to cut off the fleeing Egyptians and set up an ambush into which Sharon and Tal could push the Egyptians.

Yoffe started his next advance early on Day Three. Surprised by the speed with which the Egyptians were fleeing, he immediately directed his brigades to race ahead to the Mitla and Giddi Passes to engage the Egyptians. Upon arrival, he ordered his troops to position any bombed-out vehicles near the pass and form a man-made channel through which the remainder of the Egyptian force—thirty thousand men and three hundred tanks—would be funneled.

Once in place at Mitla, the Israelis employed a *combined arms* attack—the integration of the man-made channel, artillery, armor, direct machine gun fire, and aircraft bombing runs—to place the Egyptians in an inescapable "damned if you do, damned if you don't" situation. As the Egyptians proceeded through the pass and the man-made channel, their movement was restricted. The Israelis used armor and artillery to stall the Egyptians' forward movement and then destroyed their opponents in place with devastating direct fire and air strikes.

By the end of Day Three, Israel had essentially captured the entire Sinai Peninsula; all that remained was pursuing the retreating Egyptians and securing some of the recently vacated outposts at the far outreaches of the desert. On June 8, little more than four days after the war began, the shattered Egyptian forces agreed to a cease-fire, thereby allowing Israel to recommit forces to the northern fronts and secure quick victories over Syria and Jordan.

OUTCOME AND OBSERVATIONS

Israel's masterful prosecution of its meticulously prepared battle plan resulted in one of the most resounding victories in modern warfare. Three Israeli divisions totaling some fifty thousand men routed the equivalent of seven Egyptian divisions of more than a hundred thousand men and conquered an area approximately three times the size of Israel at a cost of fewer than four hundred of their own troops and forty-six pilots killed. While any loss of life in warfare is tragic, these losses were much, much less severe than anticipated.

At the heart of this resounding victory were the *italicized* words you saw interspersed throughout the chapter—the seven guiding principles of maneuver warfare. The Israelis knew their opponent's greatest weakness and conducted their attack with the aim of aggressively exploiting it. During the course of battle they took considerable, albeit calculated, risks and concentrated overwhelming combat power at critical points and times to achieve dramatic outcomes. A combination of speed and surprise created uncertainty and chaos within the Egyptians' ranks. The willingness of frontline commanders, such as Colonel Mendler, to make on-the-spot decisions created a rapid pace of battle to which the enemy could not respond effectively. Finally, the creative combination of complementary weapons gave the Egyptians no way out in the Mitla Pass. This series of actions represents the approach to preparing and prosecuting business plans that we hope to impart in this book, and we now turn to delineating and defining each principle.

CHAPTER 3

THE SEVEN GUIDING PRINCIPLES

"Many years ago, as a cadet hoping someday to be an officer, I was poring over "Principles of War," listed in the old Field Service Regulations, when the Sergeant-Major came up to me. He surveyed me with kindly amusement. "Don't bother your head about all them things, me lad," he said. "There's only one principle of war and that's this. Hit the other fellow, as quick as you can, and as hard as you can, where it hurts him most, when he ain't lookin'!"

—Sir William Slim[1]

At the risk of outdoing the sergeant major, we have distilled from *Warfighting* seven guiding principles of maneuver warfare: *targeting critical vulnerabilities, boldness, surprise, focus, decentralized decision making, tempo,* and *combined arms.* These principles, potent when applied individually and devastating when applied in subsets or as an integrated whole, provide a useful framework for thinking about business strategy.

In this chapter, which we offer as a stand-alone reference, we introduce each principle with an after-action review of the Israelis' actions in the 1967 War, as profiled in the previous chapter, and an illustrative example from the business world. We also preview the modern-day practices that the Marines employ to foster maneuver warfare in their organization in an effort to lay the foundation for our subsequent recommendations as to how you can foster maneuver warfare in *your* organization.

Please note the words *introduce* and *preview*. In the subsequent seven chapters, each principle will receive its own in-depth treatment, with numerous supporting examples and prescriptions to illustrate the appropriate application of maneuver warfare and selected counterexamples, to illustrate the downside associated with misapplication. But in this chapter we start with the basics.

TARGETING CRITICAL VULNERABILITIES

Targeting critical vulnerabilities—the principle of "hitting the other fellow where it hurts the most"—aims to identify and exploit those fundamental weaknesses that "will do the most significant damage to the enemy's ability to resist."[2]

As we saw in Chapter 2, Israel's resounding victory in the 1967 War began with its ability to target its opponent's critical vulnerability. Rather than attack the numerically superior and more heavily armed Egyptians head-on, Israel opted to pierce their defensive lines and disrupt their cumbersome, centralized decision-making process, thereby driving them into a debilitating state of chaos and confusion.

In a similar fashion, upstart MCI discovered in the early 1980s that incumbent AT&T's critical vulnerability was to be found in the long-distance telephone service market. The then-regulated incumbent's uniform pricing of long-distance services was based on the duration and distance of the call rather than on its cost of providing the service. Moreover, prices for long-distance service were inflated significantly to subsidize two unprofitable AT&T businesses: local telephone service, especially in rural areas, and long-distance service in remote, geographically challenging areas, like the Rocky Mountain states.

MCI exploited the vulnerability by attacking AT&T in markets that were large enough to be profitable and geographically benign enough that microwave communications technology could be deployed effectively: its first route, between Chicago and St. Louis, crossed no major mountains or other impassable geographic obstacles and was relatively easy to install. MCI also launched and won litigation that granted it to access AT&T's network: the courts forced AT&T to sell network capacity to MCI so that MCI could become a true nationwide carrier, without installing its own network connections in many locations. Targeting its opponent's critical vulnerability of uniform pricing thus afforded MCI a fundamental cost advantage in building and operating networks that AT&T could not match, and the upstart gained considerable market share at AT&T's expense.

The Marines' emphasis on targeting critical vulnerabilities can serve as a useful guide to implementing this principle in your business. They view targeting critical vulnerabilities as a top-down, bottom-up process, and all Marines, from the front line to the highest headquarters, constantly search for the enemy's fundamental weaknesses. At the same time, they are aware that their organization has its own critical vulnerabilities and constantly endeavor to prevent them from being targeted.

BOLDNESS

Boldness is the daring to seek breakthrough results rather than incremental ones.

Israel jeopardized its national security when it committed nearly its entire air force to a preemptive strike on Egypt's air bases and left only twelve aircraft in reserve to protect its skies. This calculated risk was well rewarded, as the IAF eliminated the threat of Egyptian air attack on the Israeli homeland and afforded Israel air superiority for the remainder of the war.

In the past fifty years, Boeing has twice taken bold gambles that transformed commercial aviation. To enter the commercial jet aircraft market in the 1950s, Boeing committed the equivalent of 25 percent of its entire corporate net worth to the development of a prototype for the 707. Despite a historically poor track record in commercial aviation and an uncertain market outlook, Boeing successfully launched the 707, one of America's first commercial jet-powered passenger airplanes, and became the definitive market leader.

In the mid-1960s, Boeing again "bet the company" on a new category of aircraft, the jumbo jet, in spite of highly uncertain market demand. The result was the 747, which reduced per-passenger cost of transatlantic flight by 30 percent and redefined the commercial aviation market by making transatlantic air travel available to a whole new class of customers.[3]

Emulating the deliberate efforts that the Marines undertake to encourage calculated risk taking and build self-confidence throughout the ranks will enable you to foster a propensity for boldness in your organization. The Marines encourage an *obligation to dissent* in the decision-making process and tolerate mistakes that stem from bold zeal—but never indecision, timidity, or lapses in integrity. They also train their juniors to make decisions in the face of limited information and exercise initiative with confidence. And when all else fails, they default to the venerable option that "it is better to beg for forgiveness than ask for permission"—provided their actions are in harmony with the organization's overall strategic objectives.

SURPRISE

Surprise—the principle of "hitting the other fellow when he ain't lookin' "—refers to the use of information to impair a foe's decision-making ability and a subsequent unexpected strike. It can be achieved using one of three approaches: stealth, ambiguity, or deception.

Israel's preemptive air strike on Egypt exemplifies the use of stealth to achieve surprise. Nap of the earth flight patterns were so low that Israeli aircraft could not be detected by Egyptian radar—until they wanted to be. Careful planning of departure times and approaches ensured that the attacks occurred simultaneously; consequently, none of the Egyptian air bases was able to alert the others of the strike—until it was over. The IAF also employed ambiguity to conceal the intent of its actual attack: by launching at the same time every day during the previous two years, the IAF lulled the Egyptians into believing that the takeoff on the morning of June 5, 1967, was merely another training run.

In the mid-1990s, commercial airlines established websites to provide general information to customers. As the functionality of these sites expanded, customers could reserve and purchase tickets directly from the sites. Once the number of online orders reached a critical mass, Delta, in a move quickly emulated by other airlines, surprised unsuspecting travel agents by slashing commissions, from 10 percent of the value of each ticket sold to a flat $50 (and recently $0) per ticket. While the threat to travel agents of travelers buying directly from the airlines had been evident all along, the greater threat of declining commissions had not. Because travel agents weren't aware of the power shift that the Internet enabled, they were unprepared to launch effective countermeasures.

The Marine Corps's recent articulation of and commitment to the concept of *information operations* can serve you as a useful guide to employing information to achieve surprise in the business environment. Recognizing the increasingly central role that information will play in twenty-first-century armed conflict, the Marines have dedicated personnel and resources to the management of information in support of maneuver warfare and have formally integrated this new approach into the planning and execution of all combat operations. And this high degree of commitment suggests very strongly that a disciplined follow-through must accompany every well-intended use of information to shape the rules of competitive encounters.

FOCUS

Focus—the principle of "hitting the other fellow as hard as you can"—is the "generation of superior combat power at a particular time and place" that enables "a numerically inferior force to achieve decisive local superiority,"[4] thereby providing an advantage when and where it matters most.

At the strategic level Israel endeavored to break the Arab coalition by focusing its attack on the coalition's leader, Egypt, rather than face Arab threats on three fronts and risk dilution of its limited combat power. On the tactical level Tal's decision to strike the Egyptians with "fists of armor" enabled him to inflict heavy damage to critical points in his larger opponent's defenses.

Since its initial public offering in 1999, upstart Juniper Networks has employed a focused attack to infiltrate the market for high-end Internet routers. Routers—devices that act as "traffic cops" to move data packets across the Internet—serve a wide variety of markets and command considerably different profit margins; the high-end "backbone" routers, used by telecom companies, yield the highest profits. Juniper managed to take share from Cisco, the dominant incumbent, which served all markets from high- to low-end routers; however, Cisco did not serve the telecom market with particular fervor or focus.

Sensing opportunity, Juniper committed all of its resources to building a faster, more reliable router designed expressly for these large telecom operators. It hired leading Internet protocol engineers to design a faster router and dedicated researchers to "get in the trenches" with telecom operators to determine exactly what they wanted in terms of operability. And, between 1999 and 2002, it invested nearly $450 million in research and development.[5] The result of these efforts was a router four times faster than Cisco's comparable offering and more suited to the unique needs of telecom companies. To date Juniper has gained an approximate 30 to 40 percent market share.

The Marines' high proficiency in focus can guide in your efforts to uncover lucrative opportunities, shift resources toward them, and manage the accompanying risk in business. The Marines rely heavily on information to locate lucrative targets as they arise and to commit available forces rapidly and in a coordinated fashion. In every combat engagement they designate a main effort, which can change depending on the course of battle. And they acknowledge that focusing resources in support of the main effort requires economy of force elsewhere.

DECENTRALIZED DECISION MAKING

Decentralizing decision making down through the ranks gives those closest to the action the latitude they need to take advantage of on-the-spot information unavailable to their superiors and exercise initiative without having to wait for approval.

As much as the Egyptians' inability to function in the absence of orders contributed to their defeat, a reliance on decentralized decision making contributed to the Israelis' success. Colonel Mendler's decision to attack opportunistically at Kuntilla, based on his understanding of unfolding events, exemplifies decentralized decision making. But by no means were this and countless other on-the-spot decisions like it a product of happenstance. Long before the 1967 War began, the Israelis had, through rigorous leadership training, ingrained in their troops a willingness to make decisions in the absence of complete information and an inclination to exercise initiative. More than a positive attribute, initiative was and continues to be a *duty* among members of the Israeli armed forces.

Shortly after assuming the role of CEO at Continental Airlines in 1994, Gordon Bethune symbolically burned the company's inflexible customer service manual and gave employees considerable latitude to make impromptu decisions regarding customer service. But to align employees' individual actions with the organization's overall strategic objectives, he repeatedly emphasized the need to improve in three industry-important metrics: customer satisfaction, lost baggage, and on-time arrivals.

The employees of Continental rose to Bethune's challenge. Take, for example, a flight attendant on a full flight short of meals and needing to make an on-time departure. A predetermined decision, dictated by the customer service manual, may have prescribed closing the doors before the arrival of the necessary number of meals, thereby ensuring an on-time departure. Alternatively, the resourceful flight attendant, possessing on-the-spot information, could offer free drinks to certain business travelers in lieu of a meal. Under this scenario the plane departs on time, an entire planeload of people is happy, no one misses a connection, and no one stays in a hotel at Continental's expense. Collectively, such frontline decisions were a driving force behind Continental's widely heralded turnaround.

Emulating the techniques that the Marines employ to decentralize decision making will enable you to maximize the potential benefits of unleashing the ingenuity of your people while minimizing the risks associated with a lesser degree of control in your organization. Within units Marine leaders establish a baseline of trust with those in their charge, tailor communications with the aim of arming junior leaders with the "bigger picture" into which their actions fit, and vigilantly supervise the implementation of all directives issued. At the institutional level the Marine Corps formally trains its members to make decisions in the absence of orders and uses technology to share information and therefore improve awareness among dispersed units. And as individuals, all Marines leaders keep in the back of their mind the venerable saying "You can delegate authority, but you can never delegate responsibility."

TEMPO

Tempo—the principle of "hitting the other fellow as quick as you can"—is relative speed in time: identifying opportunities, making decisions, and acting faster than one's opponent, thereby forcing him into a constant state of reaction.

From the outset of hostilities, the Egyptians struggled to react to Israel's faster tempo, and their ability to react deteriorated as the war progressed. Ultimately, the Egyptians were overcome by events. By the time the Egyptians were aware that their Air Force had been destroyed on the ground, the IDF had already launched its ground attack. After penetrating the Egyptians' first line of defense, the IDF immediately transitioned to the next stage of the attack and pressed hard into the second line. The Israelis maintained this momentum through the third line and on to the Mitla and Giddi Passes, where they intercepted the fleeing Egyptians.

Jenny Craig, the chain of weight-management centers, used rapid tempo to deliver a decisive blow to its archrival NutriSystem in the 1980s. In this market, where diet centers were deriving almost all of their profits from the sales of portion- and calorie-controlled food products, Jenny Craig engaged NutriSystem in a duel of product improvements: first freeze-dried food, then boil-in pouches, and later microwavable pouches.

Because NutriSystem was primarily a chain of franchises, each product improvement required the approval of countless franchisees. Jenny, who, with her family, owned most of her company's diet centers, was able to make companywide decisions and implement those decisions much more rapidly. Almost immediately after identifying an opportunity to sell a new line of microwavable frozen foods, Jenny Craig invested heavily in the new product line and its requisite storage capacity. NutriSystem, which struggled to gain consensus among its hundreds of independently owned franchisees to invest in yet another product improvement, failed to respond to Jenny Craig's move, lost considerable market share, canceled its IPO, and was eventually acquired. Now only the name survives.

Marines consider tempo a vital weapon, and this weapon can become part of your arsenal of business practices as well. By leading from the front and pushing decision making to the lowest levels, they endeavor to locate themselves as close to the point of decision as possible. The Marines' adherence to the *⅓-⅔ Rule*, which reserves ⅓ of the planning time remaining before a deadline for a commander and the remaining ⅔ for his or her subordinates, reveals that they discipline themselves not to monopolize precious time during the planning process. Recognizing that excessive debate can slow tempo, Marines execute their leader's decision once it has been made as if it were their own. As an institution they train decision-making speed. And they have even streamlined the formal planning process into a rapid reaction planning process (R2P2) for special situations.

COMBINED ARMS

Combined arms, the integration of complementary weapons and capabilities, increases their collective effectiveness and creates for the opponent a "damned if you do, damned if you don't" situation in which "to defend against one attack, the enemy must become more vulnerable to another."[6]

At the Mitla Pass, the Israelis' combined arms attack increased the effectiveness of the weapons they employed and systematically eliminated the options available for an Egyptian response. The steep slopes on either side of the passes denied the Egyptians lateral movement, and Yoffe's man-made channel of destroyed vehicles funneled their forward movement.

Artillery fire and a wall of tanks at one end of the pass halted the Egyptian vehicles, and air strikes and withering direct fire finished off the stationary targets with devastating accuracy.

From 1964 to 1966, IBM successfully combined marketing, sales, hardware design, software design, and service to create the System 360 computer. The System 360 (as in 360 degrees, or full-circle coverage) was unique in that it was intended to be a single-computer architecture that would support data processing for small and large businesses as well as scientific and engineering applications. Some companies might have offered better scientific computing; others might have offered more powerful multitasking capabilities for business computing. But no one could match the 360's all-embracing architecture. To increase its advantage further, IBM offered on-site services, unparalleled after-sales support, and a superior parts distribution system. One by one competitors exited the mainframe business, ceding the market to IBM for decades to follow.

The practices the Marines employ to combine arms can help you put your competitors on the horns of a dilemma, the worst of all "damned if you do, damned if you don't" situations. The Marines keep all critical functions—air, artillery, infantry, armor, and communications—"in house." All Marines undergo rigorous initial infantry training to establish a common grounding. And extensive follow-up cross-training in other specialties fosters a better understanding among the different functional areas involved in the combined arms effort. Finally, the Marines make the human investment necessary to ensure the efficient functioning of the combined arms team: the collocation of dedicated full-time experts.

INTEGRATION OF PRINCIPLES: "BRINGING IT ALL TOGETHER"

While each of the preceding principles of maneuver warfare represents a valuable concept on its own, the benefits of this combat philosophy are realized most fully when the principles are working together. Maneuver warfare is not about execution in isolation but about applying the principles simultaneously—in subsets or as an integrated whole—to determine the most decisive outcome at the least cost.

A closer look at the Israelis' experience in Chapter 2 shows how the seven principles complement and reinforce one another when applied in an integrated manner. In the air attack, surprise complemented boldness;

the Israeli pilots' ability to conceal their intentions until the moment of the attack decreased the risk associated with the bold move. And both boldness and surprise reinforced focus. The Israelis would not have been able to deliver a "knockout blow" had they not committed almost their entire Air Force and had the Egyptians been expecting an attack.

On the ground, boldness again reinforced focus. Tal would not have been able to attack with "fists of armor" had he not risked vulnerabilities elsewhere, and Yoffe would not have been able to deny Egyptian reinforcements had he not risked a crossing of the impassable sands. Boldness also reinforced decentralized decision making, which in turn enabled a rapid tempo. Countless on-the-spot decisions made confidently in the absence of complete information maintained the blistering momentum of the Israeli attack. Finally, tempo complemented targeting critical vulnerabilities. The faster the Israelis penetrated the Egyptian defenses, the more they created chaos and confusion and accelerated the collapse of the Egyptian command and control system.

Once we have provided a thorough treatment of each of the seven guiding principles, we will examine in greater detail this notion that the principles are complementary and mutually reinforcing. We will offer the concept of *reconnaissance pull*, which encompasses targeting critical vulnerabilities, focus, decentralized decision making, and tempo. Reconnaissance pull is a real-time response to opportunity, whereby an individual identifies an opportunity, directs the organization toward it, and then immediately leads in its exploitation. From there we will demonstrate the synergistic effects of the fully integrated application of all seven principles in the business environment. And we will close with a discussion of leadership—again, the backbone of maneuver warfare—without which well-intended strategy never translates into actual results.

CHAPTER 4

TARGETING CRITICAL VULNERABILITIES

"Thetis when he was born had intended to make him invulnerable by dipping him into the River Styx, but she was careless and did not see to it that the water covered the part of the foot by which she was holding him."
—THE STORY OF ACHILLES[1]

A practitioner of maneuver warfare continually analyzes a rival with the aim of identifying those fundamental weaknesses that, "if exploited, will do the most significant damage to competitors' ability to resist."[2]

Identifying the weakness that will cause the opponent to collapse— his Achilles' heel—can be achieved in one of three ways: through constant search by every member of the organization, through forward-looking planning, and through rigorous self-examination. Once the opponent's Achilles' heel is identified, resources must be marshaled rapidly and decisively to exploit it. Critical vulnerabilities are fleeting opportunities that must be targeted before the opponent is aware he is susceptible and takes steps to remedy them; otherwise they could be missed permanently. Thus minimizing the lag time between the identification of the weakness and its exploitation maximizes the effectiveness of the resources deployed in this effort.

In this chapter we offer four historical examples of targeting critical vulnerabilities and its key components, as well as present-day lessons from the Marines. Erwin Rommel's victory over the Italians at the Battle of the Isonzo in World War I and Lowe's follow-on attack against Home Depot in retail home improvement illustrate the successful identification and exploitation of a rival's critical vulnerability in warfare and in business. Shell Oil's successful use of *scenario planning*, which aims to identify, prepare for, and practice in several futures instead of predicting a single future, provides a potential means of identifying competitors' critical vulnerabilities before they do. And hesitation by the Union Army at the Battle of Petersburg in the American Civil War illustrates the adverse consequences of failing to marshal resources rapidly in the exploitation of a rival's critical vulnerability.

The Marines' experience with identifying and exploiting critical vulnerabilities can serve as a useful guide to implementing this principle in your organization. To this end, our intent in this chapter is to use their experiences and some of the lessons learned from our historical examples to suggest ways in which you can encourage a top-down, bottom-up approach to targeting critical vulnerabilities in your organization and safeguard your own critical vulnerabilities from competitors.

ROMMEL AT ISONZO

In 1918, at the 12th Battle of the Isonzo, then-lieutenant Erwin Rommel, commanding a small detachment of three companies of light infantry, targeted the critical vulnerability of his Italian opposition: a key mountain pass used as a main supply route. The capture of this pass broke the Italians' will to fight and caused the collapse of the northern part of their entire front, which consisted of thousands of well-positioned troops. To reach the pass, Rommel identified gaps in each of three defensive lines, bypassed enemy strong points, and attacked Italian defenders from the rear.

Under heavy rainfall, Rommel's detachment quickly penetrated the artillery-devastated first line and advanced up a steep slope until his lead elements encountered heavy machine gun fire. Instead of attacking through this well-fortified position, he chose to attack the Italian second line from a less obvious direction—a steep gully to his left.

At the top of the gully, he dispatched an eight-man patrol down a hidden path. The patrol, resembling Italians returning from the front, slipped through the enemy line and silently captured a dugout full of defenders huddling away from the rain. Pouring through the opening created by the

Figure 4.1 ROMMEL'S ATTACK ON ISONZO, 1918

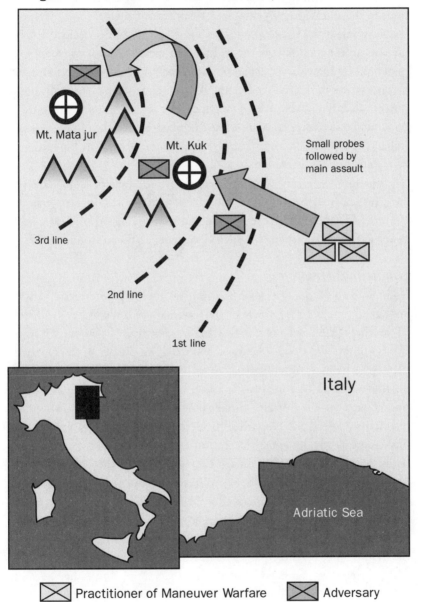

Mt. Mata jur

Mt. Kuk

Small probes
followed by
main assault

3rd line

2nd line

1st line

Italy

Adriatic Sea

Practitioner of Maneuver Warfare   Adversary

patrol, Rommel's force then defeated the remainder of the defensive positions in the second line by attacking them from the rear.

Arriving at the heavily defended third line, Rommel decided to conduct an independent attack eleven hundred meters west of the main German fighting force. Once again, he dispatched numerous patrols in search of weaknesses in the Italian defense. A small team led by one of his junior officers eventually discovered an opening, and Rommel directed the remainder of his force through it. At this point he had the option to attack Italian positions in the third line or bypass them. Within striking distance of his ultimate objective, he decided to bypass.

Leading his exhausted troops deeper into the Italians' vulnerable rear area, he reached the mountain pass shortly thereafter. In just 52 hours, Rommel's force had captured 150 Italian officers, 9,000 soldiers, and 81 heavy guns, while incurring casualties of 6 dead and 30 wounded.

Leadership Lessons

Rommel employed a top-down, bottom-up approach to targeting critical vulnerabilities, and his capture of the mountain pass illustrates the powerful psychological impact of this first guiding principle of maneuver warfare.

From the "top down," he was relentless in his pursuit of the mountain pass—the Italians' Achilles' heel—and he never lost sight of his ultimate objective. He pushed his heavily laden troops, each carrying an eighty-pound pack at high altitude, to their physical limits for fifty-two continuous hours and did not stop until his detachment captured the mountain pass. Importantly, knowing that capturing the pass would ensure victory, he made these extreme demands at the right time for the right reason.

From the "bottom up," he relied heavily on subordinates to lead him to his opponent's critical vulnerability. The identification of gaps in the Italians' defense—critical vulnerabilities at the subordinates' level—enabled him to move his forces through enemy lines with minimal contact and reach the mountain pass via the path of least resistance. Finally, once the Italians realized that they had been isolated from their supply lines, they began to believe that defeat was imminent and lost the will to continue fighting.

LOWE'S HARDWARE VS. HOME DEPOT

Not until a follow-on attempt did Lowe's successfully target the critical vulnerability of Home Depot in the U.S. retail home improvement market.

In the early 1980s, Lowe's attempted to compete head to head with Home Depot on the basis of price and failed; Home Depot's national presence and unmatched buying power rendered low price an unassailable strength. In recent years, however, Lowe's has redirected its efforts toward exploiting the seemingly invincible Home Depot's Achilles' heel—an apparent lack of user friendliness in its store format. As a result of this approach, Lowe's has emerged as, perhaps, the new market leader.

Home Depot founders Bernie Marcus and Arthur Blank long prided themselves on and even promoted the austere, warehouselike feel of their nationwide chain of home improvement retail superstores. This approach appealed to professional contractors and semiskilled craftsmen, and Home Depot's ability to offer low price and wide selection redefined the retail market for home improvement. But Home Depot failed to recognize and accommodate a shift in consumer preference as the U.S. housing market boomed in the late 1990s. Americans with little or no experience in home improvement began to undertake repairs and new construction on their own homes as professional contractors' services, in short supply, became prohibitively expensive.

In contrast to Home Depot's emphasis on catering to contractors and semiskilled craftsmen, Lowe's conducted and acted on market research that revealed that women initiated 80 percent of home improvement projects. Realizing that only 13 percent of its shoppers were women, Lowe's decided to target its own critical vulnerability: its inability to attract women who "were turned off by buying things 'in lumber shops.'"[3] It invested heavily in a "pleasurable shopping experience" and captured considerable market share from Home Depot as this new segment of nonprofessional do-it-yourselfers opted for the more user-friendly Lowe's format.

The stock market punished Home Depot's loss of sales to Lowe's, and the declining price per share of Home Depot stock produced a second-order effect—lower morale among employees. A large component of employee compensation at Home Depot was stock option–based, and a low share price meant that most of the employees' options fell "out of the money." Customer service declined with Home Depot's share price, further detracting from the incumbent's ability to provide a pleasurable shopping experience to the consumer. Said Sandy Cooper, a mother of four and formerly loyal customer of Home Depot, in 2002, "At Home Depot, you can't find anybody to help—and if you do, they just point."[4]

Leadership Lessons

Lowe's was both persistent and forward-looking in challenging Home Depot, and the success of this challenge underscores the powerful psychological impact of targeting critical vulnerabilities in the business environment. Lowe's was persistent in that its initial failure prompted it to regroup and reformulate a more creative, less defensible attack—based on an awareness of its own critical vulnerability—the second time. Lowe's was also forward-looking in that it identified Home Depot's critical vulnerability before it existed; thus it was well positioned to exploit the opportunity created by the market shift from professional contractor to do-it-yourselfer. Finally, just as the Italians lost the will to continue fighting at Isonzo once Rommel captured the mountain pass, many Home Depot employees lost the will to continue providing customer service at levels above and beyond the "call of duty" once the company's share price fell.

SHELL OIL: SCENARIO PLANNING

One could argue that targeting a critical vulnerability before it materializes—a major determinant of Lowe's success—might require clairvoyance and that imparting such a capability is extremely difficult. But Shell Oil's experiences suggest that scenario planning can be employed as a useful technique to identify not only your own critical vulnerabilities but also those of your rivals, before they are aware that they have them.

Scenario planning starts by deriving a set of strategic uncertainties, things that are both highly uncertain and highly significant. The values taken on by those uncertainties determine a set of potential outcomes and the conditions that generate them. Since they are uncertain, and since you cannot know how they will evolve or what their values are, you assume both extreme values for them and evaluate how the different combinations of these extreme values define different scenarios. Once you have defined your scenarios, you assume in sequence that each one will be the one true future, and you explore what the world would look like if this were indeed your future prediction. Then you plan, practice, and prepare for each scenario, just as you would if the condition were indeed going to develop.

Shell Oil pioneered the corporate use of scenario planning in the late 1960s to examine drastic, unexpected changes in the international oil market that could not be predicted through simple extrapolation of historical trends. When oil prices had been stable at less than $4 per barrel, Shell, unlike its many counterparts, was most interested in the seemingly improbable events that could restrict supply to the Western world and cause prices to soar to $40 per barrel. It was less interested in optimizing the allocation of crude supplies among refineries and pricing for distilled products based on $1- to $2-per-barrel fluctuations in the price of crude.

Shell's scenario-planning efforts addressed such contingencies as crises in the Middle East that could disrupt the flow of oil to the West and the emergence of regimes hostile to Western interests in the oil-producing nations most important to Shell. Shell was therefore able to identify its own critical vulnerability in 1972 and proactively prepare for what would have otherwise been a catastrophic event—the loss of oil supplies from Iran, Libya, and Algeria.

When these supplies were actually interrupted in the years between 1979 and 1981, the flow of oil—and profitability—continued without serious interruption. As a result of its extensive scenario-planning efforts, Shell had right-sized its fleet of oil tankers relative to the reduced flow of crude from the Middle East. And it had built a flexible and effective oil-trading operation that replaced the lost supplies with long-term forward contracts under which it prepurchased large quantities of oil at "locked in" prices.[5]

Leadership Lessons

Instead of trying to reason from history and data to predict what will happen in a "perfect world," scenario analysis uses intuition, experience, and introspection to delimit the range of things that might happen in a rapidly changing and disordered reality. This range of outcomes can, in turn, be analyzed and understood to identify critical vulnerabilities.

Shell used scenario analysis to identify its own critical vulnerability, but it could very easily have used scenario analysis to identify competitors' critical vulnerabilities or key customer needs that were not being served. Moreover, Shell moved quickly to act on its scenario-planning efforts, even though the scenarios identified were neither immediate nor certain, and subsequently successfully protected its own critical vulnerability.

BATTLE OF PETERSBURG

The Battle of Petersburg from the American Civil War serves as a vivid example of how sluggishness, poor planning, and indecision can cause a fleeting critical vulnerability to become a missed opportunity.

In mid-1864, Robert E. Lee's beleaguered Army of Northern Virginia built five miles of interlocked trenches and heavily fortified, sprawling earthworks to defend the city of Petersburg against the well-supplied, much larger Union Army. After numerous unsuccessful attacks and heavy casualties, a Union volunteer infantry unit composed primarily of coal miners, the 48th Pennsylvania, developed a plan to create a critical vulnerability in the Confederates' formidable defense.

Working around the clock, the 48th dug a five-hundred-foot mine shaft under the center of the Confederate lines, loaded it with eight thousand pounds of explosives,[6] and blew a hole, thirty feet deep, seventy feet wide, and two hundred feet long, in the center of the Confederate lines. The blast eliminated the Confederates' primary line of defense, destroyed many heavy guns, and buried men alive. The already-shorthanded Confederates were suddenly vulnerable at the most critical point in their defense.

But poor planning, weak leadership, and disorganized execution delayed the Union exploitation of this newly created gap. First, poorly devised Union attack plans failed to account for the need to remove the obstacles in front of the Union's own trenches, which slowed the advance of Union troops. Second, command of the attacking force was assigned to Brigadier General James Ledlie, who was reportedly drunk at the time of the attack and caught hiding in a bunker. Third, the effect of the blast was so devastating that many of the attacking Union forces were left in shock. Some stopped to help dig out their enemy counterparts who were buried alive; others simply turned and ran back to their own lines.

This delay afforded the shocked Confederates precious time to regroup, reconstitute, and bolster their shattered defense. Orienting all remaining firepower on the crater and relocating reserve cannons from other parts of the line, the defenders devastated the jumbled mass of Union soldiers attempting to breach the gap in their line. Within hours the Union, which had experienced nearly four thousand casualties, called off the attack.

Leadership Lessons

Petersburg was the last line of defense between the Union Army and the Confederate capital of Richmond. The men of the 48th Pennsylvania formulated a clever plan to crack the Confederate defense, and a timely passage through the crater would have paved the way to Richmond for the nearly-seventy-thousand-strong Union force sitting in reserve. But Union leaders failed to formulate and execute a clear, swift, and seamless plan that minimized the lag time between identification and exploitation of the Confederates' critical vulnerability and, thus, missed an ideal opportunity to end the war seven or eight months early. Again, breakthrough, the breaching of a line of defense, must be followed by breakout—follow-on efforts to exploit the initial breakthrough—and this will occur only if forces are marshaled rapidly to exploit initial success.

ANALYSIS ACROSS EXAMPLES

Taken as a whole, the examples raised to illustrate this first guiding principle of maneuver warfare offer several key insights. First, the two military examples, Rommel at Isonzo and the Battle of Petersburg, show that the process of targeting critical vulnerabilities is not only top-down but also bottom-up: in both instances subordinates led commanders to the opponent's critical vulnerability. Second, Rommel's use of the path of least resistance to reach the mountain pass shows that gaps in an opponent's defense often lead to critical vulnerabilities. Third, the Union's hesitation at Petersburg suggests that without action and, indeed, rapid action, the identification of an opponent's critical vulnerability is wasted brilliance. Fourth, Shell's success suggests that scenario planning can be an excellent technique to emulate Lowe's "clairvoyance"—targeting critical vulnerabilities before opponents become aware of them and take corrective action. Finally, Rommel's decision to attack around the ambush his force walked into, and Lowe's success against Home Depot after initial failure, emphasize the importance of persistence: when they hit a wall, they went around it.

TARGETING CRITICAL VULNERABILITIES . . . THE MARINE CORPS WAY

A top-down, bottom-up approach to identifying and exploiting critical vulnerabilities pervades the U.S. Marine Corps. All Marines, from the front line to the highest headquarters, incessantly search for rivals' Achilles' heels. And the Marines masterfully balance this outward focus with a rigorous introspection intended to safeguard their own critical vulnerabilities. These practices can serve you as a useful guide to targeting critical vulnerabilities in the business environment.

Leading from the Front

Leading from the front enables Marine leaders to observe firsthand unfolding events and possibly discover opponents' critical vulnerabilities in real time. During offensive maneuvers, Marine officers locate themselves at the front of the tactical formation—as close to the action as possible, without crowding junior leaders or losing sight of the "big picture."

Leading by Walking Around

Leadership by walking around creates invaluable opportunities to leverage the insights of those closest to the action to identify critical vulnerabilities. These firsthand observations can either lead directly to critical vulnerabilities or serve as partial information that can be compiled and synthesized—pieces of a larger "puzzle." In static defensive positions, Marine leaders visit fighting holes and machine gun emplacements to ensure that fields of fire overlap and that fighting holes support one another. When units return to base from field maneuvers, leaders visit the vehicle lot, the communications hut, and the armory to check on weapons and equipment. Whether in the field or in garrison, these visits enable leaders to interact with their Marines, solicit their ideas, and learn from their observations. Some senior commanders go as far as to check the soles of their junior leaders' boots to ensure that they have been "putting in the miles." While leaders cannot really notice if the soles have been worn, this policy reinforces the importance of getting away from the desk and walking around to spend time with their Marines.

Reconnaissance, Intelligence, and War Games

Reconnaissance activities range from sending a small patrol forward of an infantry platoon in the field to the deployment of highly skilled scouts, known as "Recon" Marines, deep behind enemy lines. The aim of these activities is to determine the location and disposition of enemy forces, probe enemy defenses, and, most important, discover weaknesses. Intelligence is the synthesis of raw information, such as satellite imagery, tips from informants, and reports from units dispersed throughout the battlefield, gathered about the enemy or surrounding environment to provide the commander with a relevant and timely picture of the battlefield. War games prepare Marines for even the most unlikely future scenarios well before they occur. Commanders may gather around a map or sand table diorama of the battlefield to rehearse their plans, debate possible enemy reactions, and then refine their plans in light of potential outcomes. This process often reveals shortcomings in their own plans or, even better, an opponent's critical vulnerabilities.

Bias for Action

Marine leaders orient those in their charge on the enemy's fundamental weaknesses and constantly demand action. Near the beginning of every tactical plan, commanders communicate a description of enemy critical vulnerabilities, and from the early days of boot camp and officer training, all Marines are ingrained with a bias for action. Marines hear the venerable "no plan ever won a battle" and "a plan executed poorly today is almost always better than a plan executed perfectly tomorrow"[7] throughout their careers. As newly minted officers "cut their teeth" during leadership assignments in initial field training, they frequently hear "What are you going to do *now*, lieutenant?" In frontline units, Marines push one another to deliver results, not excuses. The sum total of these practices concentrates the energies of highly determined Marines on an enemy's greatest weaknesses.

Rigorous Introspection

Marines balance this determined outward focus with an acute awareness that their opponents could be doing the same to them, and they are as diligent as time and battle conditions permit in their efforts to protect their own critical vulnerabilities. Indeed, the adoption of maneuver warfare in the 1980s as a means to "do more with less" was a direct result of this rigorous introspection.

APPLICATION IN BUSINESS

You can employ all of these practices in your organization to target rivals' critical vulnerabilities. Do not sit idly in the "ivory tower" that is your office. Visit the disparate parts of your organization and solicit the insights of your people on a regular basis. All too often what you learn is valuable, time-critical, and surprising. With practice your team will learn to share information without constant probing and prodding.

Reconnaissance, intelligence, and war games have their counterparts in the business environment: *market study*, *environmental scan*, and *scenario planning*. A market study can be anything from a discussion with a frontline employee or salesperson to learn from his or her firsthand observations to a brief survey intended to understand recent events and trends. An environmental scan interprets data gathered from deliberate research efforts and product reengineering to answer questions such as "What features do their products have that ours do not?" and identify existing opportunities. Finally, as we saw earlier in the chapter, business leaders can employ scenario planning to identify, prepare for, and practice in several futures and identify critical vulnerabilities before they appear.

Use your sales force as your "reconnaissance unit" to act as your eyes and ears and monitor your customers as well as your competitors. Meet with them as often as possible to keep your finger on the pulse of evolving customer preferences. Rely on your operations planning arm as your "intelligence unit" to synthesize information and build longer-term plans to exploit rivals' critical vulnerabilities. Conduct scenario analysis—war games—at all levels of management to prepare your organization for success in an unpredictable future. Focus your organization's energy outward on rivals' critical vulnerabilities through constant reminders and quiz your people to emphasize the importance of these reminders. When you identify a critical vulnerability, act as quickly as possible to exploit it, and if you hit a wall, go around that wall. Finally, periodically step outside of your own organization and examine every aspect of your business from the perspective of your competitors to prevent your own critical vulnerabilities from being targeted.

CHAPTER 5

BOLDNESS

"Touch a thistle timidly, and it pricks you; grasp it boldly, and its spines crumble. Carry the battle to the enemy! Lay your ship alongside his!"
—ADMIRAL WILLIAM "BULL" HALSEY[1]

Boldness is the daring to commit resources to endeavors with uncertain, even highly uncertain, outcomes to achieve breakthrough results and, in some instances, "blow open" frozen situations.

Such commitments usually entail considerable risk. While informed estimates of the costs and benefits of capturing, maintaining, or defending a position can mitigate this risk, sometimes the data are insufficient to make an estimate, or the information that does exist may suggest a cautious approach. Nevertheless, when the potential benefits are sufficiently high, the practitioner of maneuver warfare must be willing to take action despite data that are inconclusive or downright discouraging. What keeps this risk-seeking behavior from becoming recklessness is the thoughtful weighing of risk and reward.

In this chapter we offer five historical examples of boldness and its key components, as well as present-day lessons from the Marines. General Douglas MacArthur's amphibious landing at Inchon in 1950 during the Korean War and Lou Gerstner's successful turnaround at IBM in the early 1990s illustrate boldness in warfare and in business. From the American Civil War's best-known battle, Gettysburg, Union colonel Joshua Chamberlain's stand at Little Round Top and Confederate general George Pickett's infamous charge serve as contrasting examples of how to and how not to weigh the risks and rewards associated with acting boldly. And from business the launches of Victory Brewing Company's HopDevil India Pale Ale and Lager serve as similarly contrasting examples of how to and how not to commit resources to a new market. Finally, Warren Buffett's reluctance to invest in the technology "bubble" of the late 1990s shows that boldness sometimes requires the steely resolve to abstain from an uncertain and potentially undesirable situation.

The Marines' creation of a culture that encourages self-confidence and decisiveness can serve as a useful guide to fostering a propensity for boldness among the members of your organization. To this end our intent in this chapter is to use their experiences and some of the lessons learned from our historical examples to suggest ways in which you can use a *risk-reward trade-off* framework to increase your propensity to make bold decisions, train your people to make decisions and act in the absence of complete information, and reinforce and reward risk taking, both successful and unsuccessful, at all levels in your organization.

MACARTHUR AT INCHON

MacArthur's amphibious assault at Inchon during the Korean War in 1950 is widely regarded as one of the boldest attacks in modern military history. MacArthur himself even acknowledged, with typical bravado and embellishment, "I realize this is a 5,000 to 1 gamble, but I am used to taking such odds."[2] But this risky move was well rewarded: the successful landing at Inchon led to the capture of Seoul and isolation of North Korean forces to the South, thereby dramatically altering the momentum of the war.

By September 1950, the North Koreans had pushed the U.N. forces to the southern tip of the Korean peninsula, in what became known as the Pusan Perimeter. With the harsh Korean winter looming, MacArthur knew that he had little time to make a deep and decisive blow to break this static front. He chose Inchon, a port city on Korea's western coast, because it offered a direct route to Seoul and because it was the worst possible, and therefore least defended, location for an amphibious landing.

A landing at Inchon would be possible on only one day during the month of September—the 15th. On this day the tides, which varied by as much as thirty-one feet, would reach their extreme highs for three hours

Figure 5.1 MACARTHUR'S AMPHIBIOUS ASSAULT, 1950

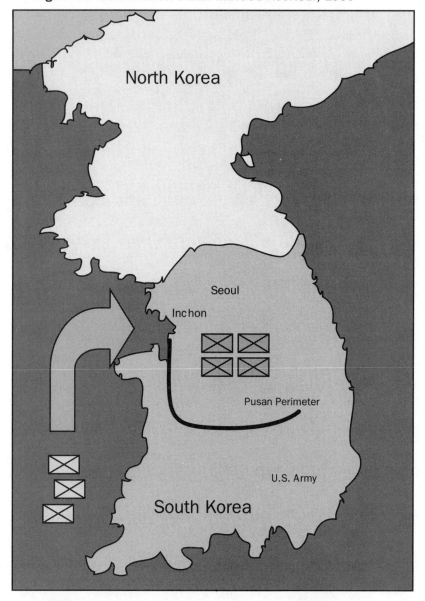

in the early morning and three hours in the late afternoon. A failure to land during these narrow windows of opportunity would leave the U.N. forces stranded helplessly on Inchon's unforgiving mudflats and exposed to enemy fire. Further complicating the landing, the narrowness of the channel would force a two-stage landing, completely eliminating the element of surprise. Finally, upon reaching the shore, the landing force would have to scale, one by one with makeshift ladders, an imposing seawall.

MacArthur faced stiff opposition from his Army, Navy, and Marine Corps counterparts in the Korean theater and from the joint chiefs of staff and political forces in the United States. Despite his history of success and his reputation for avoiding unnecessary risks, MacArthur's detractors saw Inchon as too risky and therefore advocated landing on a beach that didn't offer "nearly every natural and geographic handicap."[3] But MacArthur was steadfast in his commitment to his scheme of maneuver, which embraced these handicaps in an effort to avoid a landing opposed by strong and entrenched enemy forces. Building a brilliant invasion plan and meticulously backing it with ample tactical facts, he systematically persuaded skeptics, even President Truman, and ultimately achieved the consensus he needed.

MacArthur made every possible effort to stack the odds in his favor. Preparing for the difficult assault was no exception. To minimize uncertainties surrounding the challenge that lay before him, he assembled a team of oceanographers, cartographers, intelligence agents, and even scout swimmers that reconnoitered the Inchon Harbor a week before the invasion. As a result of the efforts of this diverse team, MacArthur knew the exact timing and duration of the tides, the location of all natural underwater obstacles, the layout and composition of the beaches, the height of the seawall (five to eight feet), the width of the channel and landing areas, the location and disposition of enemy forces at Inchon, and how long enemy reinforcements would take to arrive.

On the morning of September 15, nearly three hundred ships in the Pacific, including Japanese and American merchant ships, were pressed into service to support the seventy-thousand-strong invasion force. At 6:30 A.M., the initial assault force of U.S. Marines landed successfully and captured Wolmi-Do, the small but well-fortified island at the mouth of Inchon Harbor. The Marines held Wolmi-Do for the remainder of the day until a second wave of U.S. Marines, the main assault force, hit the beach at about

Figure 5.2 LANDING AND ATTACK AT INCHON HARBOR, SEPTEMBER 15, 1950

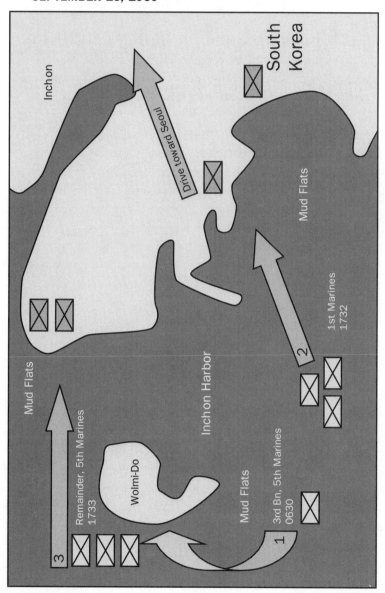

5:30 P.M. By midnight the landing force had moved inland and secured Inchon, at a cost of 22 killed and 174 wounded—far less than anyone had expected.[4]

With Inchon secured, MacArthur dispatched a giant follow-on force through the opening created by the Marines and pressed on to Seoul. Within two weeks he captured Seoul, severed the North Koreans' logistical and communications lines, and cracked the Pusan Perimeter.

Leadership Lessons

MacArthur's brilliant plan and masterful execution exemplify boldness on four counts. First, he had the courage to stand behind his convictions in the face of considerable organizational resistance and eventually managed to convince opponents of the invasion to support his plan. Second, he identified a breakthrough opportunity and acted decisively to turn it into a breakout gain. Third, his exhaustive planning efforts mitigated many of the risks associated with the huge gamble he was taking, thereby creating a more favorable risk-reward profile. Finally, the indirect attack on the North Koreans at Inchon unfroze the static front to the south at the Pusan Perimeter.

GERSTNER AT IBM

In 1993, Lou Gerstner assumed the formidable challenge of reversing the decline of computer maker IBM. Boldly basing his turnaround plan on anecdotal evidence and intuition rather than exhaustive analytical data, he successfully refocused and reinvigorated the massive company in a mere four years.

IBM was stagnating in the early 1990s. Technology players and pundits alike dismissed the mainframe computer as irrelevant in the disaggregated world of networked computing, and IBM was falling behind in the desktop revolution. Competitors such as Compaq, Dell, and NEC took over market-share leadership in the personal computer (PC) market that IBM had created, while server vendors such as Sun, DEC, and Hewlett Packard cut deeply into IBM's once-indomitable server market. Similarly, competitors such as Microsoft, Computer Associates, and Oracle controlled the enormously profitable market for software that IBM had helped to build. Nothing IBM did, with its own hardware, software, operating system, or database query languages, seemed adequate to break through the commanding position that this new generation of PC makers and software vendors enjoyed.

Beyond these technology-related challenges, relationships with customers had deteriorated. Gerstner's predecessor had initiated efforts to reorganize the company into thirteen parts. The workforce needed to be reduced drastically. Owing to a high debt burden, the company's credit rating was declining. Gerstner himself even remarked, "It just looked like it was going into a death spiral. I was not convinced it was solvable."[5]

Gerstner's original plan was to leverage IBM's services capabilities to sell more hardware and software. However, in discussions with customers, he kept hearing that large corporations still wanted a specialized outsider to formulate their technology strategies and build and operate their complex networked systems. Accordingly, he changed his plan on the fly. He abandoned efforts to turn around the company by competing directly against competitors' strengths and, instead, bet IBM's future viability on the interaction between its mainframes and services businesses—a decision that defied prevailing industry consensus.

Under Gerstner's watch, IBM invested heavily to overhaul and revive its line of mainframes, which he believed would still be necessary to tie networks together in much the same manner that servers did. And he leveraged IBM's customer relationships and well-recognized brand to expand the company's presence in higher-margin, value-added services. Both decisions were widely perceived as ill advised at the time, since industry experts believed that the demand for mainframe technology would never recover and that IBM could never compete in information technology (IT) services against established firms. Nonetheless, by late 1996, the sales of new mainframes were booming, IT services had become IBM's biggest growth business, and Gerstner was widely heralded as Big Blue's savior.

Leadership Lessons

Gerstner's confidence, decisiveness, and flexibility drove the turnaround of IBM. Owing to his conversations with key customers, Gerstner was not afraid to trust his intuition and defy the "groupthink" that pervaded IBM and the technology industry in general. As decisive as he was defiant, Gerstner made almost all of his most important decisions within ninety days of his arrival. Willing to deviate from his original plan, he listened to the insights of key customers and incorporated those insights thereby increasing the likelihood of a successful turnaround. Finally, the sum total of these efforts enabled Gerstner to unfreeze a static front: by reorienting IBM's strategic focus on mainframes and IT services, he was able to circumvent the entrenched positions of PC makers and software vendors that had stymied previous turnaround efforts.

CHAMBERLAIN AND PICKETT AT GETTYSBURG

Colonel Joshua Chamberlain's defense of Little Round Top and Major General George Pickett's charge on Cemetery Ridge, which occurred within just twenty-four hours of each other during the Battle of Gettysburg in 1863, could not be further apart in illustrating the appropriate weighing of risk and reward. Chamberlain's stand prevented the collapse of the Union line. Pickett's tragic charge was what historians often call the High Water Mark of the Confederacy—the last time the South would be a viable threat to the Union.

Chamberlain

Chamberlain's 20th Maine Regiment guarded the extreme left flank of the Union line during the Battle of Gettysburg. Greatly outnumbered by the attacking Confederates and relatively inexperienced, the 20th Maine repulsed several attacks on July 2, 1863, and denied the enemy the exposed Union flank on the rocky hill known as Little Round Top. Holding this hill was a strategic necessity for the North, as it anchored the Union line. Taking Little Round Top would have enabled Confederate forces to attack the exposed flank of the Union line. Losing the hill would have been disastrous for the Union.

By late afternoon of July 2, the 20th Maine had suffered heavy casualties, and ammunition was dwindling. Expecting yet another onslaught of Confederate troops, Chamberlain steadfastly ordered his men to "hold fire," then "fix bayonets," and, at the last second, "charge!" His motivated men formed a line and charged down the hill headlong into the advancing Confederate force. Chamberlain's bold plan risked his entire unit, and casualties were high—one-third of the remaining regiment. But the 20th Maine shattered the Confederate advance and altered the course of battle in the Union's favor.

Figure 5.3 CHAMBERLAIN AT GETTYSBURG, JULY 2, 1863

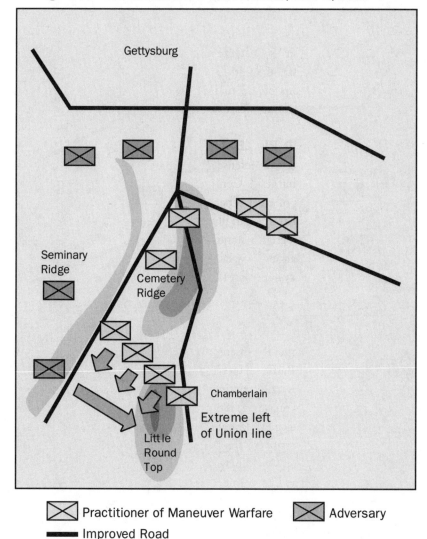

Practitioner of Maneuver Warfare   Adversary

Improved Road

Pickett

On the eve of July 3, General Robert E. Lee was exasperated after two days of unproductive sparring intended to break the Union defensive front. He therefore devised a grandiose plan to send Pickett's division en masse across an open field to strike the center of the Union line, high atop an expanse

Figure 5.4 PICKETT'S CHARGE, JULY 3, 1863

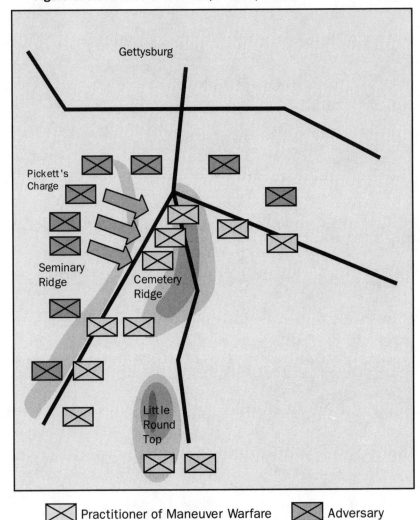

known as Cemetery Ridge. Many Confederate leaders considered the plan suicidal. Lieutenant General James Longstreet, Pickett's direct superior, pleaded with Lee, "General, I have been a soldier all my life. I have been with soldiers engaged in fights by couples, by squads, companies, regiments, divisions, and armies, and should know as well as anyone what soldiers can do. It is my opinion that no 15,000 men ever arrayed for battle can take that position."[6]

Despite Longstreet's misgivings, on July 3 Lee decided to press onward with the attack—with no credible exploitation plan should Pickett succeed. At 1:00 P.M., Pickett led his division on the fateful charge. Fully exposed to the enemy in the open grassy field through which they marched in the attack, Pickett's men faced devastating enemy fire from multiple angles and were cut down by brutal Union cannonade and sniper fire. After two hours Pickett ordered retreat and returned to the bottom of the hill to report to General Lee—with 10,000 fewer men than he had had at the outset. Immediately following the battle, Lee accepted complete blame for the disaster: "Come, General Pickett, this has been my fight, and the blame rests on my shoulders."[7] The slaughter cost Lee nearly one-third of his army, leaving him in no position to attack again and forcing him to retreat quietly across the Mason-Dixon line, never to threaten northern soil again.

Leadership Lessons

Chamberlain's decision to "fix bayonets" serves as an excellent example of a judicious risk-reward trade-off. The risk of losing most—if not all—of his remaining men had to be taken to deny the enemy access to the highly strategic Union flank. The entire Union line could have been "rolled up" from the commanding position provided by Little Round Top; instead, Chamberlain's embattled regiment turned the tide of the battle.

In contrast, even if Pickett had managed to defy the odds and take Cemetery Ridge, Confederate forces were not positioned to exploit the opening before the massive Union Army could close off the gap. There would have been no gain commensurate with the risks that Lee and Pickett were assuming. Thus Lee's acceptance of risk—the loss of an entire division in the face of insurmountable odds and with little potential gain— is a puzzling but clear example of a poor risk-reward trade-off. It is also an example of how not to unfreeze a static front: Pickett's force shattered when it was hurled headlong into the Union defensive line.

VICTORY BEER

Tiny microbrewery Victory Brewing Company is an interesting study in contrasts: its bold, brash HopDevil India Pale Ale has been wildly successful, while its safer, more mainstream Lager has not.

As at any other microbrewery, total annual production at Victory amounts to no more than a single eight-hour shift at Budweiser, and total annual sales are less than .5 percent of Budweiser's advertising budget. Rather than attempt to challenge Budweiser and other deep-pocketed industry heavyweights head-on, Victory's founder and president, Bill Covaleski, and his partner and brewmaster, Ron Barchet, chose the unique strategy of making beers that were intensely flavorful and different from anything else in the marketplace. They bet the success of the company on a number of unproven assumptions: that there existed a sufficiently large future market demand for such beers, that they could identify the demands of this market, and that their beers would not only create demand in this expected market but also sell at a premium price.

HopDevil

One of the beers in Victory's initial introduction in 1996 was HopDevil. Rated at close to 70 on the International Bittering Unit scale of beer bitterness, HopDevil is five times more bitter than and almost twice as expensive—$24 per case—as mass-marketed American standard beers, such as Budweiser. Consumers are seldom indifferent to this distinctive brew; they either love it or hate it. Those who love HopDevil buy it, praise it, recommend it, and accomplish through word of mouth what the company cannot afford to do through paid advertising: create a cult following among a select group of beer drinkers with a high willingness to pay.

Lager

Providing an interesting contrast is Victory's Lager, which Covaleski and Barchet launched concurrently with HopDevil. The Lager was formulated as a fine beer, light in color and made with the best possible ingredients. As similar to traditional American lagers like Bud and Miller as a super-premium beer could be, Covaleski and Barchet expected it to be an immediate, albeit somewhat modest, success. Unlike HopDevil, no one hated the Lager; at the same time, no one loved it, which created a problem for Victory.

While sales of HopDevil have grown approximately 40 percent per year for the last seven years and now represent over half of total sales at Victory, the Lager has been a marketplace failure.

Leadership Lessons

Victory is a story of two beers launched at the same time by the same company with dramatically different outcomes. The launch of HopDevil embraced risk and made a full commitment to capturing a market segment necessary for survival; the apparently safer Lager failed to stand out in the eyes of beer drinkers. Victory's experience suggests an interesting paradox: for a small player, boldness may very well be essential, and in many instances being conservative may prove to be an unsafe strategy.

WARREN BUFFETT'S STEELY RESOLVE

Warren Buffett's refusal to "follow the lemmings over the edge of the cliff" during the height of U.S. stock market frenzy in the late 1990s offers a simple yet powerful lesson about boldness: sometimes discretion is the better part of valor.

As valuations in equities markets skyrocketed, business reporters chastised Buffett, chairman and CEO of Berkshire Hathaway, from all angles for not investing in high-flying technology and telecommunications stocks. *Time* magazine published an article touting "The Fall of Buffett" and accused him of being out of synch with technology stocks.[8] Assaults on his value-oriented approach likewise came from overseas: the *Sunday Times* of London went so far as to suggest that Buffett break up Berkshire Hathaway, claiming it looked like "a fish out of water" in the online new economy.[9]

Weighing the potential rewards that the skyrocketing markets offered against the risk of an inability to exit a richly valued position, Buffett decided the trade-off was undesirable. In the face of mounting criticism and a lagging Berkshire Hathaway share price, he resolutely adhered to his tried-and-true method of investing in companies that he understood, that generated positive cash flow, that enjoyed strong brand recognition, and that commanded respect from consumers and the general investing public.

After the "tech bubble" burst in late 2000 to early 2001, the very same business reporters began to laud Buffett for his "steel nerves" and principled investing approach. Instead of suggesting his demise, the *Sunday Times* published an article titled "How to Be a Successful Investor,"[10] which highlighted Buffett's shrewd investment style as a model to be emulated. *Fortune* magazine proclaimed, "the world's greatest investor is back on top."[11] And in July 2002, Buffett even went so far as to add a "new economy" company to his portfolio. He led a consortium that invested $500 million in Level 3, a beleaguered telecommunications service provider with a high-quality fiber optics network.[12] At the time of his investment, Level 3's shares were priced at 3.3 percent of their calendar-year-2000 high.[13] At the time of writing the shares were priced at 5.3 percent of the same high, an appreciation of almost 60 percent.[14]

Leadership Lessons

A self-admitted "technophobe," Buffett knew his limitations and resisted temptation amid widespread euphoria. When asked in 2002 if accusations of being a "has-been" bothered him, he replied, "Never . . . You can't do well in investments unless you think independently. And the truth is, you're neither right nor wrong because people agree with you. You're right because your facts and your reasoning are right. In the end, that's all that counts." After the bubble burst, Buffett was rewarded for this independence of mind and self-assuredness with an almost unfettered ability to capitalize on distressed valuations as "the buyer [of companies] who can come up with cash over a weekend."[15]

ANALYSIS ACROSS EXAMPLES

Even more compelling than the commonalities among the experiences of MacArthur, Gerstner, Chamberlain and Pickett, Victory's HopDevil and Lager, and Buffett are the differences. MacArthur, Chamberlain, and Buffett all made appropriate, perhaps even brilliant, risk-reward trade-offs, but Lee's inexplicable decision to risk a division without either a high probability of success or a plan in place for the rapid exploitation of victory underscores the fine line between boldness and tragic desperation. Furthermore, MacArthur, Gerstner, Chamberlain, and the HopDevil launch all represent full commitments to the right strategy and commensurate benefits, whereas Pickett and Lager failed because Lee fully committed to the wrong strategy and because Lager was not a bold enough product offering. Finally, MacArthur and Gerstner illustrate successful efforts to unfreeze a static front, whereas Pickett illustrates a failed effort.

Of the three "maestros," MacArthur, Gerstner, and Buffett, only MacArthur made a deliberate effort, in the form of exhaustive, meticulous planning and information gathering, to mitigate the risks associated with his plan; Gerstner and Buffett relied on their intuition. And, of the three, Gerstner was the most flexible; his genius was his willingness to alter his plan radically on the fly as conditions changed. Buffett altered his plan, but only after a long observation period, and MacArthur adhered closely to his plan through changing conditions.

BOLDNESS . . . THE MARINE CORPS WAY

Marines view boldness as a "force multiplier," and they have created a culture that encourages, at all levels, this second guiding principle of maneuver warfare. They train their junior leaders to make decisions in the face of limited information and exercise initiative with confidence. They foster an *obligation to dissent* in the decision-making process. They tolerate mistakes—except in the cases of indecision, timidity, or lapses in integrity—and even go so far as to celebrate well-intended failure. Finally, they rely on bold action as a default when all else fails. These practices can serve you as a useful guide to fostering a propensity toward boldness among the members of your organization.

80 Percent Rule

Marines train their junior leaders to rely on the 80 Percent Rule, which states that delaying any decision so that it can be made with more than 80 percent of the necessary information is hesitation. Throughout initial training, newly minted officers are repeatedly placed in situations intentionally designed to deprive them of the full information needed to make a comfortable decision. For example, lieutenants go through an urban combat training exercise in a mock town (the FBI's "Hogan's Alley") where they have to deal with hostile "locals" and rioting crowds. The lieutenants, who have no idea what to expect and no clarity as to who is friend and who is foe, are expected to make decisions and act on limited information. Initially the individual might be nearly paralyzed when faced with such a situation, but over time he or she becomes increasingly willing to decide and increasingly able to act in the face of limited information.

Obligation to Dissent, Part I

The Marine Corps's traditional hierarchical nature does not preclude commanders from encouraging those in their charge to "speak up" during the formation of tactical plans and suggest superior courses of action. This obligation to dissent not only leverages the insights of lower-ranking and sometimes more experienced members, notably senior enlisted staff noncommissioned officers, but also signals that juniors have the latitude to form their own viewpoints and take the appropriate risks to act on those viewpoints.

Acceptance of Certain Mistakes

Marines acknowledge that boldness sacrifices precision in execution and therefore reject the dreaded "zero defect" mentality. Leaders correct, rather than punish, mistakes that stem from bold zeal, such as an inexperienced lieutenant charging off and leading his unit in the wrong direction during a night training exercise. At the same time, there is zero tolerance for indecision, lapses in integrity, and, above all, weakness—all of which can be career-ending.

Toilet Seat Awards

Marines celebrate failure almost as much as they celebrate success. Obviously, Marines receive formal awards, such as medals and letters of commendation and praise for noteworthy accomplishments in front of their peers. But one Marine commander sponsors in his organization the unique practice of handing out a monthly "toilet seat award" to the junior Marine who shows the most initiative in an endeavor with an unsuccessful outcome. The commander's Marines consider receiving the toilet seat a special honor, second only to receiving an actual medal or other form of official commendation. This form of dubious distinction reinforces ingenuity, action, and the willingness to take a chance.

The Default

Finally, when all of these practices fail to deliver breakout results, Marines learn that *it is better to beg for forgiveness than ask for permission.*

APPLICATION IN BUSINESS

You can emulate the Marines' practices to encourage boldness in your organization. During training, devise creative ways to place your people in controlled situations of uncertainty and force them to make decisions; as a result of such "practice," they will become more comfortable exercising initiative in actual uncertain situations. Encourage your people to speak up during the planning process and challenge well-laid plans with thoughtful and well-supported suggestions for improvement. Forming an independent viewpoint and challenging consensus requires considerable courage of conviction, and success in this endeavor will undoubtedly build a junior's confidence. Understand that an increased incidence of risk taking in your organization will inevitably result in a higher prevalence of mistakes; correct "honest" mistakes as quickly as possible and punish inexcusable mistakes, such as indecision, timidity, or lapses in integrity, ruthlessly. And recognize and reward both the successes and failures resulting from bold actions.

Above all, remember that boldness requires calculated risk taking: appropriately weighing risk and reward so that you avoid reckless behavior in your pursuit of breakthrough results. The following relationship will serve you well every time you evaluate a potential course of action:

$$\left(\begin{array}{c}\text{Probability} \\ \text{of} \\ \text{success}\end{array} \times \begin{array}{c}\text{Potential} \\ \text{results} \\ \text{from success}\end{array}\right) - \left(\begin{array}{c}\text{Probability} \\ \text{of} \\ \text{failure}\end{array} \times \begin{array}{c}\text{Potential} \\ \text{cost of} \\ \text{failure}\end{array}\right) = \begin{array}{c}\text{Expected} \\ \text{value of} \\ \text{outcome}\end{array}$$

The relationship itself is relatively straightforward, but the inputs themselves require considerable thought. Your experience will guide you in your estimates of these inputs, but also remember to leverage the expertise of the people with whom you work to refine your estimates and identify any considerations you overlooked. Other key factors to weigh are time to completion of the challenge at hand, the magnitude of your potential upside versus that of your downside, your ability to exit safely if events do not unfold favorably, and the cost of exiting the course of action if necessary.

When weighing risk and reward, remember to be patient and disciplined; wait for the opportune time to commit resources to decision, and, no matter how exciting the opportunity, always ask yourself, "What's the downside?" Be sure you have clear objectives and clear measures of success to quantify your outcome. If resource-constrained, pick your battles wisely. Manage the multitude of risk-reward trade-offs as a portfolio. Diversify your risk across your portfolio of risk-reward trade-offs; always pursue a handful of high-reward/low-probability breakout opportunities, but have more medium-reward/medium-probability opportunities and plenty of lower-reward/higher-probability opportunities in the queue as well. Finally, keep a journal of your past successful and failed risk-reward trade-offs to learn from your mistakes and accelerate your development as a calculated risk taker.

CHAPTER 6

SURPRISE

"Always mystify, mislead, and surprise the enemy, if possible."
—Lieutenant General Thomas J. "Stonewall" Jackson[1]

To achieve surprise, the practitioner of maneuver warfare must proactively take steps to degrade the quality of information available to the adversary. This multifaceted endeavor shapes the conditions that govern competitive encounters and creates an inequality in situational awareness, "the ability to determine the relevance of unfolding events."[2] Once the adversary's decision-making process and ability to deploy resources are impaired sufficiently, striking him in an unexpected manner can ensure that his response comes too late to be effective.

Surprise can be achieved using one of three approaches: stealth, ambiguity, or deception. *Stealth* "denies the enemy any knowledge of impending action."[3] Denying such critical information to the enemy minimizes or even eliminates the threat of retaliation by keeping rivals in a state of unawareness until sudden, unexpected action is taken. *Ambiguity*, "acting in such a way that the enemy does not know what to expect,"[4] involves sending an overt signal that confuses rivals and requires them to commit resources in a dispersed fashion to counter a number of potential combat scenarios. Attempting to prepare for every possible contingency spreads those resources so thin that the enemy becomes vulnerable on any number of fronts and the attacker can target the most attractive opportunity.

Deception, "convincing the enemy that we are going to do something other than what we are actually going to do,"[5] is designed to cause a rival to deploy resources inappropriately, in defense of a target removed from the actual point of attack. Such a signal can take the form of a deliberate release of misinformation or the more subtle form of distorted information left "on display," with the anticipation that the opposition will observe it.

In this chapter we offer six historical examples of the three means to achieving surprise as well as present-day lessons from the Marines. To illustrate stealth, we offer Sam Houston's attack on Mexican general Santa Anna during the Texas War for Independence in 1836 and PepsiCo's launch of Mountain Dew Code Red in 2001. To illustrate ambiguity, we describe the Coalition's attack in Operation Desert Storm in 1991 and Microsoft's strategy of offering across-the-board upgrades for new releases of its products. To illustrate deception, we recount Allied diversionary efforts during the Normandy invasion in World War II and Merrill Lynch's successful efforts to delay competitors' responses when it introduced its cash management account in the late 1970s.

The Marine Corps's recent articulation of and commitment to the concept of *information operations* can serve you as a useful guide to managing information to achieve surprise in the business environment. To this end our intent in this chapter is to use their experiences and some of the lessons learned from our historical examples to suggest ways in which you can safeguard critical company information, use the media and other available channels as means to influence the perceptions and behavior of competitors, and create teams within your organization that are directly responsible for information-centric activities.

SAM HOUSTON AT SAN JACINTO: STEALTH

On April 21, 1836, at the Battle of San Jacinto, General Sam Houston and his roughshod band of Texans used stealth to achieve a decisive victory over Santa Anna's Mexican Army and secure Texas's independence from Mexico.

Following a devastating defeat at the hands of Santa Anna at the Alamo on March 6, 1836, the Texan Army was beleaguered but hungry for vengeance. Given that he had only 783 men, most of whom were poorly equipped and without uniforms, Houston needed to choose the most opportune time and place to engage Santa Anna. That time and place came on April 20, on a small peninsula located a few miles from what would become Houston, Texas. Arriving shortly after their opponents, the Texans crossed the San Jacinto River and assembled in secrecy just three quarters of a mile to the north of the fifteen hundred Mexican soldiers. Noted Houston, "Our situation afforded us an opportunity of making the arrangements preparatory to the attack without exposing our designs to the enemy."[6]

Figure 6.1 SAM HOUSTON AT SAN JACINTO, 1836

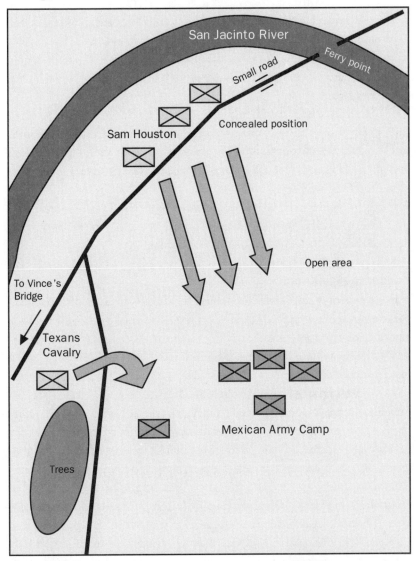

 Practitioner of Maneuver Warfare   Adversary

Houston knew he possessed the element of surprise and decided that a one-battle, winner-take-all strategy at San Jacinto was his best chance to win the War for Independence outright.[7] On the morning of April 21, he ordered his cavalry to destroy the only access to the marshy peninsula, Vince's Bridge, thereby isolating Santa Anna's army—and his own—on the peninsula.

At exactly 3:30 P.M., the invariable time of the Mexican siesta, Houston gave the order to attack. The Texans had to leave the cover of the stand of trees and march across a wide-open field, fully exposed to Mexican fire. To avoid signaling their approach, Houston's men held their fire until they were within arm's length of the sleeping Mexican army. Then crying, "Remember the Alamo! Remember Goliad!" the Texans opened fire at point-blank range.

The entire battle lasted only eighteen minutes; the Texans captured the 730 survivors and all of the Mexicans' equipment, weaponry, and livestock. Santa Anna, found in the woods not far from the battlefield, was brought to Houston. Knowing that his scattered forces were leaderless, disorganized, and helpless without him and fearing for his own life, Santa Anna diffidently agreed to withdraw his army from Texas. His surrender thus marked the birth of the Republic of Texas, and Sam Houston later became the independent republic's first president.

Leadership Lessons

The essence of stealth, which enabled the Texans to overcome resource constraints and emerge victorious, is to attack an enemy who does not see a need to defend himself. Like the Egyptian Air Force in 1967, Santa Anna knew that he was at war, but he did not expect the Texans to appear when or where they did.

By delaying action that would announce his intentions until the last possible moment, Houston caught the Mexicans off guard. Almost totally unprepared for the arrival of Houston's troops and in a position that they believed to be secure, the Mexicans were unable to respond, defend themselves, or mount a counterattack. Furthermore, Houston's ability to maintain silence among his vengeful troops is a testament to his strong leadership capabilities and their discipline. One early shot, one overzealous war cry by a Texan soldier could have announced the attack to the Mexicans and allowed them to prepare a defense, thereby resulting in an entirely different outcome—a slaughter of Houston and his men in the open field they had to cross. Finally, Santa Anna's inability to imagine that his weaker opponent would have the audacity to mount a "winner-take-all" attack made Houston's attack considerably more difficult to detect.

PEPSI: THE "CODE RED" STEALTH LAUNCH

In the long-waged cola wars between market giants PepsiCo and Coca-Cola, Pepsi used stealth in 2001 to introduce its Mountain Dew Code Red soft drink to its target market while camouflaging its intentions from its rivals.

Carbonated beverages were losing ground to a growing field of teas, coffees, and sports drinks. Pepsi, led by CEO Steve Reinemund, a former Marine captain and 1970 U.S. Naval Academy graduate, sought to respond by developing a drink that would increase consumption by capitalizing on the Mountain Dew brand, the long-standing number-one noncola carbonated drink. Pepsi strategists went to the "war room" with the goal of creating an edgy, high-energy, bold drink to target a younger, largely urban crowd. The result of these sessions was Mountain Dew Code Red—a caffeine-laden, cherry-flavored brand extension.

Typically, soda launches at Coke and Pepsi are multiyear, multimillion-dollar events with big-splash national media coverage. The downside of these carefully staged, highly visible efforts is that they signal the intentions of the launching company and allow competitors sufficient time to counter. But to reach a mass market, you have to mass-advertise, conduct national taste tests, and systematically build wide-scale public awareness, right? Not so. In launching Code Red, Pepsi "went underground" and, with overwhelming success, managed to reach a large, diverse customer base.

Pepsi deliberately kept the details of the launch hushed, leaving consumers and competitors to speculate. Initially, Pepsi hit the streets to advertise in stealth mode and promoted at "alternative" venues such as the Winter X Games. At the games, Pepsi deployed an "ambush patrol," which gave out gifts and promotional material but not the drink itself. Said Bart Casabona, Pepsi spokesperson for the launch, "People might have thought it was something related to Mountain Dew but couldn't be exactly sure." Additionally, Pepsi "street teams" infiltrated urban teen hangouts, shopping malls, skate parks, and city basketball courts with similarly stealthy tactics. Pepsi also built a slick website with "teaser ads" that didn't divulge many details about the drink but provided sufficient information to pique consumers' interest: the site included a challenging interactive game called "Mission Code Red

High Score," where the fifteen hundred highest scorers could win cases of Code Red several weeks before the official product launch.

Pepsi adhered to a short ten-month product launch campaign. The product was conceived in July 2000, launched in May 2001, and sold only in single-serve sizes in convenience stores, where kids and teens, not parents, bought soft drinks. Despite the limited size and channel offerings, Code Red saw tremendous growth: Pepsi achieved its seventeen-million case goal within five weeks instead of thirty-four weeks, and by July Code Red was already the fifth-best-selling twenty-ounce soft drink.[8] Stores couldn't keep enough in stock, and soda machines were reported to sell out in minutes—in some cases consumers were following trucks to the stores just to get their hands on the drink.[9] A pleasing by-product of this grass-roots effort was big savings: Pepsi delayed running otherwise-costly TV ads until October 2001, long after the product was already flying out of convenience store coolers. In 2001, Pepsi sold seventy-five million cases of the drink.[10] And in 2002, its first full sales year, it sold a hundred million cases.[11]

Coke and the rest of the competition were taken by surprise. According to Casabona, "Typically Coke would have at least put up road blocks to challenge Pepsi's launch, but in this case it appeared Coke didn't see it coming because no blocks were put in Pepsi's way . . . the competition likely didn't realize something big was coming until it was too late."[12] Moreover, Coke didn't have any product to immediately counter Code Red. A few follow-the-leader flavored carbonated beverages eventually pursued Pepsi, including Cadbury Schweppes's Dr Pepper Red Fusion and Coke's cherry-flavored Mello Yello, but none penetrated the market significantly. In early 2003, Coke announced the upcoming launch of a fruity version of Sprite, in which it is using underground tactics similar to those used by Pepsi.

Leadership Lessons

The primary motivation behind Pepsi's stealth marketing tactics was to appeal to a select teen customer base, but the by-product of keeping Code Red off competitors' radar screens proved to be an enormous additional benefit. Stealth enabled Pepsi to reach its target audience without overtly revealing its future moves to competitors. It also enabled Pepsi to build a sizable customer base before competitors could mount an effective response. And Pepsi's short time-to-market campaign helped it maintain a greater level of secrecy before Code Red hit store shelves, a difficult task when attempting to introduce a product to a national market.

COALITION ATTACK IN OPERATION DESERT STORM: AMBIGUITY

In Operation Desert Storm, the direction of the Coalition Forces' attack was so ambiguous to the Iraqis that they did not know what to expect, and their defense became too widely dispersed to be effective.

The Coalition's activity prior to the attack forced Iraqi president Saddam Hussein and his generals to allocate their combat resources to three fronts, all of which were possible avenues of attack. Although Iraq maintained the fourth-largest land army in the world at the time, preparing for every eventuality inevitably created a weakness, the lightly defended western end of the Iraqi line, which the Coalition ultimately exploited.

Initially the Coalition Forces, consisting of an alliance of thirty-five countries and commanded by U.S. general Norman Schwarzkopf, deployed on the ground in two general formations to the southwest of Iraq. First, a force of about fifty thousand ground troops, massed due south of Kuwait City in the Saudi desert, posed the most immediate threat: an attack "right up the middle" could immediately break Saddam's grip on the oil-rich lands of Kuwait. A second ground force, consisting of highly mobile armor, air assault, and mechanized infantry units and five times larger than the first, assembled in the Saudi desert and threatened Iraq's western flank.

Already presenting two credible attacks, the Coalition then began to assemble a third—the largest amphibious force since the 1950 invasion of Inchon—in the Persian Gulf.[13] U.S. Navy battleships bombarded coastal targets with massive projectiles, up to two thousand pounds, and U.S. Navy cruisers, destroyers, and submarines launched devastatingly accurate "Tomahawk" missiles. Additionally, eighteen thousand troops were positioned to "hit the beach" aboard amphibious personnel carriers and high-speed hovercraft under the cover of carrier-based jets and helicopters.

Eventually Saddam "showed his hand" and moved about eighty thousand of his troops—mostly units from the vaunted Republican Guard—from strategic reserve to the south to defend against the possible amphibious assault. This commitment weakened Iraq's available defenses elsewhere and placed Schwarzkopf in a position to dictate the terms of the contest.

Figure 6.2 COALITION ATTACK, OPERATION DESERT STORM, 1991

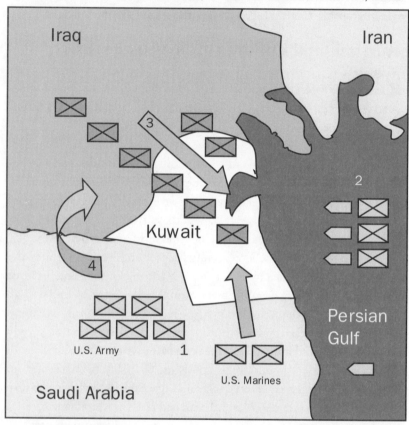

Practitioner of Maneuver Warfare ⊠ Adversary

1. Army and Marine units build up to the south.
2. Navy ships move north into the Persian Gulf.
3. Iraqis respond by moving ground units south to "defend against everything."
4. The smaller Marine force drives up the middle, while the main blow comes from the U.S. Army's "left hook" into the weakened Iraqi western flank.

The Coalition immediately responded with a ground-based attack from the west. Schwarzkopf's plan called for a quick strike "up the middle" from the Marine-led force in the south and a fast-moving, powerful "left hook" from the XVIII Corps into Saddam's depleted western flank. This one-two punch crushed the once-formidable Iraqi Army and ended the war exactly a hundred hours after the launch of the ground attack.

Leadership Lessons

Because the defender is assumed to have built entrenched, fortified positions and have had time to lay away munitions and other supplies, defense is generally considered the stronger form of combat. But this maxim rests on the assumption that the defender knows when the attack will occur and from which direction it will come. By creating multiple credible threats and obscuring its intentions, the Coalition was able to seize the advantage from the confused and overextended Iraqi defenders and pick the most vulnerable point to attack. Generally speaking, an attacker can use ambiguity to maintain maximum flexibility and avoid committing resources until the defender exposes a significant weakness in his own preparation and deployment of resources, thereby rendering the offense the stronger form of combat.

MICROSOFT PRODUCT UPGRADES: AMBIGUITY

Microsoft creates ambiguity for competitors when it publicly announces plans for a large set of potential upgrades, changes, or additions to its software or operating systems.

Competitors, whose software products must offer an array of features that at least match those offered by Microsoft, have little choice but to respond to every possibility. Microsoft's caginess about the ultimate configuration of its new products gives it a tremendous cost advantage over competitors: because it never implements all of the potential changes, it incurs costs only for those it actually upgrades, while competitors scramble.

Ambiguity at Microsoft has been highly publicized: journalists have coined the phrase "vaporware" to describe the uncertainty that its product announcements create, and many articles have highlighted Microsoft's use of ambiguity to confuse competitors. A representative article stated, "Microsoft Inc. is particularly adept at this tactic and frequently announces new products that either never appear on the market or appear long after the announced date of introduction."[14]

Microsoft's use of ambiguity can be seen in its recent ".NET" umbrella initiative. .NET is evidently a set of web-based services that allow data to be exchanged seamlessly and efficiently online—between customers and a small business or between that small business and its suppliers. Microsoft's difficult-to-interpret announcements say .NET covers a wide range of products, from its database and Internet servers to its Windows XP operating systems to its productivity software.[15]

Though competitors are doubtful that .NET will actually encompass all these products, they have little choice but to respond to the *possibility* that this will be the case. Thus, by forcing the competition's hand, Microsoft places itself in a position to gauge competitive response and then pursue its optimal course of action.

Leadership Lessons

Nothing about ambiguity implies a breach of integrity or a violation of the law. But, by merely announcing a large set of plausible product features, Microsoft effectively impairs rival firms' decision-making abilities and preserves maximum flexibility for itself. Of course there are potential costs associated with such actions—customers can become as confused as the competition, and courts may not look favorably on such dubiousness. Microsoft's ambiguous practices surfaced in the *United States v. Microsoft* proceedings in 2001,[16] and though U.S. courts ruled that its behavior was not anticompetitive, Microsoft's defense of its enigmatic behavior proved to be quite costly. In short, Microsoft shows us that forcing an opponent to respond to numerous threats, all plausible but only some real, causes him to spread himself so thinly that he deploys resources that could have been better used elsewhere in order to defend against threats that never materialize.

ALLIES BEFORE D-DAY: DECEPTION

In 1944 the Allies used deception to convince the German High Command that Pas de Calais, France—not Normandy—was the most likely location for the colossal D-day amphibious landing.

Code-named "Operation Fortitude," the deception effort began with the construction of a "force" of dummy tanks, oil storage depots, airfields, and landing craft located in Dover, England, directly across the English Channel from Calais. The troops involved in the operation were all closely

Figure 6.3 ALLIED DECEPTION BEFORE D-DAY, 1944

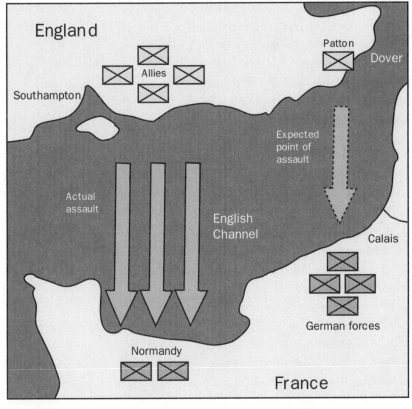

screened, highly trained, and constantly reminded of the need for secrecy. The "tanks" and "boats," made of rubber balloons, and the "aircraft" and "buildings," made of plywood, were all intentionally left on display for German reconnaissance aircraft. And Allied Supreme Commander General Dwight D. Eisenhower went so far as to place one of his top generals, George S. Patton, "in charge" of the fictitious landing force.

The Allies used Patton's public actions, false radio traffic, double agents, and misleading bombing attacks to further the deception. First, conducting phony troop inspections and visiting Eisenhower's headquarters at times when the Germans were likely to observe such actions, Patton masterfully brought considerable attention to himself. Second, the

Allies transmitted false radio traffic that mimicked the communications typical of a large army and created the illusion that the Allies were marshaling an invasion force at Dover. Third, to convey misinformation to the Germans, the Allies deployed a complicated and extensive network of double agents; one agent, Spaniard Juan Pujol-Garcia, even had direct access to Hitler and convinced the führer that Normandy was nothing more than a diversion. Fourth, in preparation for the D-day attack, the Allied forces bombed the Calais region more severely than the Normandy area; for every bomb dropped in Normandy, two were dropped on Calais.

With the German main defensive effort firmly fixed on Calais and the German High Command duped into believing that the invasion force totaled ninety divisions, the Allies attacked Normandy on June 6, 1944, with thirty-nine divisions. While the defenses at Normandy were formidable, they were soft enough that the Allies were able to build a beachhead on the French coast and later push inland.

Even after the Allies invaded Normandy, the German High Command, still convinced that Patton and a more sizable force lay in wait at Dover, refused to ferry forces to Normandy. And, in an effort to reinforce the Germans' erroneous beliefs, the Allies continued the deception efforts into mid-July. These measures were so effective that the Germans were not convinced that Normandy was the site of the main Allied attack until almost one month *after* the D-day landing, far too late to mount an effective counter to the invasion.

Leadership Lessons

The Allies' deceptive efforts were effective because they were credible, mutually reinforcing, and ongoing. Eisenhower's willingness to commit one of his top generals to the fictitious landing force and the heavy expenditure of precious bombs at Calais made the threat of a landing there very real in the eyes of the German High Command. Moreover, the multiple sources that German intelligence cross-referenced—the observations of their spies in England, the whispers of double agents close to the High Command, the results of German aerial reconnaissance, the interception of false radio traffic, and the bomb damage assessment reports at Calais—reinforced one another beautifully. Finally, the deceptive efforts at Calais continued long after the attack on Normandy commenced and fixated the Germans' attention on Dover even longer.

MERRILL LYNCH'S CMA: DECEPTION

Anecdotal evidence indicates that Merrill Lynch employed deceptive measures to deter competition from other securities firms when it introduced the cash management account (CMA) in the late 1970s.

The CMA was an innovative all-purpose money management account that offered a brokerage account, money market fund, checking account, and credit card. The CMA infringed on activities traditionally reserved for commercial banks, and because it offered an interest rate of 12.5 percent, compared with the 5.0 to 5.5 percent that regulations allowed banks to offer on traditional savings accounts at the time, Merrill Lynch seized considerable market share from retail and commercial banks.

The banks retaliated with numerous lawsuits alleging violation of the Glass-Steagall Act. A commercial banking group filed the first of many lawsuits almost immediately after Merrill Lynch advertised the CMA in a Denver newspaper. Shortly thereafter, commercial banking leaders called for organized opposition at the national level, and the state of Utah tried unsuccessfully in 1981 to prohibit the CMA. Even the chairman of the Federal Reserve, Arthur Burns, expressed skepticism about the legality of the CMA.

Viewing this controversy as an opportunity to deceive would-be competitors as to the actual attractiveness of the CMA market, Merrill Lynch deliberately drew media attention to the lawsuits. On the surface this was a seemingly reckless move. But Merrill Lynch knew that the likelihood of an unfavorable ruling was low, because the CMA had been designed specifically not to violate federal securities laws. Merrill Lynch also correctly surmised that rival brokerage firms were unlikely to devote the time, effort, and expense necessary to follow the outcomes of each and every lawsuit and that rivals were even less likely to invest in systems for competing products as long as the CMA's legality was in question.

While the trials and tribulations of its experiences with the CMA received considerable coverage, Merrill Lynch barely mentioned the fact that it never lost even one of these lawsuits. This selective communication of information created a taint of litigation and helped deter would-be competitors from offering similar products and gave the company a five-year lead in the lucrative CMA market. Citing the launch of the CMA as one of the most noteworthy U.S. business events in the twentieth century, the *Wall Street Journal* noted, "By the time other brokerage firms caught on in 1982, Merrill Lynch had sold 533,000 CMAs with assets of $32 billion."[17]

Leadership Lessons

Merrill Lynch cunningly used the media as a means to capitalize on its rivals' reluctance to undertake the costly process of gathering their own firsthand information. Rivals assumed the media to be an accurate and unbiased source of information, and Merrill Lynch used selective release of entire accurate reports through this reliable source to convey to competitors the information that it wanted them to see and hear. While Merrill Lynch never explicitly released incorrect information or explicitly misrepresented inflated estimates of the cost of the CMA development or its assessment of the likelihood that the product would ultimately survive judicial review, it also never corrected a competitor's estimate of costs, if too high, or probability of success, if too low. These tactics, along with the negative light cast on the CMA by the coverage of the lawsuits, lulled its rivals into believing that development of their own CMA offerings was not optimal and thus protected the lucrative opportunity that Merrill Lynch had created.

ANALYSIS ACROSS EXAMPLES

While each of the aforementioned examples represents a slightly different approach to achieving surprise, the commonalities among them offer several key insights into this third guiding principle of maneuver warfare. All of the examples involve the management of information to shape competitive encounters by impairing opponents' decision-making capabilities, obscuring friendly intentions, and deferring the commitment of resources until the most opportune moment. Five of the examples—Houston at San Jacinto, Pepsi's Code Red, the Coalition in Desert Storm, the Allies at D-day, and Merrill Lynch's CMA—show that controlling information can be extremely effective when mounting an offense. The sixth example, Microsoft, illustrates the power of obscuring accurate information in the defense within a barrage of noise that requires a careful response. The Battle of San Jacinto and the activities prior to the D-day landing underscore the importance of maintaining discipline and secrecy among the members of the organization when attempting to achieve surprise. Finally, the release of information into the public forum to achieve surprise by Microsoft and Merrill Lynch suggests that the media can be an extremely effective means to influence the behavior of rivals.

SURPRISE . . . THE MARINE CORPS WAY

Acknowledging the increasingly central role that information will play in twenty-first-century armed conflict, the Marine Corps recently articulated a structured, formalized approach to the management of information in support of its maneuver warfare efforts. Known as *Information Operations* (IO), this approach employs multiple information-based activities "to deny, degrade, disrupt, destroy, or influence an adversary commander's methods, means, or ability to command and control his forces and to inform target audiences."[18] These activities include deception, electronic warfare, psychological operations, physical destruction, information assurance, public affairs, civil-military operations, and computer network operations.

While broader in scope than the topics covered in this chapter—that companies would jam each other's signals or launch computer viruses against one another seems unlikely—IO can, nevertheless, serve as a useful guide to achieving surprise in the business environment. Like surprise, IO involves the management of information to shape competitive encounters. Beyond this basic similarity, IO is noteworthy to the aspiring practitioner of maneuver warfare because of the degree to which the Marine Corps has committed to it. The Marines have dedicated personnel and resources to IO and have formally incorporated it into mission planning and execution. As a result, the management of information in support of maneuver warfare has become more than just the articulation of a good idea; it is now an integral part of all Marine Corps combat operations.

IO Cell

IO starts with the dedication of personnel and resources to an "IO cell" in support of a larger combat operation. Led by a full-time IO officer, the IO cell consists of a diverse group of individuals with backgrounds in operations planning, intelligence, electronic warfare, fire support, communications/information systems, and public affairs. These individuals may or may not be fully dedicated to the cell, but they have core responsibilities as part of it.

IO Plan

Based on the commander's guidance for shaping the conditions of the operation at hand, the IO cell selects an appropriate subset of information-based activities and formulates a preliminary plan for their employment. Working closely with the other constituencies involved in the planning of the operation, the IO cell then refines this plan and ensures that it is fully integrated into the operation's overall scheme of maneuver. Among the requirements for successful integration: extensive coordination with the other constituencies and participation in interactive war games that test the IO plan's flexibility and adequacy.

The IO plan that survives this rigorous process is then incorporated into the overall operations order (OpOrd). To symbolize its importance, IO even has its own section in the OpOrd.

IO Implementation

The responsibilities of the IO cell extend well beyond the completion of the IO section in the OpOrd. During the execution of the operation, the IO cell monitors the effectiveness of its efforts, reacts to changing events as necessary, and makes the appropriate adjustments. Thus, from start to finish, the IO cell is intimately involved in all aspects of the operation.

APPLICATION IN BUSINESS

With regard to achieving surprise in the business environment, the Marines' experience with IO, while maybe not 100 percent applicable to your immediate situation, strongly suggests that a disciplined follow-through should accompany every well-intended use of information to shape the rules of the competitive encounter(s).

Consider the following strategies for achieving stealth, ambiguity, and deception, respectively, which will allow you to act when your opponent is unprepared or otherwise confused and off balance:

- Conceal your intentions or coordinate your efforts so that your first moves do not announce the timing or direction of your initial attack or block your later efforts.

- Announce a list of plausible courses of action and make a selection among them only after your opponent attempts to prepare for all of them; in this manner, you create options for yourself while he is confused.

- Use all channels available to you when deliberately conveying selected information to influence the behavior of your rivals; perhaps the most effective channel is the media.

Only through painstaking effort will you be able to surprise your competitors. The slightest slipup can spell disaster for even the best of plans.

Stealth, ambiguity, and deception have become more difficult to maintain in warfare as military formations have become larger and more dispersed and as electronic surveillance and other forms of intelligence gathering have become more effective. Similarly, the three means to achieving surprise have become more difficult in the business environment because of the widespread proliferation of information technology, requirements for full disclosure of financial information, and frequent staff turnover. Nevertheless, these are not excuses to make your competitors' intelligence gathering efforts easier or more fruitful through the sloppy management of information on your part.

Every time your organization makes a public announcement, creates a web page on the Internet, attends a trade show, or even calls on a customer, you are making available to snooping competitors information that could telegraph your next move. How meticulously do you scrutinize this information leakage? If you do not scrutinize it all yourself—and you cannot—your guidance for and supervision of the release of information via these channels must be thorough. You should also spend more time contemplating how you can use these channels to create ambiguity or deception in the minds of your competitors.

Remember to remind your people constantly of the need to maintain secrecy about new initiatives. The creation of your own IO cell could be the most effective means to safeguard your organization's intentions and devise methods to degrade the quality of information available to competitors. Finally, stealth, ambiguity, and deception should have their own section in your OpOrd.

Surprise, it seems, is difficult to achieve, but with an increasing reliance on information and information technology come increased opportunities to use information to your advantage.

CHAPTER 7

FOCUS

"The essence of strategy is, with a weaker army, always have more force at a crucial point than the enemy."

—Napoléon Bonaparte[1]

Focus, the "generation of superior combat power at a particular time and place, enables a numerically inferior force to achieve decisive local superiority"[2] and provides an overwhelming advantage when and where it matters most.

Military commanders achieve focus on the battlefield by massing resources—men, materiél, and firepower—at critical points and times. The business equivalent of this activity is the commitment of maximum resources—information, capital, personnel, and physical equipment—in pursuit of market opportunities. But concentrating resources in one area requires reducing them elsewhere, which invariably exposes weakness. Moreover, shifting certain types of resources is more difficult in some cases than in others. Given these constraints, effective focus requires considerable balance and creativity on the part of the practitioner of maneuver warfare. In addition to balance and creativity, effective focus requires the astute management of information; information can be employed to uncover previously overlooked but lucrative opportunities and commit maximum resources with greater accuracy.

In this chapter, we offer four historical examples of focus and its key components, as well as present-day lessons from the Marines. The German invasion of France in 1940 and Lexus's entry into the U.S. luxury automobile market in the mid-1980s illustrate focus in warfare and business, respectively. British admiral Lord Horatio Nelson's classic naval victory at the Battle of Trafalgar in 1805 shows how the willingness to assume certain risks and the use of information enable focus. And the emergence of Harrah's Entertainment in the 1990s as a leading U.S. casino operator exemplifies how the sophisticated use of information can maximize the effectiveness of resources committed to a particular market opportunity.

The Marines' high proficiency in focus can help you bring overwhelming resources to bear on the customer's wants and needs. Our intent in this chapter is to use their experiences and some of the lessons learned from our historical examples to suggest ways in which you can dedicate resources to lucrative market opportunities more effectively, manage the accompanying risk, and use information to understand and anticipate customer behavior better than your competitors do.

GERMAN INVASION OF FRANCE

Despite being outnumbered by almost one million soldiers and by a ratio of three to two in artillery pieces and tanks in the invasion of France in 1940, the German Army smashed through the weakest point in the Allied line and brought the primarily French army to its knees. The Germans achieved this overwhelming victory by focusing fifteen hundred aircraft and forty-five infantry and tank divisions against nine French divisions in the lightly defended Ardennes forest.

The Germans' original plan, to strike France in the North through Belgium and Holland, was compromised three months prior to the intended invasion date, and the French moved the large majority of their forces north to defend against the expected attack. The commitment of thirty Allied divisions to a heavily defended line from southern Holland through Belgium left only a small contingent to the south to defend the Meuse River, which lay on the western side of the Ardennes, a wooded area that they believed difficult for tanks to navigate. In fact the French were so confident that the Germans would steer clear of the Ardennes that they manned large portions of the defensive line with overaged, undertrained reservists.

The forward-thinking German general Heinz Guderian, who had developed and proven the efficacy of a fast-striking armor concept during the 1930s, was adamant in his belief that any attack on France should be conducted through the Ardennes. After all, Guderian reasoned, the forest provided ideal camouflage, and passage through it was much easier than widely believed. The High Command of the Germans' western front shared these innovative views and eventually convinced Hitler of their merits. With the original plan compromised and German intelligence sources confirming French weakness in the South, Hitler gave the order for his army to deliver a massive "power punch" through the weakest point in the French line via the "impenetrable" Ardennes.[3]

The Germans' plan brought almost all available armor, infantry, and artillery forces and every available aircraft to bear on the thinly held

Figure 7.1 GERMAN INVASION OF FRANCE, 1940

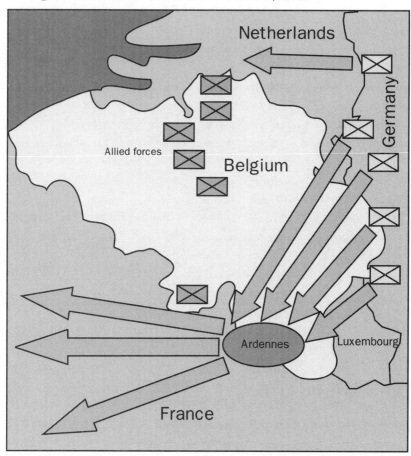

Ardennes forest. The lead tank division, commanded by none other than Erwin Rommel and supported for the first time in combat by low-flying German dive bombers, smashed through the French defenses. Guderian, in command of the XIX Panzer Corps—the most formidable armored unit in the German Army—poured through the opening shortly thereafter. In short order, breakthrough—breaching the line—became breakout—an advance at breakneck speed behind and around the French defenders.

Focus was not limited to the strategic level. German tank commanders used radios to fight in packs, a tactic that Guderian had pioneered against the newer, faster, more heavily armored French Somua tanks, which normally operated individually. While the twenty-ton French Somuas were superior to the ten-ton German Panzer II's on all counts (save the radio), a single Somua was no match for a pack of Panzers coordinated by radio. In the air the German Luftwaffe massed its planes in huge waves to defeat individual Allied fighters systematically and annihilate the poorly concealed French forces on the ground.

Within four days of crossing the Meuse, Guderian's corps reached the English Channel. Behind him, the remainder of the German Army created a forty-mile gap in the French defense and swarmed through the French countryside. Though France did not officially surrender until June 21, the battle was essentially over once the French line was breached.

Leadership Lessons

The outnumbered Germans focused their strength against the weakest point in their opponent's line. And that focus pervaded the entire attack, from Hitler's strategic commitment of "all operational strength of the Luftwaffe" to tactical "pack fighting" by the German Panzers.[4] This overwhelming commitment did, however, expose some risk; the Germans' positions in the North were highly vulnerable to counterattack. But given the low probability that the French defenders would leave their static defensive positions, Guderian accepted this risk as an inevitable by-product of his plan.

LEXUS'S ENTRY INTO THE U.S. AUTO MARKET, PART 1

In the mid-1980s, Toyota focused $500 million and its engineering might on an emerging market segment of upwardly mobile, price-sensitive luxury car buyers in the United States and quickly established itself as a premier marquee among luxury automobiles.

"Baby boomers," a disproportionately large segment of the population in the United States who were previous owners of Japanese cars, were entering their forties and growing more affluent. Ready to "graduate" from a practical vehicle to a luxury automobile, many baby boomers were not willing to pay the substantial premiums that European automakers, such as BMW, Jaguar, and Mercedes, commanded. This class of customer also wanted a level of quality, reliability, image, and performance that the U.S. luxury brands, such as Cadillac and Lincoln, were not able to offer.

To "meet . . . the heightened needs" of customers "moving up in life," Toyota chairman Eiji Toyoda decided in 1983 that he wanted " 'to develop the best car in the world' " and committed resources accordingly.[5] A team of top engineers, assembled under Ichiro Suzuki, received the chairman's full financial backing and began designing a fuel-efficient, 150-mph, four-door sedan with the smoothest and quietest possible ride.

To guide the efforts of his engineering team in Japan, Suzuki sent twenty specialists to the United States to conduct market research and hired a U.S.-based cultural anthropologist. The specialists conducted focus groups, interacted with dealers, and gathered insights into the traits and preferences of prospective buyers. The cultural anthropologist identified specific buyer traits, such as age, willingness to pay, brand loyalty, and desired image to convey. Moreover, once it was determined that many consumers who could afford *any* luxury car would buy a Lexus to demonstrate that they were savvy, rather than an equivalent but more expensive Mercedes to show that they were wealthy, the anthropologist was able to identify the most effective means to reach these prospective buyers: a strong review in the magazine *Consumer Reports*. The anthropologist then determined the metrics most decisive in achieving *Consumer Reports'* highest ratings: wood trim, stereo, seat heaters, and cup holders; surprisingly, engine performance was not one of them.[6]

Suzuki's investment in market information, while significant, paled in comparison to the investment he made in development, manufacturing, and quality control. His team made eight design proposals to senior management before approval, and prototypes covered twice as many test miles than normal before full-scale production commenced. Assembly occurred in a state-of-the-art facility with the world's most advanced automation, and inspectors performed five additional quality-control checks to minimize the incidence of even the smallest defects.

Six years, 2.5 million test miles, and $500 million after Chairman Toyoda's decision, Lexus's flagship model for its new luxury car line, the LS 400, rolled off the assembly line with a sleek design, world-class performance, impeccable quality—all at a $35,000 base price. In its first year the LS 400 scored extremely well on customer satisfaction surveys and quickly gained share in the luxury car market. Ever since, Lexus has enjoyed considerable success as a premier luxury automobile. It has been consistently ranked number one in terms of quality and driver satisfaction[7] and was the top-selling U.S. luxury brand for three years prior to this writing.[8]

Leadership Lessons

Chairman Toyoda identified a market opportunity and decisively committed to it an enormous budget, the world's most advanced automation, and a team of his most talented professionals. And his lieutenant, Suzuki, wisely used information to guide this focused effort. But, as we will see in Chapter 10, focus was not the only principle of maneuver warfare that Lexus employed in its successful launch of the LS 400; combined arms also played a major role.

NELSON AT TRAFALGAR

At the Battle of Trafalgar in 1805, British admiral Lord Horatio Nelson crushed the Combined French-Spanish fleet off the coast of Spain by focusing his combat power at two critical points in French admiral Pierre-Charles Villeneuve's line.

Nelson was outnumbered and outgunned thirty-three ships to twenty-seven but possessed key advantages in seamanship and short-range gunnery. Accordingly, he devised a plan to breach the combined fleet's line and engage at close quarters, where his forces held the upper hand. Defying conventional naval tactics, which would have had the opposing fleets line up parallel and bombard each other's broadsides, Nelson divided his smaller force into two columns and attacked in a perpendicular direction, which brought overwhelming combat power to bear where it mattered most.

Owing to an advance warning he received from his frigates, fast-moving scout ships, Nelson occupied an advantaged position—upwind[9] and to the west relative to his opponent—in the waters outside the Straits of Gibraltar on the morning of October 21. Upon spotting Nelson's fleet, Villeneuve ordered his fleet, which had been sailing in a southeasterly direction, to change course 180 degrees, re-form its line, and head back

Figure 7.2 NELSON AT TRAFALGAR, 1805

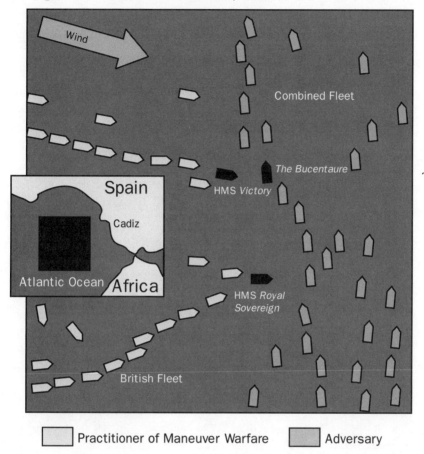

to Cadiz in a northwesterly direction. Because of light winds, this was a jumbled process, and Villeneuve's line bowed in the center.

Using flags to signal the now-famous guidance "England expects that every man will do his duty," Nelson unleashed his attack.[10] Aboard the HMS *Victory*, he led one of the British columns toward Villeneuve's *Bucentaure*, the tenth ship in the combined fleet line. To the south of Nelson, Admiral Cuthbert Collingwood, aboard the HMS *Royal Sovereign*, led the second column toward the twelfth ship in the combined fleet line.

During this final approach the British were most vulnerable. Nelson's ships were fully exposed to the broadsides of the combined fleet, and their own side-mounted, outward-facing cannons were limited in their ability to fire forward. Nelson had to take this risk to focus his limited combat power, breach the combined fleet's line, and capitalize on his sailors' superior seamanship and gunnery skills. Fortunately, both British columns were sailing with the wind.

In the final stages of the approach the lead British ships began taking heavy fire. Nevertheless, they smashed through the combined fleet's line and inflicted heavy damage. *Victory* devastated the decks of the *Bucentaure* with a large sixty-eight-pound gun that fired grapeshot at point-blank range. And the remainder of Nelson's column effectively isolated the combined fleet's vanguard—the first nine ships in the line—from the conflict. Collingwood's column smashed into the second point in the combined fleet's line with a wedge-shaped formation and attacked the Spanish and French ships from the rear.

After five hours of intense fighting and heavy casualties on both sides, fifteen combined fleet ships were captured, four were destroyed completely, and fourteen were fleeing. No British ships had been lost; although many had been damaged. Villeneuve had been captured, but Nelson had suffered a mortal wound—a rifle shot from a sniper—in his moment of triumph. "Thank God I have done my duty" were his last words.[11] And do his duty he did: Nelson's victory asserted the British navy as the preeminent sea power in the 1800s and contained Napoléon's campaign within continental Europe.

Leadership Lessons

Nelson knew that he would have little chance of victory if he were to line up parallel to the numerically superior combined fleet and engage in a contest of firepower. Accordingly, he willingly exposed a vulnerability and used focus to break Villeneuve's line, thereby changing the nature of the engagement to a contest of seamanship and close-range gunnery, areas in which the British were far superior. His unorthodox yet brilliant approach removed the first nine ships in the combined fleet's line from the battle and positioned his forces to attack the Spanish and French ships from the rear, where they were weakest.

HARRAH'S ENTERTAINMENT

By focusing maximum resources on an underserved segment of "low roller" gamblers, Harrah's Entertainment has grown in the past decade from a four-property, second-tier casino operator with limited finances to a twenty-six-property gaming industry leader with a market capitalization of $4.4 billion.[12]

In the early 1990s, Harrah's lacked the financial resources to engage larger casinos, such as MGM, Mirage, and Park Place Entertainment, in contests of one-upmanship to see who could build glitzier, more glamorous casinos to attract a small base of superwealthy gamblers. Its CEO, Phil Satre, thus decided to forsake this approach, which aimed to attract free-spending high rollers, and instead pursued closer relationships with low rollers—middle-market patrons who gambled away a few hundred dollars per visit on a repeat basis.

Harrah's market research revealed that this low-roller segment, neglected by the larger casinos, accounted for nearly 100 percent of the company's profits, despite representing just 30 percent of its customers.[13] Accordingly, the company invested heavily to identify, attract, cater to, and retain the low roller. It built a world-class customer information system, recruited top managerial talent from outside the industry, and provided its frontline workforce with extensive customer service and system operation training.

The point of departure for Satre's strategy was the development of the gaming industry's first centralized patron database system, a single repository of information linked electronically to all of Harrah's properties. The three-year development process cost a hefty $65 million,[14] but when complete, the system enabled Harrah's to track the characteristics and habits of its patrons and perform sophisticated statistical analyses that provided insights into customer behavior. Harrah's marketers could use the system to tailor incentive offers to individuals' particular tastes and preferences, cross-promote its numerous properties, and estimate each gambler's expected lifetime profitability. Harrah's casino operators, for example, could use the system to provide customized services to a visiting patron and optimize game offerings to maximize profits at their respective properties.

Satre knew that his world-class system needed a world-class management team, and he paid handsomely to attract outside talent with advanced analytical capabilities and extensive information technology experience. Bucking the industry norm of hiring casino veterans, he hired Harvard Business School professor Gary Loveman as chief operating officer, and he recruited management consultants from world-class firms and graduates from top-tier business schools.

Satre also invested substantially in training his frontline employees, who would be operating the system, recording interactions with customers, and, it was hoped, encouraging more return visits. Hotel managers, pit bosses, restaurant workers, and marketing personnel received extensive instruction in the use of the complex information system and in how to leverage its capabilities to provide superior customer service. And *every* employee went through rigorous customer service training, a program Harrah's ran twenty-four hours a day to ensure all employees on all shifts were able to attend.

Satre thus made a commitment to obtain the best available management team to improve service, even though he was competing for individuals whose service needs had not been deemed worth meeting by other casinos. Additionally, he invested heavily in training his entire staff to use this information to focus on attracting and retaining this target segment with service well beyond that which they would have received from competitors.

This strategy of bringing maximum resources to bear on the low roller delivered dramatic results. By 2002, Harrah's customer base more than doubled, to more than twenty-five million gamblers, endowing the company with the most extensive and widespread customer database in the industry. Customer retention skyrocketed, and with more repeat business, customer acquisition costs plummeted. The number of customers playing at more than one Harrah's property jumped by over 70 percent, and over half of the company's Las Vegas profits came from patrons who normally gambled at Harrah's casinos outside the state of Nevada.[15] Owing to this tremendous success with the customer, Harrah's has enjoyed the widest profit margins, fastest earnings growth, and greatest appreciation in share price in the casino industry since 1999.[16]

Leadership Lessons

Harrah's strategy exemplifies focus on two counts but is atypical on a third. First, Satre wisely avoided the strengths of his competitors and focused his limited resources on an overlooked yet lucrative segment of the market. Second, Harrah's maximized the effectiveness of the resources it committed to this segment by using information to match product offerings to customers' wants and needs with greater accuracy. Third, this application of focus is unique because Harrah's made a disproportionately large commitment of resources not to a specific market opportunity but to an intangible end—gaining superior insight into customer wants and needs and building customer loyalty. This commitment in turn enabled the company to deploy its scarce resources at the most critical points and times.

ANALYSIS ACROSS EXAMPLES

When examined together, the examples raised to illustrate this fourth guiding principle of maneuver warfare offer several key insights. In the cases of the German invasion of France, Nelson at Trafalgar, and Harrah's, we see the selective application of strength against opponents' weaknesses and the use of overwhelming local superiority to overcome an overall resource disadvantage. In the cases of Lexus and Harrah's, we see a heavy reliance on information to guide the commitment of resources. In the two warfare examples, both Guderian and Nelson willingly exposed a weakness in an effort to achieve focus. In the two business examples, Harrah's made a disproportionately large commitment to information-based activity with an immeasurable outcome, whereas Lexus made a disproportionately large commitment to a particular market opportunity. Finally, Chairman Toyoda and Admiral Nelson directed the focused deployment of resources from the top down, while focus pervaded the German ranks and the Harrah's organization at all levels.

FOCUS . . . THE MARINE CORPS WAY

The need to overcome equipment, personnel, and funding constraints has driven the Marines to develop a high degree of proficiency in focus—both in peacetime and in combat. Understanding the practices they employ can help you uncover lucrative market opportunities in the business environment, shift resources more effectively, and manage the accompanying risk.

Recon, UAVs, and SigInt

Marine commanders rely on multiple sources to feed them information on the location and disposition of lucrative battlefield targets. From the front lines, artillery forward observers include with every target location a target description, such as "platoon of tanks in the open," in an effort to provide a landscape of the battlefield for intelligence specialists at headquarters units in rear areas. Forward of the main fighting force, highly skilled reconnaissance Marines, mentioned in Chapter 4 and described more fully in Chapter 11, and scout snipers serve as the commander's "eyes" by sending back detailed reports of their observations. Beyond the range of human sight, the Marines deploy unmanned aerial vehicles (UAVs), remotely piloted drone aircraft, deep into enemy territory to take high-resolution photographs and record enemy locations. And Marine Signals Intelligence (SigInt) units use sophisticated monitoring equipment to "eavesdrop" on enemy communications, pinpoint the locations from which enemy signals emanate, and estimate the volume of traffic coming from those locations.

Shuffling of Personnel

In peacetime the Marine Corps maintains a constant state of readiness around the world by rotating its limited personnel in and out of units sent overseas on 6-month "tip of the spear" deployments. Twenty-four hours per day, 7 days per week, 365 days per year, there are three 2,000-member rapid reaction contingency forces, known as Marine Expeditionary Units (MEUs), on station in the Mediterranean Sea, in the western Pacific, and on Okinawa, Japan. These units deploy at 100 percent strength but are drawn from undermanned active duty units that are normally staffed at only 60 to 80 percent strength. To reach full strength from seemingly depleted sources, the deploying units "borrow" personnel from "sister" units and quickly relinquish those personnel upon return. While this never-ending "shell game" presents challenges for unit cohesion and continuity, Marines accept it as a necessary means to project maximum combat power with a minimum footprint.

Main Effort

When the Marines commit to a focused attack, they designate a *main effort*, which can shift depending on the course of battle, and allocate resources accordingly. The main effort receives the highest priority in the allocation of air, artillery, and armor support, among other resources. For example, the commander may dedicate resources to a particular offensive or defensive effort: "1st Tank platoon is hereby attached to Alpha Company, the main effort, until further ordered." Alternatively, the commander may assign "front-of-the-line privileges" to the main effort for all requests for artillery fires and low-level aircraft bombing runs: "Alpha Company is the main effort and has priority of fires from artillery and air, until further ordered."

Clear Communication of Intentions

The phrase "until further ordered" signals to the members of the fighting force that the commander reserves the right to shift the main effort at any time during the course of battle, depending on where the concentrated deployment of resources will have the biggest impact. In certain instances the commander may even alert his Marines to the likelihood of a future shift in the main effort: "Alpha Company is the main effort during the first phase of the attack, but be prepared to shift priority of fires to Bravo Company during the second phase." The execution of the order to shift the main effort is a complex endeavor that requires considerable coordination. Consequently, during peacetime maneuvers and training, the Marines endlessly practice shifting the main effort so that the commander may be able to bring overwhelming force to bear on battlefield opportunities as they emerge.

Economy of Force

The Marines are well aware that concentrating resources in support of the main effort reduces combat power elsewhere, and they proactively take measures to mitigate the accompanying risk. *Economy of force*, the first means to mitigating this risk, refers to the deliberate reduction of resources in less critical areas. To prepare the leaders of units in those areas to "do more with less," the commander communicates where and when he expects economy of force to be required. While all Marines pride themselves on their ability to react to rapidly changing situations, advance warning from the commander lessens the difficulty associated with the inherently difficult task of economy of force.

Another way in which the commander may mitigate the risks associated with focus is varying the degree to which he commits resources to the main effort, which has implications for the commander's ability to shift resources to protect exposed weaknesses, should the need arise. Consider the difference between dedicating a platoon of tanks to Alpha Company and assigning Alpha Company priority of fires. The first alternative is the greater commitment of the two—Alpha Company effectively assumes control of the tank platoon—but is also the less flexible. Moving the platoon of tanks to another unit is more difficult and time-consuming than altering the direction of low-level bombing approaches or shifting the direction in which artillery guns fire.

APPLICATION IN BUSINESS

Applied in the business setting, the Marines' practices promise to take the venerable concept of "focus on the customer" to a new level. Indeed, shuffling personnel to the most critical areas of your business, using information to understand and anticipate customer behavior, designating and redesignating a main effort, and proactively managing the challenges associated with economy of force will enable you to bring overwhelming resources to bear on the customer's wants and needs.

Focus your personnel in the most critical areas of your business and do not limit the scope of this activity to mere numbers. Move your star performers into frontline leadership roles to supervise directly the focused application of resources. Shuffling people around the organization may take them out of their respective "comfort zones," but they will be more well rounded, and you will be able to maintain a greater market presence with a smaller footprint.

Use information to guide the focused application of resources in pursuit of market opportunities. You may not have UAVs, SigInt, and Recon Marines at your disposal, but you can apply statistical analysis to customer demographics and purchasing activities, and you can leverage the insights of frontline employees. Information gleaned from these activities will enable you to anticipate customer behavior more effectively than your rivals are able to. Moreover, this information will enable you to identify the most profitable customers and target their needs selectively.

Designate a main effort and be prepared to shift it when a more lucrative market opportunity arises. Designating a main effort ensures that focus is a formalized process and resolves potentially conflicting claims on your organization's resources. Being prepared to shift maximizes your ability to bring maximum resources to bear on changing market conditions, but it extends well beyond your own preparedness. You must train your people so that they are accustomed to shifting, and you must communicate your intentions to them in advance of any shift so that your *organization* is prepared to bring maximum resources to bear on emerging market opportunities.

Finally, proactively manage the risk associated with focus by communicating with your people and building flexibility into your plans to commit resources. Ask the leaders of the business units from which you take resources what they need to continue operations and monitor their progress, either through ongoing dialogue or through real-time information systems, so that you may rapidly respond to an exposed weakness. And just as you ask yourself, "What is the downside?" when weighing risk and reward; ask yourself, "How hard will it be to shift these resources back when needed?" when committing to a focused strategy.

CHAPTER 8

DECENTRALIZED DECISION MAKING

"Never tell people how to do things. Tell them what to do, and they will surprise you with their ingenuity."

—GENERAL GEORGE S. PATTON[1]

Decentralized decision making—the delegation of significant decision making authority down through the ranks—allows a military force "to cope with the unforeseen events and confusion that are inherent in competitive encounters, to generate a superior tempo of operations, and to exploit opportunities as they arise."[2]

The aim is to give those closest to the action the latitude to take advantage of on-the-spot information unavailable to their superiors. While midlevel and frontline leaders are strongly encouraged to make decisions on their own and act on them, their actions must be consistent with the organization's overall objectives. To this end decentralized decision making relies heavily on the commander's *intent*—the leader's desired final result—to define the scope of initiative that subordinates can exercise.

A risk-reward trade-off in its own right, decentralized decision making can deliver breakthrough results by increasing the likelihood of nonlinear accomplishments—situations in which an extraordinary act by an individual disproportionately determines the course of large-scale competitive encounters. But it also carries considerable risk: distributed authority is, by nature, chaotic and can result in a higher prevalence of mistakes, especially when overzealous junior leaders do not act in concert with the commander's intent. To reap the full rewards of decentralized decision making, the leader must be willing to trust the capabilities of his or her subordinates, relinquish some degree of control, and resist the temptation to intervene when execution is not as precise as he or she would like. At the same time, to mitigate the risks inherent in distributed authority, leaders must obtain accurate factual assessments quickly, correct mistakes on the spot, and be ever-vigilant for anything that could cause catastrophic failures.

In this chapter we offer four examples of decentralized decision making and its key components, as well as present-day lessons from the Marines. George Patton's Normandy Breakout in 1944 illustrates successful decentralized decision making in warfare. London-based Smith Newcourt's management of its trading business illustrates not only successful decentralized decision making in a high-stakes, fast-paced business environment but also the absolute importance of correcting mistakes on the spot in a positive, reinforcing manner. U.S. Marine colonel (ret.) John Ripley's heroism at the Bridge at Dong Ha in Vietnam in 1972 exemplifies how a nonlinear accomplishment can be a potential outcome of decentralized decision making. Finally, the fall of Applied Energy Systems (AES) over the last three years serves as an unfortunate example of decentralized decision making gone wrong.

In stark contrast to its widely held image as a rigid, top-down military hierarchy, the Marine Corps has embraced decentralized decision making as indispensable to battlefield success. Emulating some or all of the Marines' practices can enable you to unleash the power of this fifth guiding principle of maneuver warfare in your organization. Our intent in this chapter is to use their experiences and some of the lessons learned from our historical examples to suggest ways in which you can establish a baseline of trust in your organization, train your people to make decisions confidently in your absence, communicate in a manner that provides your people with the "bigger picture," supervise the implementation of your directions, and use technology to share information throughout your organization.

PATTON'S BREAKOUT FROM NORMANDY 1944

During the Normandy Breakout in France in August 1944, General George S. Patton relied heavily on decentralized decision making to push the German front 150 miles inland from the Normandy coast, south to the Loire River, west into Brittany, and east to Argentan in a mere two weeks, ultimately encircling the German 7th Army.

In the two months following the June 6th D-day invasion, the American-led Allies successfully established a strong foothold on the beachhead at Normandy but stalled in their efforts to move farther inland. By August 1, Patton unleashed his recently formed 3rd Army on a multidirectional attack across the French countryside with one general order to his army: "Seek out the enemy, trap him, and destroy him."[3]

Figure 8.1 PATTON'S NORMANDY BREAKOUT, 1944

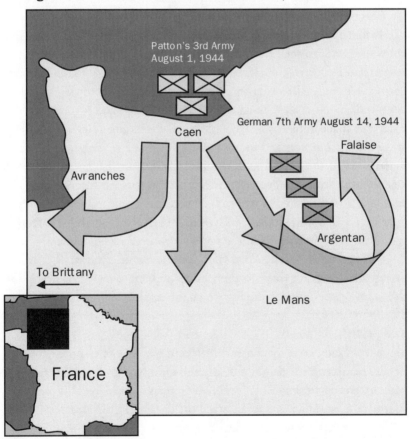

This initial communication was the first of many brief orders—often verbal and rarely exceeding a few sentences when written—that Patton would issue. In stark contrast to his peers, who normally communicated tactical plans to their large forces through lengthy documents, Patton opted to lead his 3rd Army with short mission orders that stated *what* needed to be done and left the *how* to subordinate unit commanders.

Believing that in-person visits afforded commanders ideal opportunities to communicate intent directly and inform their troops of the larger context into which their actions fit, Patton also reduced the number of cumbersome written reports that flowed upward. And when it came to supervising his subordinates, he never hesitated to ask tough questions or provide more explicit direction when necessary. At one point he went so far as to personally direct snarled traffic.

Patton split his four-corps-strong Army into three main prongs—one corps sped west to seize the Brittany Peninsula, two corps drove south to Angers and Le Mans to liberate a series of German-held towns, and another corps traversed east to trap the German 7th Army. Patton's reliance on decentralized decision making unlocked the energy and ingenuity of his men, who made decisions based on their understanding of unfolding events at the point of action and eagerly exercised initiative. Subordinate commanders ranged as much as a hundred miles from his command post, enabling his army to cover a remarkably expansive geographic area and causing Hitler to think he was facing an enemy twice its actual size. The attack caused chaos within the German Army, which had grown accustomed to strategic fighting in the previous two months of static fighting.

In two weeks, Patton's Army encircled one hundred thousand Germans in a giant loop from Caen to the Falaise Gap and recaptured nearly ten thousand square miles of the French countryside.[4]

Leadership Lessons

Some historians jokingly contend that Patton issued brief orders because he suffered from dyslexia. Indeed, after his untimely death in 1945, the U.S. Military Academy at West Point, his alma mater, positioned his memorial statue on the campus grounds to face the library. To this day, West Point Cadets joke that Patton faces the library because he never cracked a book there.

No historian denies, however, that Patton's willingness to push decision making to the lowest possible levels was a key determinant of his success during the Normandy Breakout. Knowing that each battlefield situation presented a unique set of challenges, he wisely delegated to the commanders facing those challenges in the field and trusted them to do their jobs. He also surmised correctly that he could accelerate the pace of his attack by issuing brief orders that oriented his forces on objectives and freed his subordinate leaders to proceed as rapidly as unfolding events allowed. Finally, by minimizing the amount of written correspondence between field units and higher headquarters and by pushing his commanders to visit frontline units in person, Patton dramatically improved the flow of communication within his organization.

SMITH NEWCOURT

Partners at the British trading firm Smith Newcourt[5] managed to deftly balance the risks and rewards of decentralized decision making by placing their trust in their junior traders, demanding honesty in return, and correcting mistakes on the spot.

Like any other large market-making firm in Britain in the mid-1980s, Smith Newcourt was a partnership. If a member of the firm were to make a really bad trading decision and then fail to work off his or her position, the partners, who were personally liable, would share in the losses. And if the mistake were large enough to consume all the capital the partners had, they would all be individually bankrupt. As one senior partner liked to joke, this was not U.S.-style bankruptcy but "real, old-fashioned British bankruptcy. None of this keep a house, keep a car, keep some clothes comfortable bankruptcy. This was live in a station on the London Underground, walk around in a barrel bankruptcy."[6] This high degree of personal liability could have resulted in very conservative behavior on the part of the partners and in suffocating control over all decisions made by junior personnel.

But trading decisions needed to be made quickly, often nearly instantaneously. If interest rates were to rise, Smith Newcourt traders would need to reduce their holdings of long bonds before everyone else did. If a window for equity arbitrage were to open, Smith Newcourt traders would need to short cash immediately and write a futures order in a minute or two.

There simply was not sufficient time for junior traders to ask for permission before making a decision.

Clearly, the need for speed necessitated decentralized decision making and absolute trust among junior traders. By virtue of their limited experience, they did make mistakes, which caused losses, sometimes significant, for the firm. But if juniors did not trade, they would never earn money, nor would they ever gain the experience or confidence they needed to become effective traders. To balance risk and reward, speed and safety, short-term losses and the long-term value of experience, partners at Smith Newcourt started junior traders with smaller position limits and taught them that only cowardice, dishonesty, and a failure to ask for help when in trouble were unforgivable.

In 1988 a junior trader interrupted a meeting and approached Smith Newcourt's head of equities trading, Tony Abrahams. Looking sheepish, the junior trader explained a mistake he had made seconds before. Abrahams looked at him, pretended to throw a punch, laughed, and said "Oy, meshugena" (which loosely means "Woe, silly one" in Yiddish). He then put an arm around the young trader's shoulder, walked over to the desk, and worked him out of his difficult trading position.

The young trader had gotten into a difficult position because of his lack of experience, but he was not punished because had done exactly what he had been asked to do. He saw an opportunity and acted; when it turned out badly, he went to a senior trader for help. This incident, while featured here in isolation, was indicative of an overall culture of candor and mutual trust at Smith Newcourt. Individuals could act rapidly to exploit opportunities consistent with their understanding of their objectives, and the firm could respond rapidly to manage any risks that might arise as a result.

Leadership Lessons

The partners' willingness to place their trust in juniors while maintaining firm yet forgiving vigilance reinforced the right behavior throughout Smith Newcourt. Junior traders knew they could trade aggressively without being punished, provided that they immediately informed their seniors of slipups; at the same time, they knew there would be zero tolerance for timidity, indecision, or lapses in integrity. Partners, in turn, knew that they could free junior traders to make the rapid decisions necessary to capitalize on market opportunities without fearing that small mistakes of inexperience would become firm-threatening mistakes.

RIPLEY AND THE BRIDGE AT DONG HA

During the North Vietnamese Easter Offensive in 1972, then-Captain John Ripley, U.S. Marine Corps, single-handedly destroyed a key bridge near the village of Dong Ha and halted the advance of a North Vietnamese Army (NVA) regiment of thirty thousand troops and two hundred tanks.[7] The results Ripley achieved were nonlinear in the sense that they were disproportionate to the effort made by one man and almost unbelievable in their ability to modify the tactical situation he faced. The impact came from his extraordinary physical efforts in the face of extreme adversity but also from his willingness to act decisively in the absence of guidance from higher headquarters.

Rapidly advancing in a southerly direction toward Hue City, the NVA regiment aimed to cross the Cam Lo River via a small but sturdy bridge near the village of Dong Ha. Ripley realized that the South Vietnamese unit to which he was attached as an adviser could do little to stop the NVA regiment and quickly devised a daring plan to destroy the bridge, the only available river crossing for miles.

Exposed to heavy enemy fire and armed with little more than a backpack, Ripley traveled hand-over-hand along the bottom of the bridge and ferried explosives to its key structural points. Making approximately twelve trips over the course of three hours and crimping the detonators with his teeth, Ripley secured hundreds of pounds of explosives to the bridge's girders. He detonated the bridge just prior to the arrival of the NVA regiment, and the regiment's sudden stop caused a pileup among its vehicles. Sensing vulnerability, he then called in an intense, steady barrage of aircraft and naval gunfire support, which inflicted heavy damage on his tangled opponent. For his heroic actions, which played a major role in thwarting the NVA Easter Offensive, Ripley later received the Navy Cross, his nation's second-highest award for valor.

Leadership Lessons

Ripley understood the larger context into which his actions fit and aggressively exercised initiative to achieve breakout results; he did not ask for permission. His heroism suggests that individual actions can make an impact at the strategic level, and organizations can unlock this potential by affording their people the latitude they need to "crimp detonators with their teeth."

THE FALL OF AES

Maverick electric power producer AES's aggressive decentralized approach to managing, developing, and acquiring generation and distribution facilities resulted in a spectacular rise—and fall—from 1996 to 2002. At the heart of the fall was a failure on the part of senior management to provide clear commander's intent, supervise adequately, and hold individuals accountable for transgressions of integrity.

Roger Sant, a former university professor, and Dennis Bakke, a career public official, decided when they founded the company in 1981 to forsake traditional corporate checks and controls and, instead, placed their full, if not blind, trust in their people. AES plant managers, who were closest to day-to-day operations, enjoyed unprecedented autonomy to oversee their plants as self-contained businesses; all decisions were made at the plant level under their supervision. Newly minted MBAs negotiated multimillion-dollar project loans and fuel procurement contracts. And in the 1990s AES power plant developers received free reign to invest aggressively in opportunities in the United States and developing areas, such as Latin America, southern Asia, and the former Soviet Union. Owing to this unique decentralized approach, AES was widely heralded as a new paradigm in the historically stodgy electric power and utilities industry.

But electric power markets in the United States and around the world failed to develop as economists had predicted, and AES's high-flying stock price tumbled from $70 per share in October 2000 to $5 per share in June 2002. Investors had lost faith in the assumptions underlying the company's earnings guidance and in the ability of AES senior management to address the challenges that the depressed power markets presented.

This loss of faith was well justified. As evidenced by remarks such as "We don't have a grand central plan at AES. We're pretty much opportunists,"[8] Bakke was not providing his company with a unifying strategic direction beyond the articulation of AES's core values of integrity, fairness, social responsibility—and *fun*. Project developers and regional managers received no clear, overarching guidance as to how to diversify risk across

AES's burgeoning portfolio of assets, and as a result bottom-up opportunism caused disproportionate growth in areas with high local risk, notably Latin America and California. Even at the operational level, AES lacked consistent policies for activities such as purchasing, which hurt the company's relationships with suppliers and contractors and eroded benefits from scale. According to one consultant, suppliers objected to "'a lot of people in the project structure doing things the way they want to.'"[9]

Furthermore, basic supervision at AES was woefully inadequate at multiple levels. Said Sant, "We have no sign-offs. None whatsoever. Zero."[10] The tough questions were not being asked. No one was double-checking inexperienced MBAs as they negotiated multimillion-dollar deals with industry veterans. As project developers made final decisions to build or acquire plants, the assumptions underlying the projections used to justify their multimillion-dollar commitments were not scrutinized rigorously. Not asking tough questions himself, Bakke was far removed from these and other major decisions. In one instance he did not learn about AES project developers' successful $1 billion tender offer for Chilean power company Gener, S.A., until, in his words, "after the fact."[11] Even worse, he failed to punish adequately a breach of integrity at AES's Shadypoint plant in Oklahoma, where workers had falsified emissions data. Finally, AES's board of directors failed to ask their CEO tough questions, demand greater diversification in the AES portfolio, and challenge the assumptions underlying AES's opaque consolidated financial projections.

Under pressure from disgruntled investors, Bakke resigned as CEO in June 2002. And in January 2003 the company announced a $2.7 billion noncash charge related to the reduction in the value of certain assets in the United States, United Kingdom, and Brazil.

Leadership Lessons

Among the litany of factors that contributed to AES's spectacular rise and fall, decentralized decision making played a central role. The company's unorthodox, freewheeling philosophy inspired higher levels of performance throughout its ranks, released the creativity and ingenuity of its employees, and afforded plant managers and project developers ample latitude to capitalize on market opportunities as they appeared. But without unifying intent, adequate supervision, and accountability, operations unfortunately degenerated into little more than a collection of individuals pursuing personal objectives.

ANALYSIS ACROSS EXAMPLES

The commonalties and differences among the examples raised in this chapter reveal three valuable insights regarding decentralized decision making.

First, successful decentralized decision making requires not only trust and open communications but also clear commander's intent and supervision. In the cases of Patton and Smith Newcourt, both successes, all four traits were present. Leaders willingly placed their trust in those who were closest to the action and who possessed superior local information. Communications flowed freely throughout the organizational structure. Those closest to the action clearly understood the larger context into which their actions fit and acted in accordance with the commander's intent. And leaders were able to maintain an adequate level of supervision without squelching individual initiative. In the unsuccessful case of AES, however, clear commander's intent and supervision were notably absent.

Second, decentralized decision making can be employed to increase decision making speed, and in rapidly evolving situations on-the-spot decision making may be the only way to achieve sufficient speed of response. Patton and Smith Newcourt both delegated significant decision-making authority because they knew that requiring subordinate leaders to ask for permission at every critical juncture would result in missed opportunities. By not waiting for orders from higher headquarters, Ripley was able to destroy the bridge at Dong Ha just before the North Vietnamese attempted to cross. We will see in the next chapter how decentralized decision making begets another principle of maneuver warfare, tempo.

Third, while commander's intent originates from the top, it is actually a mutual agreement between the leader and the members of the organization. The leader agrees to provide a vision and to integrate the actions of subordinates, while subordinates agree to act in a manner most likely to obtain results that support this vision. When one party does not honor the agreement, decentralized decision making falters. Bakke's failure to provide his people with clear commander's intent undermined AES's decentralized approach, whereas the junior Smith Newcourt traders' willingness to ask for help in difficult situations averted disaster and no doubt resulted in invaluable lessons learned.

DECENTRALIZED DECISION MAKING . . . THE MARINE CORPS WAY

Many of the techniques the Marines employ to decentralize decision making can be generalized to other environments and applied in your organization to inspire a higher level of performance at all levels, while minimizing the risks associated with a lesser degree of control.

Trust Tactics

The Marines' successful employment of decentralized decision making begins with the notion of *trust tactics*, which represents an implicit agreement between junior and senior Marines that is not to be violated. The senior places his or her trust in the junior, expects the junior to be actively involved in all decision-making efforts, and gives ample latitude to the junior during the execution of operations. The junior, in turn, makes decisions without asking for permission, keeps his senior informed of unfolding events, and exercises initiative that is within the limits of commander's intent without constant supervision.

Specific Decision-Making Training

With an inviolable agreement between seniors and juniors reached in principle, Marines receive specific training to ensure the success of decentralized decision making in actual implementation. At Officer Candidates' School (OCS), a ten-week "boot camp" for aspiring officers, the on-the-spot decision-making abilities of officer candidates are put to the test in the *Leadership Reaction Course* (LRC). A series of problem-solving exercises that force participants to lead their peers under simulated conditions of uncertainty, the LRC provides candidates with a dramatic introduction to the demands of decentralized decision making and weeds out weak, indecisive candidates.

Immediately after a team of candidates completes an LRC problem, they each receive candid and constructive feedback on their performance. Indeed the main purpose of the LRC is to test candidates not on their ability to solve the problem but on *how* they went about solving it: how clearly

Figure 8.2 Demonstrating the widespread applicability of the Marine Corps' Leadership Reaction Course in Quantico, MBA Students from the Wharton School work together to negotiate an obstacle.

the plan was communicated, how long they deliberated before acting, whether all team members were involved, and who emerged as the leader of the group.

Teach-Ins
In the active-duty Fleet Marine Force (FMF), unit commanders at all levels regularly conduct *teach-ins*, interactive sit-down discussions with their Marines, to convey their leadership philosophy and give junior Marines perspective on how they think about tactics and operations. The aim of these teach-ins is to enable the Marines to better anticipate and act in accordance with their leader's plans.

Commander's Intent "Two Levels Up," Mission Orders, and Explaining the Why
In actual implementation decentralized decision making requires the communication of commander's intent, mission orders, and "the why." Com-

mander's intent issued "two levels up" defines the scope within which junior Marines may exercise initiative and serves as the all-important first step the leader takes toward arming his Marines with the "bigger picture"—the larger context into which their actions fit. Leaders deliver to their Marines not only their own commander's intent but also that of their direct superior—two levels above the Marines receiving the order. And, like Patton, Marine leaders communicate their plans with *mission orders*, which state *what* needs to be done without prescribing *how* it must be done. And, going one step further, Marine leaders explain "the why." To those who perceive the Marine Corps as a rigid, top-down hierarchy, explaining "the why" is a surprisingly democratic communication technique in which the leader provides his subordinates with the rationale for his plan and for the operation as a whole. Democratic considerations aside, explaining "the why" to junior Marines reinforces the larger context into which their actions fit and provides additional rationale not covered in commander's intent.

The *S* in BAMCIS

Marine leaders remain ever-vigilant of their subordinates' activities, without interfering unduly in those activities. Supervision is a never-ending task, and Marine leaders know that the *S* in *BAMCIS*—a well-known acronym that stands for "Begin the planning, Arrange for reconnaissance, Make the reconnaissance, Complete the plan, Issue the order," and "*Supervise*,"—is the most important letter. Marine leaders, who adhere to the saying "Inspect what you expect," continually walk the lines, ask tough questions, correct mistakes on the spot, and counsel underperforming subordinates. Mistakes that stem from bold zeal or inexperience are treated as learning opportunities, provided they are in the scope of commander's intent, but indecision, timidity, and lapses in integrity are punished swiftly and forcefully.

Ultimate Responsibility

In a similar vein, all Marine leaders personally accept responsibility for the actions of the subordinates to whom they delegate authority. Indeed the Marine Corps's equivalent of Harry Truman's venerable "The buck stops here" is "The leader is ultimately responsible for everything his or her unit does or fails to do."

Common Tactical Picture

Always seeking to hone its proficiency in decentralized decision making, the Marine Corps has turned to technology in recent years to enable better-informed decisions among its frontline units and accelerate the upward flow of information within its fighting forces. The *Common Tactical Picture* (CTP) initiative, under development since the late 1990s, promises to link several previously disparate tactical systems and provide all Marine commanders—from general to captain—with a common, current, and relevant picture of the battlefield and, therefore, improved awareness of unfolding events. To access the system, frontline leaders carry portable computers, which provide alerts of key events, track reports of enemy sightings, call for supporting fire, and offer larger views of the battlefield than otherwise available. These portable computers connect to field headquarters units via distributed collection devices, and field headquarters units use CTP to tailor information available to frontline commanders and track the locations and actions of frontline units. While CTP has the undesirable potential side effect of excessive supervision of frontline units by overly nosy higher headquarters, the system does enable pervasive information sharing and enhanced decentralized decision making.

APPLICATION IN BUSINESS

To employ a decentralized approach reminiscent of that of the Marine Corps in your organization, first establish clear guidelines for the degree of trust to be shared between seniors and juniors. With these guidelines in place, prepare your people to make decisions in the absence of direction. Devise creative ways to train them to make decisions and lead under simulated conditions of uncertainty and provide them with real-time feedback on their performance in these exercises. When possible, complement this bottom-up training with teach-ins, which reinforce your philosophy from the top down, and encourage your junior managers to do the same in their respective groups.

Prior to communicating detailed instructions, orient your people on the objectives you wish to achieve by issuing an accompanying statement of your commander's intent. And make your people aware of the objectives that your supervisor wishes to achieve by mentioning his or her commander's intent. Moreover, remember that commander's intent cannot be imposed solely from the top down; it requires the willing consent of those in your charge.

Once your people are oriented to the goals you wish to achieve, communicate to them what needs to be done and explain to them the larger context into which their actions fit; no one can exceed expectations that he does not understand. Then give them the latitude they need to use their judgment and initiative to deliver the desired results. But be sure to follow this delegation with vigilant supervision and a willingness to intervene where necessary, for, as previously noted, "you can always delegate authority, but you can never delegate responsibility." Correct mistakes on the spot and punish violations of trust to reinforce honest, open behavior in your organization.

Finally, to increase the information available to and, thus, the decision-making capacity of those in your charge, develop systems that share information both vertically and horizontally throughout your organization. Many enterprise resource-planning systems, like SAP, already provide a common picture of sales, revenues, and expenses throughout an organization. Other systems integrate management support and route or network management data, to enable real-time pricing and capacity allocation decisions. Devise new and creative ways to leverage these systems.

CHAPTER 9

TEMPO

"Things may come to those who wait, but only things left by those who hustle."

—ABRAHAM LINCOLN[1]

Tempo is *relative speed* in time—identifying opportunities, making decisions, and acting faster than one's opponent, thereby forcing him into a constant state of reaction.

Speed is clearly central to maneuver warfare, but the relevant measure for tempo is not absolute speed or hustle: the aim of tempo is to plan and initiate the next action while the opponent is still observing and reacting to previous moves. Seizing the initiative allows the practitioner of maneuver warfare to dictate the time, place, and nature of each competitive encounter, thereby assuring a superior state of preparedness and a position of relative advantage. As the opponent attempts to comprehend the action and muster a response, the practitioner of maneuver warfare imagines and prepares for that which might happen next and plots his or her next moves. Ideally, in a multiperiod encounter, the opponent will fall increasingly behind and will end up responding inappropriately to events that have already occurred. Alternatively, in a multiple-arena encounter, the practitioner of maneuver warfare can move among the arenas so rapidly that the enemy is never sure where he is being engaged.

In this chapter we offer five examples of tempo and its key components, as well as present-day lessons from the Marines. U.S. Air Force colonel John Boyd's breakthrough analysis of the differences in decision-making speed exhibited by U.S. pilots and their North Korean and Chinese opponents during the Korean War illustrates tempo in warfare. And Cisco Systems' ascent in the networking equipment market since its initial public offering in 1990 illustrates tempo in business. Lieutenant General "Stonewall" Jackson's leadership in the Shenandoah Valley in the U.S. Civil War in 1862 exemplifies tempo in a multiarena encounter in warfare. In the very same year, hesitation by Union general George McClellan cost the Union a valuable opportunity at the Battle of Antietam—and McClellan his job. Finally, a rapid-fire sequence of interrelated customer service and scheduling innovations at corporate travel agency Rosenbluth International in the early 1980s exemplifies tempo in a multiperiod encounter in the business environment.

The Marines consider tempo a weapon, and this weapon can become part of your arsenal of business practices. Based on the techniques they employ and on some of the lessons learned from our five historical examples, we will recommend ways in which you can increase your own decision-making speed, promote rapid tempo throughout your organization, and use technology to accelerate operations and prevent catastrophic halts.

F-86 V. MIG-15 AND BOYD'S OODA LOOP

In the skies above Korea, North Korean and Chinese fighter pilots in Soviet-made MiG-15 planes were no match for their American counterparts, who flew F-86 Sabre jets, from 1951 to 1953. Colonel John Boyd dedicated the subsequent thirty-five years to analyzing reasons for the Americans' success, and his groundbreaking theories brought considerable emphasis to relative decision-making speed as a key determinant of success in combat.

Despite the Soviet-made aircraft's superior capabilities in turning, climbing, and acceleration, American pilots shot down ten MiG-15s for every F-86 lost. The Americans achieved this impressive kill ratio by adjusting their aerial tactics to exploit the two key advantages that the F-86 enjoyed relative to the MiG-15: visibility and responsiveness. First, the F-86's "bubble" canopy afforded its pilot an unobstructed view in nearly every direction, whereas the MiG-15's canopy sacrificed the pilot's field of vision for superior aerodynamics and performance. Second, the F-86's fully powered hydraulic flight controls, which were highly sensitive to the pilot's inputs, required far less physical and mental exertion during aerial maneuvers than did the MiG-15's hydraulically boosted mechanical flight controls, thereby allowing faster execution and sequencing of actions as the combat unfolded.

Together a better field of vision and a more responsive set of flight controls enabled the F-86 pilot to transition more quickly and more effortlessly between individual maneuvers, and American pilots engaged the MiG-15s with a series of sudden, quick moves to which the MiG-15s could not respond. For example, if a MiG-15 were pursuing an F-86 and the F-86 started a turn in one direction and then quickly reversed its move, the MiG-15 would not be able to follow without falling slightly behind in the chase. As this series of moves and counter-moves repeated, the MiG-15 would fall farther and farther behind in time until the F-86 assumed the firing position (behind or perpendicular to the MiG-15) and shot the MiG-15 down.

Boyd disaggregated these aerial duels into discernible steps, which he believed could be generalized to all competitive encounters. He articulated these steps as the *OODA loop*, a continuous, time-competitive cycle in which each opponent: *Observed* the other's behavior, *Oriented* himself or herself to unfolding events, *Decided* on a best possible course of action, and *Acted*. The articulation of the OODA loop became the forerunner of many studies that Boyd would conduct, and these studies, particularly his 1986 *Patterns of Conflict*, have left an indelible impression on modern maneuver warfare theory. Not only did Boyd go on to teach warfare theory at the Marine Corps University in Quantico, Virginia, but there were also more Marine Corps officers present at his funeral than there were Air Force officers.

Leadership Lessons

The opponent that proceeds through the four-step OODA loop in less time operates inside the other's decision-making cycle and seizes the upper hand. And, given that OODA loops flow together in time, such rapid decision making in one OODA loop leads to success in others. If an opponent is already struggling to cope with the situation at hand when the other opponent's action begins an entirely new situation, effective response becomes increasingly difficult. Eventually, the effects of rapid decision making accumulate, and the slower-moving opponent is overcome.

CISCO SYSTEMS—"THE FAST BEATS THE SLOW"

Embodying CEO John Chambers's mantra, "It is not the big that beats the small in the new world; it is the fast that beats the slow,"[2] Cisco Systems has employed rapid tempo in product development, acquisitions, and internal operations to outpace its rivals and become the premier provider of Internet networking equipment.

Pre-Internet telecommunications equipment was generally designed to last several years or more, and products had correspondingly long sales and development cycles. Correctly anticipating the accelerating pace of technological change in the Internet age, Cisco turned to decentralized decision making to shorten these cycles from years to months and ushered high-quality products to market faster than competitors were able to. Cisco organized its product managers around market segments and gave them considerable authority to make design, budgeting, and marketing decisions based on their particular segment's needs; there was no waiting for approval from layers of bureaucracy far removed from evolving market dynamics.

In stark contrast, product introductions and changes at other telecommunications equipment companies, notably Lucent Technologies, muddled through a cumbersome product review and approval process, often resulting in multiyear product development cycles. Owing to such methodical review, Lucent and other would-be competitors fell behind as Cisco raced forward.

Although Cisco developed an estimated 70 percent of its products internally, the remainder came from acquisition; to this end the company acquired seventy-one small companies from 1990 to 2000 alone.[3] Beginning with the due diligence and decision-making process, speed was a central element in Cisco's acquisition strategy. While competitors typically approached due diligence deliberately, fumbled through multiyear integration efforts, and relied heavily on outside advisers, Cisco appointed in-house mergers and acquisitions (M&A) teams to analyze targets and complete acquisitions. These teams relied heavily on predefined frameworks and procedures with specific technical, strategic, financial, and cultural guidelines to structure their efforts and incorporate lessons learned from previous acquisitions. And immediately after transaction closings, Cisco would dedicate internal cross-functional "SWAT" teams to oversee the full integration of the acquired companies, a process that was generally completed in a mere 120 to 180 days.

The 1994 acquisition of Kalpana Inc., a 150-employee provider of Ethernet switching equipment, exemplifies Cisco's blistering tempo in acquisitions. IBM had been considering acquiring Kalpana for several months. But during one of the weekends that IBM was conducting, of all things, soil tests at the Kalpana site, a Cisco M&A team completed an analysis of Kalpana's strategic fit and valuation, made the decision to acquire the smaller company, and snatched it from IBM's grasp.[4]

To facilitate breakneck speed in internal operations, Cisco has embraced the power of the Internet. Systems that are closely networked together have maximized the amount of timely information that can be shared throughout the company. Digital "dashboards" have enabled managers to monitor all aspects of the company's operations in real time and make better-informed decisions more quickly. And Cisco's chief financial officer claimed in 2000 that the company could "close the books"—reconcile and aggregate the financial statements of its far-flung global operations—using online software system *in a day*.[5]

Rapid tempo has resulted in rapid growth for Cisco, whose revenues have increased from $69 million in 1990 to $19 billion in 2002.

Leadership Lessons

Cisco could very well have served as an excellent example of decentralized decision making in Chapter 8. But Cisco appears in this chapter because the company was deliberately configured to support a strategy of rapid decision making. Product development decision-making authority was positioned as close to the market segments Cisco served to maximize responsiveness to changing conditions. The company's leaders brought M&A capabilities in-house and adopted a highly structured approach to create internal expertise and facilitate rapid execution in an inherently uncertain and complex endeavor. And Cisco senior management invested in the infrastructure necessary to arm decision makers with real-time information and streamline internal operations.

STONEWALL JACKSON—"PRESS ON"

Embodying *his* mantra of "Press on. Press on, men," Lieutenant General Thomas "Stonewall" Jackson led his Confederate troops on a series of quick strikes in the Shenandoah Valley between May 23 and June 9, 1862, and forced the much larger Union Army into a constant state of off-balanced reaction to his initiatives.[6]

During the Spring of 1862 three separate Union armies, outnumbering Jackson's forces by three to one, occupied several outposts throughout the valley. Undaunted, Jackson devised a brilliant plan to strike these outposts in succession, destroy the larger Union Army in detail, and deny the Union a southerly route through the valley into the heart of the Confederate States.[7] The key to his transitory "hit and move strategy" was rapid movement between points, which would enable his forces to attack with local numerical superiority before Union reinforcements from adjacent outposts could arrive.

Given the importance of mobility to his plan, Jackson memorized the distances between the towns in the valley to estimate travel time between points, and he located every improved road to identify the quickest marching routes for his troops. Moreover, he used trains to ferry troops from one attack site to the next and marched his men at breakneck speed, sometimes with nothing more than a bare minimum of food, clothing, and ammunition.

Beginning with a battle in the small western valley town of McDowell on May 8, Jackson crisscrossed the valley on a whirlwind series of attacks. With all the speed he could muster, Jackson ferried six thousand of his troops by foot and train to McDowell to defeat an isolated Union force of twenty-three hundred men. This victory, though seemingly small, set the tone for a series of sluggish Union reactions to his unpredictable moves.

He then advanced 120 miles to the northeast to strike Front Royal on May 23, where his forces inflicted more than 900 casualties on a 1,000-man Union force, and north to Winchester on May 25, where his forces routed a force of more than 6,000 men. After reaching Harpers Ferry and posing a threat to northern soil, which further distracted the Union from the Confederate States, Jackson then turned south and raced 100 miles to strike the Union at Cross Keys on June 8 and Port Republic on June 9.

During this whirlwind series of attacks, Jackson's forces repeatedly routed their Union opponents and on more than one occasion used speed to narrowly escape envelopment from reinforcements. In five weeks Jackson's Army covered more than 600 miles, captured 3,500 prisoners, inflicted 6,900 casualties, at a cost of fewer than 2,500 casualties, while safeguarding both the valley and the Confederate States from the Union.[8]

Figure 9.1 STONEWALL JACKSON'S VALLEY CAMPAIGN, MAY–JUNE, 1862

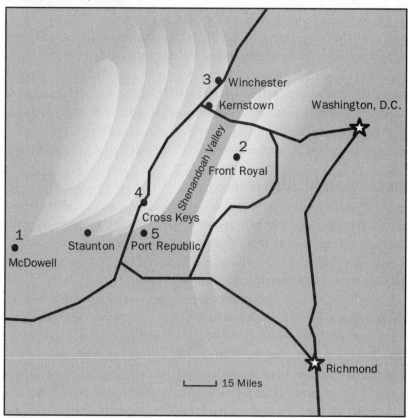

Approximate Distances
Winchester – Port Republic 80 mi
Staunton – McDowell 34 mi
Front Royal – Kernstown 22 mi
McDowell – Front Royal 113 mi

Leadership Lessons

Jackson's campaign embodies tempo in a multiarena encounter because he kept his opponent off balance by striking at multiple points in rapid succession. The much larger Union Army never knew where or when the next attack would come, thereby enabling Jackson to dictate the terms of battle. By the time his opponent reacted to one of his strikes, he was already moving in another direction, rendering the response inappropriate and ineffective.

Jackson knew that he could not withdraw from his much larger opponent without jeopardizing the very survival of the Confederacy. He also knew that, given his numerical inferiority, he could not allow the Union to gain the initiative, maneuver into a position of advantage, and bring its overwhelming strength to bear on his forces. Thus he chose to seize the initiative, isolate the Union forces unit by unit, and defeat them in detail. In so doing, he used familiarity with the local geography and transportation infrastructure—roads and railroads—to accelerate his rate of maneuver.

MCCLELLAN AT ANTIETAM

Standing in stark contrast, Stonewall Jackson's classmate at West Point General George Brinton McClellan failed to seize two key opportunities at the Battle of Antietam in September 1862 and a third in the months that followed. His hesitation serves as an excellent example of how the human decision-making process can limit tempo.

McClellan's first failure to seize the initiative occurred four days prior to the battle, when Union soldiers found Lee's battle plans. By midday September 15, McClellan had already amassed seventy-five thousand of his ninety thousand troops at the town of Sharpsburg, directly in front of Lee, whose army included only eighteen thousand troops at the time.[9] Lee's forces were split and vulnerable: he lacked a readily available reserve, and he had minimal supporting artillery or cavalry. Despite knowing Lee's precarious disposition, McClellan, making the excuse at approximately 2:00 P.M. on the 15th that it was too late to move, opted to wait before striking. Then stalling again on the 16th, McClellan blamed his delay on "obtaining more information, rectifying the position of troops, and perfecting the arrangement for attacks."[10] These two delays resulted directly in the standoff that followed at Sharpsburg; Lee used the lapse in time to bring twenty-two thousand additional troops from the South. What ensued was the bloodiest single day of fighting on American soil—Lee lost nearly eleven thousand of his men, while McClellan lost more than twelve thousand—without a decisive victory for either side.

McClellan's second failure to seize the initiative occurred after the battle. Although still outnumbering Lee by nearly fifty thousand men, he refused to press the attack on the beleaguered southerners. This time he cited a lack of complete information and inadequate strategic reserves for his inaction. Through the 18th, the Confederate forces were backed against the Potomac River. After realizing that McClellan was not in pursuit, Lee understood that the difficult strategic withdrawal across the river could be accomplished safely without drawing enemy fire, and he was able to slink slowly across the single river crossing back into West Virginia.

For nearly two months following the battle, McClellan declined to give chase and remained rooted at Sharpsburg, even as President Abraham Lincoln pleaded that he renew the attack. For this third and final reluctance to act, which gave Lee valuable time over the fall and winter, to regroup, reconstitute his army, and avoid further contact until he had assembled a more formidable force, Lincoln officially relieved McClellan of his command.

Leadership Lessons

McClellan failed to make decisions and act until he possessed "perfect information" or until he outnumbered his opponent by a wide margin. Accordingly, he ceded the ability to seize the initiative and dictate the course of events in the encounter. Had he attacked earlier on the 15th, on the 16th, or in the months following the battle, he would have done so from a position of relative strength, and he would have been much more likely to overwhelm the reeling Confederates. Counter to the maneuver philosophy of pressing the attack to accelerate tempo, McClellan favored taking a "strategic pause" to regroup, think, and await near-perfect information that, given the fog of war and independence of human will, never came.

ROSENBLUTH INTERNATIONAL

In the early 1980s, Rosenbluth International, a Philadelphia-based corporate travel management company, initiated a series of customer service improvements that identified and satisfied customer needs before dozens of competitors, who were slow to realize what was happening and even slower to mount an effective response, recognized that those needs existed.

The deregulation in the U.S. airline industry in the late 1970s created tremendous complexity in air travel where rigid simplicity had previously existed. Corporate clients needed considerable help in choosing among myriad routes and fares. A strategy based on reducing complexity was an ideal response to deregulation *if* an agency was able to see the need.

From 1980 to 1981, the period of time during which the change that accompanied deregulation was most intense, then–vice president Hal Rosenbluth, now president and CEO, assigned himself to duty as a travel agent rather than a corporate officer. Witnessing firsthand customers' anger and confusion and his own agents' inability to help, Hal devised and implemented a strategy to reduce complexity for his target market of corporate clients through superior information management.

His first move was a system for managing travel expenses called *Readout*, which enabled his agents to describe flights based on price first and departure time second. Business doubled the day that Readout was introduced, and before competitors were aware of this first move Hal introduced *Vision*, a system that enabled his corporate clients to track expenses incurred by individual, department, or project. Then came *Uservision*, which enhanced the capabilities of Vision by enabling corporate clients to download and analyze information as they saw fit. These system introductions had an added advantage, which further enhanced customer service: Rosenbluth International could actively capture customer profile information and record the preferences of hundreds of thousands of customers—window or aisle seat, smoking or nonsmoking room, high floor or low floor, Marriott or Hyatt.

Competitors that might not have noticed each of these innovations could not miss their impact—Rosenbluth International was large and growing larger. Caught off balance but desperate to participate in the new market for corporate travel that Rosenbluth had created, many competitors initiated knee-jerk responses, such as rebates that were relatively insignificant to travelers but devastating to agencies' profits. These rebates ultimately undermined other agencies' ability to compete: to retain business in the face of the superior Rosenbluth service, competitors had to increase rebates further, and a vicious circle of increasing rebates and decreasing service quality resulted.

While competitors floundered in their response to his initial moves, Hal launched yet another innovation. Designed with the close cooperation of United Airlines and the Apollo computer reservation system, computer codes, known as scripting languages, automatically combined airline, hotel, and rental car reservations and automatically featured offerings from preferred providers. Scripting languages effectively eliminated the possibility of reserving a flight into New York City's JFK Airport and accidentally reserving a car at nearby Newark Airport. Scripting languages also provided greater assurances that a corporate client that enjoyed a preferred relationship with an airline would make a reservation with that airline whenever possible, thereby maximizing discounts for clients and rebates for Rosenbluth.

With these steps in place Hal began to negotiate reduced fares for his largest accounts, and he was able to achieve discounts of 10 percent or more on many routes. Moreover, as the volume of Rosenbluth International's ticket purchases increased, the airlines rewarded Hal with commission overrides, which increased the amount his firm was earning even if the cost of tickets was lower. Reduced fares attracted more business, which increased Hal's ability to negotiate fares, and his business grew further. This virtuous circle, based on tight coupling among service improvement, growth in market share, and increased investment in technological support, stands in stark contrast with the vicious circle that competitors faced.

Once again Hal's moves caught competitors off balance. Most had neither the market share to justify requesting a discount nor the systems in place to assure that customers shared in the benefits of scripting languages. Indeed, although scripting languages were available to all agencies, only Rosenbluth International had participated in their development, and only Rosenbluth International was fully positioned to benefit from them.

Rosenbluth International's array of offices was once fewer than a dozen, tightly clustered around Philadelphia. Today more than fifteen hundred offices span the globe, and the company remains privately held, with no debt and no dilution of the original family's equity position.

Leadership Lessons

Rosenbluth International exemplifies tempo in a multiperiod encounter because Hal Rosenbluth unleashed not just one but a series of rapid moves on opponents, who fell further and further behind. Hal's willingness to lead from the front enabled him to observe market trends as they emerged. Long before executives at competitors sensed how deregulation would impact customers and agents, Hal had already identified the appropriate strategy—reduce customers' complexity. Rosenbluth succeeded by identifying customers' true preferences and delivering better service and lower fares, while making firm commitments that the customer would always receive the best available fare for any ticket. While most of us cannot replicate this management style and assume the job of a frontline, first-level employee, all of us can certainly learn to listen to those closest to the action.

Although Hal was acting as an agent, he still had the authority of a corporate vice president, and he was still the CEO's son. When he made a decision, he did not have to wait for approval, and he was able to impact a broad scope of his company's activities. His decisiveness and propensity to act matched his speed in identifying market trends. Competitors could not hope to match his blistering tempo.

ANALYSIS ACROSS EXAMPLES

Taken as a whole, the examples raised to illustrate this sixth guiding principle of maneuver warfare offer several key insights. First, Cisco, Jackson, McClellan, and Rosenbluth International can all be examined from the perspective of Boyd's OODA loop. Cisco shortened the time required to *o*bserve and *o*rient by locating *d*ecision making authority close to unfolding events and exploited the slow *d*ecision making of its rivals. And its investment in information sharing further enhanced its decision makers' ability to *o*bserve and *o*rient, thereby facilitating sound and timely decisions throughout the organization.

Jackson exploited the lack of communication and long travel time between Union outposts to operate inside the Union Army's OODA loop. Dispersed Union forces could not begin their OODA cycle until Jackson *a*cted. By the time reinforcements arrived and *a*cted in response, Jackson was already focused on the next engagement and in the midst of a subsequent OODA cycle.

McClellan, in addition to taking a painfully long time to *o*bserve and *o*rient, was reluctant to *d*ecide and *a*ct.

Rosenbluth dramatically accelerated the *o*bserve and *o*rient process by assigning himself to a travel agent's desk, and he used his authority in the company to ensure that *a*ctions matched his rapid *d*ecision-making speed; competitors were only beginning to *o*bserve and *o*rient as he proceeded through multiple OODA cycles. Cisco, Jackson, and Rosenbluth all operated inside opponents' OODA loops.

Second, Boyd's analysis of aerial combat, Jackson's campaign in the Shenandoah Valley, and Rosenbluth International's rapid-fire sequence of perfectly timed moves illustrate the cumulative effects of not permitting an opponent to recover from previous actions. In contrast, McClellan's willingness to let his reeling opponent regroup eliminated any momentum his forces could have generated in the attack.

Third, while Jackson illustrates how an individual can drive tempo from the top down, Cisco and Rosenbluth International illustrate how an individual can foster rapid tempo in an organization from the bottom up. Cisco decentralized decision making as a means to achieve tempo; Hal Rosenbluth located himself and his considerable decision-making authority where he could "keep his finger on the pulse of the market" and react to unfolding events in real time.

TEMPO . . . THE MARINE CORPS WAY

Emulating the techniques that the Marines employ to promote rapid tempo can enable you to *move at the speed of decision* and preempt competitors in the business environment.

Training Decision-Making Speed

From the day they enter the Corps, Marines relentlessly strive to increase decision-making speed. One of the greatest challenges for enlisted recruits and officer candidates in initial training is having too much to do and not enough time to do it. By design, overly ambitious daily routines artificially introduce stress into the training environment, but more important, they inculcate a constant sense of urgency, which is intended to stay with Marines throughout their careers.

At The Basic School, newly minted lieutenants participate in hypothetical combat exercises on sand table dioramas with unrealistically short time limits. In front of their peers and competing against an instructor, lieutenants must formulate the best possible plan in the time period allotted. With repetition under increasingly challenging conditions, the lieutenants become more accustomed to the demands of decision making under pressure, and they begin to understand that, more often than not, unforgiving real world situations do not afford sufficient time to formulate complete plans.

In another time-sensitive exercise, lieutenants receive descriptive reports via radio from a notional "sniper" observing notional battlefield events forward of friendly lines. The lieutenant must determine how much information is enough and when to act. In the exercise the sniper acts as a scout until he is ordered to fire. The sniper's reports continue until the lieutenant keys his handset—the signal to fire—at which point the lieutenant must formulate a tactical plan for his or her unit based on the information received. Lieutenants, who key the handset early in the report, risk insufficient information for the formulation of their plans but are usually rewarded for acting quickly. Those who wait too long to key the handset might develop a better plan but are penalized severely for hesitation by instructors. The personal balance taught by this exercise reinforces the notion that decision should occur sooner rather than later.

The *OO* in *OODA*

Knowing that proximity to unfolding events minimizes the time required to *o*bserve and *o*rient, Marine commanders strive to locate themselves as close to the action as possible. As mentioned in Chapter 4, they always lead from the front. And when they reach the point at which their proximity to unfolding events begins to impede their ability to see the "big picture," they delegate ample decision-making authority to their subordinate leaders who are closest to the action.

⅓–⅔ Rule

The *⅓-⅔ Rule* requires that the leader allocate only one-third of the time available before a deadline for his or her own planning and reserve the remaining two-thirds for his or her subordinates, so that they may plan and coordinate at their respective levels. Marines' strict adherence to this rule reveals that they discipline themselves not to monopolize precious time during the planning process, thereby minimizing the incidence of decision-making bottlenecks.

Obligation to Dissent, Part 2

In Chapters 5 and 8, we saw that the Marines encourage the *obligation to dissent* during the decision-making process to foster boldness and decentralized decision making. But they also realize that this practice can inhibit tempo past a certain point. Accordingly, once the decision has been made, Marines execute that decision as if it were their own. Such discipline enables the Marines to leverage the insights of junior Marines and encourage buy-in during planning while avoiding the potential paralysis that can result from consensus-based decision making during implementation.

R2P2

Two-thousand-member Marine Expeditionary Units (MEUs) have institutionalized the Rapid Reaction Planning Process (R2P2), which enables a task force to launch from the ships that carry them and respond to calls for combat, evacuation, humanitarian assistance, or disaster relief ashore within six hours. R2P2 compresses the normal Marine Corps planning process into six steps: mission analysis, course of action (COA) development, COA war gaming, COA comparison and decision, orders development, and transition to execution—an impressive feat given the size of the MEU and number of constituencies involved.

Within the first hour the MEU commander and his battle staff receive the mission, gather available intelligence, and provide initial planning guidance. Within an hour and a half the battle staff evaluates possible courses of action, conducts war games, and recommends a preferred COA to the commander, who makes a final decision. Within three hours the battle staff refines its intelligence preparation and prepares a full written operations order. Within four hours the MEU commander and the battle staff brief the operations order. And in the remaining two hours before launch, ground combat, air, and support units conduct briefs, final preparations, and rehearsals.[11]

To meet the demanding time requirements of R2P2, the MEU commander and his battle staff rely heavily on exhaustive practice, continuity in working relationships, and, above all, standardized operating procedures (SOPs), which "allow units to carry out familiar tasks effectively and efficiently with minimal or no higher-level guidance or communications."[12]

Network Operations and Systems Security

The Marine Corps, like most organizations today, relies heavily on information systems to accelerate the pace at which it operates. But an increased reliance on technology creates new vulnerabilities: a downed server, virus, hacker, or major system failure could cause the Corps's high tempo of operations to grind to a halt.

To mitigate systems vulnerabilities, the Marines build a great deal of redundancy and security into their data systems. Every network path has at least three routes, sometimes many more. Redundancy, which entails building and placing more systems online, is inherently expensive, but systems failure is more costly in the long run. Additionally, Marines build a layered defense to protect against security breaches and virus attacks. They install high-tech security hardware and software at all entry points and inside the network, closely monitor systems for intrusion, and work vigilantly to secure all outgoing data.

APPLICATION IN BUSINESS

Constantly push yourself to make sound decisions as rapidly as possible so that your tempo is greater than that of your competitors and be your own harshest critic when evaluating your own decision-making speed. Position decision-making authority as close to the action as possible. Use the ⅓-⅔ Rule to avoid monopolizing your people's precious time. Treat competitive encounters as multiperiod or multiarena contests; strive to think several steps ahead, as Rosenbluth did in the corporate travel market, or engage competitors on different fronts rapidly, as Jackson did in the Shenandoah Valley. Above all, do not let your competitors use superior tempo to get inside of your OODA loop and short-circuit your decision-making process.

Just as you constantly push yourself, constantly push your people to follow the example that you set so that rapid tempo pervades your organization. Prepare your people to make quick decisions under pressure through practice, perhaps by posing dilemmas related to your business and working with them to formulate and articulate plans in real time. Provide them with feedback so that they may sharpen their decision-making skills on an ongoing basis. Encourage vigorous debate in the decision-making process—until the decision has been made. Consider making the investment—in terms of time, money, and personnel—necessary to institutionalize an R2P2 capability in your organization.

Realize that a growing reliance on information technology creates new opportunities—and new vulnerabilities—for rapid tempo. In the age of cell phones, E-mail, and the Internet, which enable near-instantaneous and near-ubiquitous transmission of information, the human decision-making process becomes the primary factor that limits tempo. Instead of relying on the aforementioned technological innovations as a crutch that allows you to recover from wasting time and deferring decisions, use them to get a product to market ahead of schedule or submit a presentation early. Finally, invest in systems security and redundancy to prevent a virus or communication breakdown from causing your high-tempo organization to come to a grinding halt.

CHAPTER 10

COMBINED ARMS

"The challenge for every organization is to build a feeling of oneness, of dependence on one another because the question is usually not how well each person works, but how well they work together."
—Vince Lombardi[1]

Combined arms is the integration of complementary weapons in a manner that creates a synergistic effect and places an opponent in an inescapable, hopeless situation, otherwise known as the *horns of a dilemma.*

Given that the capabilities of certain weapons reinforce one another, a commander's arsenal can be considerably more lethal when deployed as a coordinated, synchronized whole than it would otherwise be if the weapons were deployed individually. And the commander's arsenal becomes exponentially more lethal when the coordinated, synchronized deployment of weapons creates a situation in which "to defend against one attack, the enemy must become more vulnerable to another."[2] As the opponent's potential responses are systematically eliminated, he becomes paralyzed with fear and despair, loses the will to resist, and inevitably finds himself "impaled on the horns of a dilemma."[3]

While devastatingly effective, combined arms is an inherently complex and difficult endeavor that demands the utmost cooperation, practice, communication, and implicit understanding throughout an organization. To this end the various constituencies involved in the combined arms effort must set aside their competing interests, strive to understand and antici-pate the actions of other team members, and think and act as one.

In this chapter we offer four examples of combined arms and its key components, as well as present-day lessons from the Marines. English king Henry V's integrated deployment of archers, spikes, and terrain at the Bat-tle of Agincourt in 1415 illustrates combined arms in early warfare. In busi-ness Lexus's successful integration of design, manufacturing, marketing, and service enabled it to offer a product that neither German nor U.S. lux-ury automakers could match, and this successful use of combined arms made its focused attack on the U.S. luxury car market all the more effec-tive. A series of raids conducted by U.S. Marines from the 5th Battalion, 11th Marine Regiment (5/11), a Marine Corps artillery battalion, during Operation Desert Storm in 1991 exemplifies combined arms in modern warfare. And NetJets' employment of combined arms enabled it to pioneer the concept of the fractional ownership of private jets and maintain a dom-inant position in the market niche it created, even as numerous competi-tors attempted to replicate its business model.

Emulating the Marines' combined arms practices could help you put your competitors on the horns of a dilemma. Based on the techniques they employ and on some of the lessons learned from our four historical exam-ples, we will recommend ways in which you can form the optimal com-bined arms team, employ its capabilities in the most effective manner, and encourage maximum cooperation among the various constituencies in your organization.

HENRY V AT AGINCOURT

At the Battle of Agincourt on October 25, 1415, Henry V, king of England, rallied his weary army with his now-famous St. Crispin's Day speech, as immortalized by Shakespeare, "We few, we happy few, we band of broth-ers; for he today that sheds his blood with me shall be my brother,"[4] and used combined arms to rout the French Army—four times larger than his own army—that opposed him.

With approximately thirty thousand French troops in hot pursuit of his seven-thousand-man army, Henry decided to make a stand near the town of Agincourt in northern France. On a muddy field surrounded by woods and only nine hundred yards wide, the French formed for battle in three ranks, with heavy infantry in the center and armored, horse-mounted cavalry on either side. Henry correctly observed that their formation would be compressed tightly on the relatively narrow field and that individual or unit maneuver in the ankle-deep mud would be difficult.[5] He therefore arrayed his troops in an open-U-shaped single line, with heavy infantry in the middle and archers, facing inward at a forty-five-degree angle, on either side. The archers' oblique orientation was intended to enable them to provide either direct fire into the French lines or supporting fire for Henry's heavy infantry in the center of the English line. Henry also anchored the extreme left and right of his formation to the woods to prevent the French

Figure 10.1 HENRY V AT AGINCOURT, 1415

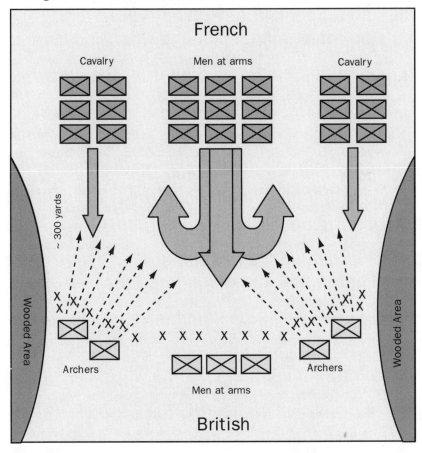

cavalry from riding around the ends of his line and attacking his vulnerable flanks.

Henry marched his forces within longbow range of the French, took a defensive position, and waited for the French attack. Renowned for their prowess, the English archers could fire their powerful longbows up to ten arrows per minute at a range of up to 300 yards.[6] These arrows had tremendous knock-down power and were lethal to infantry and horses alike at great distances. Still Henry's foot-mobile troops were vulnerable to a charge by horse-mounted heavy cavalry, which was imminent. To counter this weakness, Henry ordered his men to carve eight-foot-long wooden stakes and drive them into the ground at forty-five-degree angles; his reasoning was that the approaching horses would either stop out of instinctual fear of the stakes or be impaled. And he needed to protect his archers, who would no doubt be the first target of the charge.

At 11 A.M. on October 25, the French cavalry charged. As the horses reached the stakes, they did exactly what Henry thought they would—they stopped short, often throwing their riders. Horses that were not killed by the archers bucked their riders and frantically ran back to French lines. Heavily armored riders who had been thrown from their mounts became inescapably stuck in the mud, and the U-shaped English formation funneled the French formation into the middle of the field.

As the second wave of the French attack began, advancing troops collided with the frantic horses, creating disarray in the French ranks, and a steady hail of deadly arrows from the English longbows quickly turned disarray into mass confusion. The U-shaped English formation continued to funnel the newly committed French troops into the already compressed field, where they were held nearly motionless, exposed to English archers. The second French wave failed to make a measurable advance, while the third wave never materialized. The French foot soldiers from the initial charge that did manage to reach the English lines were too exhausted to fight effectively; the English heavy infantry defeated them with ease.

The outnumbered English handily won the day, and Henry saved his army from near-certain obliteration. The French lost an estimated 7,000 soldiers, while the English suffered a relatively low 150 casualties. On October 29, Henry and his army reached the coastal city of Calais, France, and safely returned to England.[7]

Leadership Lessons

Henry's tactics demonstrate an early yet highly effective example of combined arms. Without the stakes the horses easily would have overrun his archers. Without the archers the armored attackers could have dismounted and circumvented the stakes to annihilate his heavy infantry. And without the clever use of terrain the French cavalry could have bypassed the ends of his lines and attacked his vulnerable flanks. Moreover, the stakes triggered an instinctual reaction in the French horses, which, in turn, created pandemonium in the waves of attacking French soldiers. Though use of the stakes was somewhat common during Henry's day, Henry used them in a uniquely deadly combination with his other assets. A withering cross fire of arrows exploited this pandemonium and created a deteriorating situation for exhausted and disoriented French survivors with only one apparent way out—by attempting to fight through fresh, well-armed English infantry. The French were indeed caught in the horns of a dilemma.

LEXUS'S ENTRY INTO THE U.S. AUTO MARKET, PART 2

As we saw in Chapter 7, Lexus brought overwhelming resources to bear on an emerging segment of buyers to take the U.S. luxury automobile market by storm. But focus was merely one of the keys to Lexus's success. The successful combination of design, manufacturing, marketing, sales, and service functions created a luxury automobile that American automakers could not match in terms of quality and performance and that European automakers could not match in terms of price and service.

When Chief Engineer Ichiro Suzuki sent twenty specialists from Japan to the U.S. to conduct market research in 1985, only fifteen returned. Five remained in California, the heart of Lexus's target market, to design the LS 400's exterior and set up shop in a rented house in Laguna Beach. Suzuki's intent was to align the LS 400's look with the tastes and preferences of young, affluent, and price-sensitive U.S. buyers while maximizing aerodynamics and trunk space.

While Suzuki opted to relocate the design function in the heart of the target market, he kept the manufacturing function in a state-of-the-art, automated facility as close as possible to his engineering team in Toyota City, Japan. His intent was twofold. First, he wanted his team to work in close cooperation with manufacturing personnel to maximize the efficiency of the production process and ensure the highest standards in quality. The oversight of and responsibility for Flagship Quality groups, cross-functional teams responsible for the development and production of the LS 400's various components, started with engineers on Suzuki's team and were later passed to manufacturing as components progressed from development to production. Second, he wanted to leverage Toyota's most advanced, cutting-edge automation facilities to mass-produce a level of quality superior to that of German-engineered automobiles while avoiding the Germans' costly, labor-intensive assembly processes. Said one observant junior engineer, "Suzuki-san understood the spirit of Lexus. He is a well-respected engineer who knew what it would take to build a quality, luxury vehicle that could compete right out of the box with such historic marques as Mercedes Benz and BMW."[8]

To reach its target market in the most effective manner, Lexus hired a U.S.-based cultural anthropologist and a New York image consulting firm: the anthropologist identified the characteristics most important to U.S. buyers, and the image consulting firm coined the Lexus name. The strategy was not to produce a better Mercedes but to design a car that many Mercedes buyers would see as offering better value. To sell to this new class of discerning luxury car buyers in the most effective manner, Lexus created an entirely new dealer network: franchisees invested $3 to $5 million per dealership and received extensive instruction in customer service at a Lexus training facility in Scottsdale, Arizona. And to rival the service programs of its U.S. competitors, Lexus relied on a network of independent service providers where local dealers were not yet available: after the LS 400's first recall for three minor flaws, any Lexus owner who lived more than one hundred miles from the nearest dealer received an at-home visit from a certified Lexus mechanic.

As a result of Lexus's combined arms approach, polished and refined dealers were able to offer prospective buyers a luxury automobile with an unrivaled set of features: California-inspired design, the performance, reliability, and quality of Japan's most advanced manufacturing processes, the convenience of nationwide U.S. service and support, and a base price of just $35,000. American automakers haplessly tried to respond with rebates on their lackluster offerings, while German automakers, after disassembling the LS 400 and determining that producing a comparable automobile would then cost twice as much, could only quip, "They have no tradition."[9] No matter where American and German automakers turned, Lexus had an answer.

Leadership Lessons

Lexus's relocation of its design function and heavy reliance on indigenous partners first show us how a company can use combined arms to enter a foreign market successfully. Moreover, Lexus's colocation of its engineering team and manufacturing facility in Japan enabled the highest degree of cooperation among personnel across functions—a key determinant of success in any combined-arms effort. Finally, Lexus aligned the impression its sales force made on prospective buyers with the quality of the product its manufacturing process produced by investing significantly in customer service training for its dealer franchisees.

5/11 IN OPERATION DESERT STORM

In the days preceding the ground phase of Operation Desert Storm in 1991, then–Lieutenant Colonel James L. Sachtleben, commanding officer of 5th Battalion, 11th Marines, combined artillery, air, direct fire, and electronic warfare to disrupt and demoralize Iraqi defenders located along a fifty-kilometer section of the border between Saudi Arabia and Kuwait.

Sachtleben's seniors chose his artillery battalion to conduct a series of raids prior to the beginning of the ground phase because they needed a force that could emplace and withdraw quickly, deliver a decisive blow to Iraqi positions, and reach the enemy from the Saudi Arabian side of the border. Artillery, long known as the "King of Battle," could deliver 155mm and 203mm projectiles that weighed 100 pounds and 200 pounds, respectively, and that ranged 11 and 18 miles, respectively.

But Sachtleben realized during his unit's preparations that "it was apparent that these raids would truly be a combined arms effort."[10] Accordingly, he assembled a fighting force that was custom-tailored for the demanding requirements of his mission. In addition to his artillery units, F/A-18 Hornet fighter-bomber jets were on-station, ready to drop Rockeye cluster bombs on targets of opportunity. Eight-wheeled light armored vehicles (LAVs), which fired high-explosive or armor-piercing rounds from a twenty-five-millimeter cannon and traveled at speeds up to sixty miles per hour, provided forward and lateral security on the ground. Electronic warfare assets, including EA-6B Prowler aircraft, were employed to detect enemy radio traffic and jam enemy ground surveillance radar, which was capable of pinpointing the location of Marine artillery fire.

The assembled force possessed a formidable set of capabilities, but equally impressive was the high degree of coordination that existed among its component parts. Sachtleben and his staff enjoyed a close working relationship with the LAV commander, who had played an integral role in mission planning and execution since Operation Desert Shield, the precursor to Operation Desert Storm. And a forward air controller (FAC), an actual Marine pilot who rode with the LAVs, directed the F/A-18 and EA-6B aircraft from his position on the ground as they made their final approaches.

In all, Sachtleben's force conducted four raids—all under the cover of darkness. During the first raid the LAVs provided security as the artillery moved toward the border, fired several volleys on an Iraqi police post, and hastily withdrew upon receiving mortar fire. To cover the artillery's withdrawal, the FAC called in F/A-18s to bomb the enemy positions.

During the second raid the artillery returned the favor and covered the LAVs with an umbrella of reinforcing fires as the speedy eight-wheeled vehicles conducted a "drive-by," direct-fire attack on a second Iraqi police post.

During the third raid the artillery fired on Iraqi ground surveillance radar sites while EA-6Bs jammed the very same sites from the air to prevent Iraqi radar from locating the Marine artillery's firing location and directing accurate counterfire.

During the fourth and final raid artillery continued to rely on the LAVs for security, opted to forgo jamming support from the EA-6Bs, and fired more rounds on two Iraqi artillery units for an extended period of time. The intent was to goad the Iraqi artillery to return fire, and when flashes revealed the Iraqis' positions, F/A-18s swooped in and dropped Rockeye bombs with devastating accuracy.

As Sachtleben correctly observed, the cumulative effect of unexpected artillery and direct-fire strikes and near-instantaneous punishment from F/A-18s disrupted and demoralized Iraqi defenders: "put yourself in the place of the Iraqi rocketeers: they fired a counter-battery volley in response to our artillery fires, and within seconds of their first and only volley, they were hit by very effective aviation ordnance. Their morale undoubtedly suffered."[11]

Leadership Lessons

Sachtleben realized early on that combined arms would enable him to project maximum combat power, and his tactics grew increasingly innovative with each raid. The first three raids illustrate the complementary nature of

FIGURE 10.2 A modern-day Marine Corps combined arms team—
F/A-19 Hornet jets, Light Armored Vehicle with AH-1 Cobra
overhead, and an M198 howitzer (heavy artillery). Photos courtesy
of United States Marine Corps, www.usmc.mil, July 15, 2003.

combined arms; the fourth illustrates the horns of a dilemma. First, direct
fire from the LAVs covered the artillery's attack, and air protected the
artillery at its most vulnerable point—withdrawal. Second, the artillery
covered direct fire's attack. Third, electronic warfare prevented artillery's
attack from being detected. And fourth, artillery presented the Iraqis with
two undesirable alternatives: displace from their positions, thereby weak-
ening the overall Iraqi defense, or return fire, thereby revealing their locations to F/A-18s circling overhead.

Sachtleben also realized early on that a close relationship among the
units brought together would greatly enhance the effectiveness of his combined arms approach, and he made a concerted effort to include the leaders of those units in both planning and execution to the fullest extent
possible.

NETJETS—"IT'S MORE THAN JUST AN AIRPLANE"

In NetJets, former Goldman Sachs leasing specialist Richard T. Santulli has combined a fleet of high-quality aircraft, state-of-the-art information systems, well-trained, highly skilled employees, and an unfettered access to capital to create a time-share system for private planes that competing offerings cannot match.

NetJets offers shares, ranging from one-sixteenth to one-half, in a variety of private planes. Customers bear fixed costs proportionately and pay incrementally only for the variable costs they incur, such as the flight hours utilized. For example, a one-eighth share in a seven-seat Cessna Citation V guarantees a hundred hours of use and costs $664,000 up-front, plus $8,800 in monthly maintenance expenses and $1,373 for every occupied flight hour.[12] For most of us this is a rather expensive travel alternative. But the option to pay only for capacity used while retaining the "feel" of full ownership has become wildly popular among wealthy individuals seeking periodic access to private planes and corporations seeking to supplement normal lift requirements.

NetJets' combined arms approach begins with a world-class fleet of five hundred aircraft, ranging from seven-seat Cessna light-cabin models to more luxurious eighteen-seat Boeing business jets. All planes are completely refurbished every thirty months, and many come equipped with amenities such as DVD players, desks, telephones, kitchenettes, and wet bars.[13] In addition to a comfortable ride, NetJets provides near-ubiquitous access to airports and landing strip services at five thousand airports on three continents—North America, Europe, and Asia.

Balancing available fleet capacity with wide swings in demand and coordinating the myriad activities necessary to support shared ownership requires a second arm—sophisticated information management capabilities. IntelliJet, NetJets' comprehensive aviation management system, seamlessly connects administrative, operations, and support functions, matches planes to customer reservations, and shuffles crew assignments. Managers can use the information the system collects to develop advanced schedules, order aircraft, optimize pricing, and structure leasing plans. Finally, an advanced customer relationship management system (CRM) that tracks each customer's plane usage allows NetJets to pinpoint each customer's particular needs and preferences. With this information crews can custom-tailor meal offerings and cabin setup to meet individual tastes.

To complement its world-class fleet and state-of-the-art systems and ensure the highest levels of service, safety, and reliability for its discriminating customers, NetJets relies heavily on a third arm—a skilled, trained, and motivated workforce. Dedicated service teams are assigned to specific customers in an effort to cultivate and maintain ongoing relationships. NetJets personnel closely track and cater to their clients' specific needs and proactively reach out to clients in case of any flight or aircraft changes. Operations personnel at the company's two-hundred-thousand-square-foot aviation center in Columbus, Ohio, vigilantly guard against unexpected contingencies, such as bad weather and airport delays, to ensure that planes arrive to clients within the guaranteed four- to six-hour window.[14] Pilots have, on average, eight thousand hours of flight experience, fly just one jet model, and receive an additional twenty-three days of simulator training per year, double that of a typical airline. And all mechanics hold certifications from the aircraft manufacturer whose jet they service.

As heavyweight competitors, such as Raytheon and Bombardier, have challenged his company's lead in the market he created, Santulli has added a fourth arm—access to capital. Satisfied NetJets customer Warren Buffett—sticking to his tried-and-true practice of buying companies whose concept he understands and whose management he admires—bought the company in 1998 for $725 million and kept Santulli as CEO. With financial backing from Buffett's Berkshire Hathaway, Inc., Santulli has been able to maintain his lead by upgrading and expanding his fleet at will and investing "in *whatever is necessary* to provide the safest and most reliable travel management service for our customers."[15]

Since the genesis of its time-share system of ownership in 1986, NetJets' combined arms approach has enabled the company to amass thirty-five hundred clients and become the world's largest operator of private business jets, with a presence in about a hundred countries. Boasting an enviable list of satisfied customers, among them Buffett, Tom Hanks, Tiger Woods, and Arnold Schwarzenegger, NetJets enjoys the lowest customer turnover rate and highest customer satisfaction rates in its industry.

Leadership Lessons

By virtue of Santulli's masterful combination of mutually reinforcing arms—planes, information systems, personnel, and capital—NetJets has tapped previously unrealized market potential and placed established rivals on the horns of a dilemma. Large commercial airlines cannot compete with NetJets on the basis of convenience or timeliness; NetJets' clients never have to worry about transferring planes, waiting in airports, or going through long safety checks. Nor can charter airlines, which typically require considerable advance notice to reserve and do not offer comparable flexibility of ownership. Full ownership of a private plane cannot compete on the basis of cost, service, or ease of use; NetJets minimizes the idle time of unutilized aircraft and removes the anxiety and expense associated with maintaining a plane and managing a full-time crew. And would-be imitators lack the capital, management savvy, advanced information systems, or scale to topple NetJets from its market-leading position.

ANALYSIS ACROSS EXAMPLES

Common to the four examples raised in this chapter is the allocation of complementary resources in such a way that, no matter where the opponent turns, the practitioner of maneuver warfare has an answer. Less readily apparent is what it takes to make this principle of maneuver warfare work: combined arms is an inherently complex undertaking that requires the utmost trust and coordination throughout an organization.

In the face of a charging French cavalry at Agincourt, Henry's infantrymen had to trust the archers' aim; likewise, the archers had to trust the infantrymen's resolve. Lexus management in Japan had to trust the guidance it received from its representatives and partners across the Pacific in the United States, and engineers and manufacturing specialists at the Lexus plant had to trust one another's competence as the leadership of Flagship Quality groups changed hands. On multiple occasions Marines in 5/11 had to trust the accuracy and timeliness of the bombs dropped by their brethren in the air. And NetJets service teams, operations personnel, pilots, and maintenance crews all depend implicitly on one another to deliver a comprehensive, world-class service offering where the slightest disconnect can be deemed unacceptable by an unforgiving customer.

For the English at Agincourt and Lexus, coordination of the combined arms effort was centralized—in the leader himself. Henry V orchestrated the actions of his archers and infantry, and Ichiro Suzuki orchestrated all design, manufacturing, marketing, and sales activities. In contrast, the coordination of the combined arms effort for Marines and NetJets is decentralized, and technology serves as the unifying factor. IntelliJet, the backbone of NetJets' combined arms offering, allows previously independent-functioning groups to work in harmony. And the Marines—as you will see below—rely heavily on standardized operating procedures and multiple communications means to coordinate attacks between geographically diverse, fast-moving, and highly lethal units.

COMBINED ARMS . . . THE MARINE CORPS WAY

The Marines originally adopted combined arms because of the possibility that, as "America's 9-1-1 Force in Readiness," they would have to face more heavily equipped foes. Owing to its efficacy, combined arms quickly became a pervasive way of thinking throughout the Corps, and Marines continue to innovate and refine this interdisciplinary approach to maximizing combat power. Many of the techniques they employ are transferable to the business environment and can be implemented in your organization.

SEAD

The suppression of enemy air defense (SEAD)[16] mission epitomizes how Marines think about combined arms at the tactical level. SEAD comprises simultaneous direct-fire, artillery, and air attacks, synchronized by artillery forward observers (FOs) and forward air controllers (FACs), to create shock, terror, and chaos among opposing forces.

Upon identifying a target of opportunity, the FO calls in high-arching artillery fire, which fixes the enemy in place by forcing him to seek shelter from projectiles falling from above. During this initial attack, which lasts several minutes, maneuver forces—infantry, tanks, or LAVs—position themselves for a direct-fire attack, and the FAC brings aircraft, fixed-wing jets like the F/A-18 or helicopters like the AH-1 Cobra, into position for a strike. At a predetermined point in time the artillery fire pauses and aircraft deliver bombs or missiles on the target. With "bombs away," the artillery resumes firing to cover the aircraft's withdrawal, and the maneuver forces unleash their direct-fire attack.

For an enemy receiving overwhelming accurate fire from multiple directions, all hell might as well be breaking loose. He cannot expose himself to defend against the air attack with a surface-to-air missile (SAM) because of the "steel rain" of artillery fire. He cannot run because he will be cut down by direct fire. He cannot return fire because he has no cover. With nowhere to run, nowhere to hide, and no way to fight back, he withdraws inward, and his will to continue the fight collapses.

Organic Critical Functions

The Marine Corps is unique among the U.S. armed forces in that it is almost entirely self-contained. Thus all critical combined arms functions—air, artillery, maneuver, electronic warfare, and engineers—are kept "in-house." This policy is crucial to the Marines' success with combined arms; breakdowns stemming from interservice rivalries, different operating procedures, or miscommunications are minimized. As an institution the Marine Corps can set overarching policies and standards that ensure consistent performance. And in the field Marine commanders can ensure that the various component parts of the combined arms team are working together in an optimal manner by maintaining unified control.

Task Organization

Like Sachtleben in Desert Storm, Marine commanders frequently assemble their forces on an ad-hoc basis, based on the requirements of the missions they must accomplish. This process of mixing and matching, known as *task organization*, enhances the employment of combined arms by bringing the best possible team with the skills most closely matched to the challenge at hand.

"Every Marine a Rifleman"

Combined arms requires that individual Marines place an incredible degree of trust in one another, even if they have never met, and the foundation for this trust is laid in initial training. All enlisted Marines are trained, first and foremost, to be riflemen, and all Marine officers are trained, first and foremost, to be infantry platoon commanders. This common initial grounding ensures that all Marines share a mutual understanding, meet the same high standards, and endure similar hardships. It is therefore much easier for a Marine on the ground to trust that a diving aircraft will deliver its bombs accurately if another Marine is piloting that aircraft. Likewise, it is easier for a Marine in the air to trust that an artillery unit will deliver its rounds on time, on target if other Marines are manning the howitzers.

Colocation and Cross-Training

Marines make the human investment necessary to ensure the success of the combined arms approach. Artillery officers and pilots, the principal orchestrators of combined arms, frequently rotate into and out of the infantry units they support. The purpose of these temporary assignments, which last anywhere from a few hours during a tactical operation to a full twelve-month tour, is twofold. First, physically colocating key personnel from artillery, air, and infantry facilitates the execution of combined arms missions enormously; any unexpected contingencies or differences can immediately be resolved in person. Second, when not directly involved in the execution of combined arms missions, artillery and air representatives can cross-train their infantry brethren to call in artillery missions and air strikes, thereby increasing the combined arms capabilities of the supported infantry units and promoting increased mutual understanding.

Communications

Combined arms relies heavily on reliable communications systems, without which the various Marine entities simply could not coordinate a given battle. And communications Marines relentlessly practice responding to system outages, failures, and network attacks. These intense drills aim to ensure that communication disruptions are minimized and hopefully mitigated altogether, because, after all, lives hang in the balance.

CAST and CAX

Marines practice combined arms relentlessly, and they have invested heavily, in terms of both money and time, to institutionalize structured exercises to this end. Multimillion-dollar combined arm staff trainers (CASTs) enable Marines to convene and practice combined arms missions regularly via computer simulation. But the ultimate in combined arms training is the three-week, live-fire combined arms exercise (CAX), held in the harsh Mojave Desert in Twentynine Palms, California. CAX is extreme training under increasingly challenging conditions. Units run countless live SEAD missions. Ever-vigilant evaluators, known as "coyotes," monitor these missions closely, to ensure safety and provide thorough, immediate feedback. CAX scenarios reach levels of difficulty and complexity greater than that which could be expected in actual combat so that Marines are prepared for any possible contingency.

O-Calls

The officers' call—Marine parlance for "happy hour"—adds a personal dimension to, and therefore increases the effectiveness of, the combined arms effort. Marine officers capitalize on every opportunity to have drinks, talk shop, and tell tall tales at the Officers' Club, but these social events serve an additional practical purpose: Marines sometimes can match a name and a face to the voice on the other end of the radio. Such personalization serves as a surprisingly powerful means to foster trust among the various combined arms constituencies.

APPLICATION IN BUSINESS

To instill a combined arms mentality in your organization, follow the Marines' lead. Bring those functions that you deem most critical to your intended combined arms efforts—research and development, manufacturing, marketing, or information technology—in-house and remember that what you have under your control determines what you can combine. Create multifaceted, custom-tailored teams to capitalize on new market opportunities. Rely on indigenous partners to enter foreign markets, as Lexus did. And use information to create entirely new capabilities for physical assets, as NetJets did. Also, ensure communications systems offer the flexibility and reliability needed to meet the task at hand and ensure a disaster recovery and backup plan is in place—terrorism and network attacks have crippled many organizations that didn't adhere to such policies.

With regard to your people, invest heavily in initial and ongoing training to provide them with a shared sense of identity and common perspective. Never underestimate the power of bringing them together, whether in planning, implementation, or even a social setting. Move them around frequently to familiarize them with your organization's various capabilities and to share knowledge across functional areas. Above all, reward cross-functional cooperation with recognition, compensation, or promotion and constantly reinforce the combined arms mind-set.

CHAPTER 11

RECONNAISSANCE PULL

"Pull the string, and it will follow wherever you wish."
—DWIGHT D. EISENHOWER[1]

While each of the preceding seven principles represents a valuable concept on its own, maneuver warfare is most effective when targeting critical vulnerabilities, boldness, surprise, focus, decentralized decision making, tempo, and combined arms are employed together—either in subsets or as an integrated whole. In this chapter we feature the employment of a subset of these principles.

Perhaps the most compelling subset we have observed is *reconnaissance pull*, a real-time response to opportunity, whereby an individual identifies an opening, orients the greater organization toward it, and assumes a leadership role in planning and executing its exploitation. Reconnaissance pull encompasses four of maneuver warfare's seven principles—decentralized decision making, targeting critical vulnerabilities, tempo, and focus. Decentralized decision making is the first component: the leader of the organization must entrust highly skilled scouts with considerable authority to decide when and where to exploit opportunities. Targeting critical vulnerabilities is the second: a scout may identify an environmental shift or a rival's critical vulnerability and then immediately initiate an effort to exploit it. Tempo is the third: a timely response to the identification of an opportunity requires rapid decision making on the part of the leader. And focus is the fourth: a scout can locate an opportunity and lead the larger organization to it, but the leader must be willing to commit maximum available resources to the exploitation of the opportunity at hand.

In this chapter we offer two examples of reconnaissance pull and its key components, as well as present-day lessons from the Marines. From warfare we recount the Marine Corps's amphibious landing and decisive victory at Tinian during the storied Pacific Island-Hopping campaign of World War II. From business we feature the instrumental role that Richard A. Hackborn played in conceiving and building Hewlett Packard's printer business in the early 1980s.

The Marines have institutionalized the process of reconnaissance pull. Based on the techniques they employ and on some of the lessons learned from our two historical examples, we will recommend ways in which you can encourage frontline employees to orient your organization toward valuable opportunities by fostering a flexible, decentralized culture, investing in personnel training, and developing information and human intelligence support systems.

THE MARINES' AMPHIBIOUS ASSAULT ON TINIAN

In July of 1944, on the small island of Tinian in the South Pacific, U.S. Marines used reconnaissance pull to guide an amphibious assault that smashed through the weakest point in Japanese defenses and ultimately paved the way for the construction of an air base on the island that was within bombing range of the Japanese mainland.

Tinian was part of an island pair that would have to be assaulted in succession. The Marines' plan was to take its sister island, Saipan, which was more heavily fortified and well within artillery range, first. After twenty-five days of brutal fighting and six thousand casualties on Saipan, the Marines turned their attention to Tinian, which was already home to one of the longest airstrips in the region and therefore the more strategically significant target. Under the command of Major General Harry Schmidt, the V Amphibious Corps's Second and Fourth Marine Divisions spearheaded the fighting. Seeking a decisive victory without the heavy casualties incurred at Saipan, Schmidt deployed multiple reconnaissance elements to *pull* his two divisions through "gaps" in the Japanese defenses.

Figure 11.1 MARINES' AMPHIBIOUS ASSAULT ON TINIAN, JULY 10–11, 1944

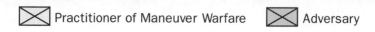

Saipan, 3 miles

Small beaches—
frogmen and Marine
reconnaissance area

4th Marine Division
shore-to-shore assault

Japanese defense

Tinian

Diversionary force

Practitioner of Maneuver Warfare   Adversary

The Opportunity. The Japanese surmised incorrectly that the Marines could not land in sufficient strength on Tinian's narrow northern beaches and therefore assumed a defensive posture to the south. Leaving the northern area of the island largely unguarded, the 8,350-man Japanese force built hardened pillboxes, constructed mazelike obstacles, and scattered mines in the southern area in the hope of denying the Marines the 39-square-mile island.

Decentralized Decision Making and *Targeting Critical Vulnerabilities.* Schmidt entrusted Navy and Marine Corps reconnaissance elements to identify the enemy's critical vulnerability, verify the activity and location of defensive forces, assist in the formulation of an attack plan, and select the openings through which the main invasion force would flow. During frequent aerial reconnaissance missions in the months preceding the landing, Navy and Marine Corps pilots discovered the critical vulnerability of the formidable Japanese defenses—susceptibility to northern attack. And Marine infantry forces on Saipan confirmed this finding when they captured valuable Japanese planning documents that revealed the Japanese believed an amphibious assault on Tinian could come only from the south.

These initial discoveries prompted Schmidt to dispatch Navy underwater demolition teams and Marine Corps reconnaissance teams to swim ashore under the cover of darkness and examine the feasibility and safety of a northern landing. The Marines conducted beach reconnaissance and harbor surveillance, while the Navy conducted hydrographic surveys to identify beaches suitable for a division-sized landing. Together the teams inspected Tinian's sharp coral reefs, recorded mine locations, mapped attack routes, and provided eyes-on assurance that the North was indeed unoccupied by enemy forces. The teams ultimately selected two beaches, which were but 60 and 150 meters wide, respectively.[2] Upon returning from the mission, the relatively junior officers in charge reported the details directly to Schmidt and his naval counterpart, Admiral Richmond Kelly Turner.

Tempo—Planning. Initial landing plans called for a southerly invasion; however, in light of his reconnaissance elements' findings, Schmidt made a timely command decision and changed his entire amphibious assault plan. Within two weeks of the reconnaissance teams' report, Schmidt, along with Turner, reoriented the invasion to the north and marshaled enough troops, ships, vehicles and supplies to make a major landing.

Focus. On July 24, 1944, Schmidt fully committed his two Marine divisions to the assault. Before the actual landing, the Second Marine Division and U.S. Navy conducted a full-fledged feint to the south, going as far as releasing assault craft from navy ships and heavily bombing the expected southern route to reinforce the Japanese belief that the attack would come from that direction. Then the Fourth Marine Division launched in landing craft from Saipan in the first shore-to-shore operation in Marine Corps history. The "Fightin' Fourth" jammed more than fifteen thousand men, tanks, artillery, supplies, and vehicles through the two dangerously narrow beachheads. According to the Fourth Marine Division Association historical record, "Never in the course of the Pacific war had a unit of division strength tried to land on any beach smaller than twice the size of these two beaches combined."

Tempo—Execution. Schmidt's tempo rippled through his fighting force. Within nine hours of its landing the Fourth Marine Division cleared the beachhead. On the second day the Second Marine Division poured through the opening and joined the Fourth to fight off a series of Japanese counterattacks inland. Together the two divisions compressed the retreating Japanese to the south side of the island. After just eight days of fighting, the Marines claimed complete victory.

Incurring far fewer casualties—327 killed and 1,771 wounded—than they had on Saipan, the Marines totally overwhelmed the Japanese defenses and captured Tinian. On the Marines' heels, "Can-Do" Navy Seabees built a strategic air base with six landing strips and turned the island into a staging point for follow-on Pacific campaigns and bombing raids on key Japanese targets.

Leadership Lessons

The Marines' success at Tinian illustrates how decentralized decision making, targeting critical vulnerabilities, focus, and tempo can be combined to achieve reconnaissance pull. Schmidt's willingness to decentralize decision making allowed his pilots, reconnaissance teams, and infantrymen to act independently and identify the enemy's critical vulnerability to the north, thereby improving the odds of a successful landing. Moreover, his ability to react in real time to new information ensured that the emerging opportunity in the North did not slip through his grasp, and a willingness to overhaul his entire plan displayed remarkable flexibility on his part. Finally, his decision to send two entire divisions across two narrow beaches ensured maximum exploitation of the opportunity.

HEWLETT PACKARD PRINTERS

In the early 1980s then-senior Hewlett Packard (HP) engineering manager Richard Hackborn identified a promising market opportunity in desktop and office printers and convinced HP senior management to move quickly to capitalize on it. The actions he took and decisions he made in leading HP toward the opportunity and building HP's printer division from scratch into a multibillion-dollar operation exemplify reconnaissance pull and its four components in the business environment.

The Opportunity. Impact-style dot-matrix and daisy-wheel printers that were clumsy, slow, loud, and messy to change and that generally produced poor-quality documents dominated the market for affordable desktop printers in the early 1980s. Incumbent competitors NEC, Epson, and Panasonic were enjoying fat profit margins for an altogether outmoded technology. Moreover, the dramatic proliferation of personal computers in the early 1980s would eventually require higher-resolution graphics and color printing, features not possible with dot-matrix or daisy-wheel printers.

Targeting Critical Vulnerabilities and *Decentralized Decision Making.* Observing low-cost Canon ink-jet printer technology for the first time in 1981, Hackborn sensed a great opportunity:[3] he surmised correctly that the potentially huge market for desktop printers was critically vulnerable to new printers, made possible by new technology that offered capabilities at lower costs than previously possible. Incumbent competitors were unlikely to abandon or cannibalize their entrenched positions and equally unlikely to risk losing existing sales by adopting an unproven technology. Said Hackborn in a 1993 interview, "The impact vendors were sitting atop a fortified hill, and I knew we couldn't attack it directly and expect to win. The key was to change the basis of battle."[4] Instead of conducting a frontal assault on the hill, Hackborn sought to circumvent incumbents' entrenched positions by introducing new laser and ink-jet technology at a relatively low price.

Hackborn developed the unconventional idea that HP deviate from its existing high-end business strategy and begin designing, producing, and marketing inexpensive, mass-produced printers that could connect directly to personal desktop computers. While these printers were not truly inexpensive, they allowed individuals and small businesses to acquire world-class technology that had been previously unaffordable or in some cases unavailable. He acquired the rights to the technology from Japanese camera and printer maker Canon, which failed to see the market opportunity and in 1982 presented his plan to then-CEO John Young. Young gave him the go-ahead and the latitude he needed to build the business, thereby pulling HP in an entirely new direction.

Knowing that the business would require sweeping changes in marketing, sales, and manufacturing, Hackborn secured approval from Young to headquarter the business in Boise, Idaho, far removed from company headquarters in Silicon Valley. HP had long been heralded for its entrepreneurial spirit and decentralization, and Hackborn's printer business was no exception. Consistent with the "HP Way," he established business groups in dispersed nontraditional technology locales throughout the western United States, and he gave the managers of these dispersed locations the same latitude to run their operations that Young had afforded him. Division headquarters and LaserJet groups were located in Boise, the inkjet line in Vancouver, Washington, and supporting departments in San Diego, California, and Corvallis, Oregon.

Tempo. With Young's rapid-fire approval of Hackborn's plan, the printer division was off to a fast start. Hackborn in turn created a constant sense of urgency among his people and decentralized decision making, which further accelerated tempo. While building a completely new global business out of an unproven technology was fraught with uncertainty, he confidently made quick decisions and set ambitious time-to-market goals. He then stepped back and relied on his dispersed operations to build and introduce products before incumbents could respond effectively with comparable offerings.

Within a mere three years of its conception, Hackborn's printer business rolled out the first HP LaserJet in March 1984. This model sold for $3,495 and printed 300 dots per square inch (dpi) at 8 pages per minute. Two months later the group launched the first-ever ink-jet printer offered in the United States, the HP ThInkJet, which printed 96 dpi (today's standard is 600 dpi). Though the products were initially far from perfect, HP aggressively filed patents on the technology, thereby creating formidable barriers to entry for the competition.

Preempting the competition and erecting barriers to entry were not the only benefits of tempo. The rapid establishment of a sizable installed base of customers also contributed significantly to the success of Hackborn's strategy, which relied heavily on sales of high-margin printer peripherals such as printer cartridges, paper, and cables. Given that a printer's purchase price implied a multiyear commitment and that most peripherals were not interchangeable among brands, selling a large number of printers quickly enabled HP to lock up almost all of the customer's expected purchases during the printer's lifetime. To illustrate, an HP inkjet cartridge currently offers a 60 percent margin on a $25 sale price, and the average customer replaces the cartridge several times each year.

Focus. CEO Young committed hundreds of millions of dollars to Hackborn's idea. HP built new facilities, initiated an ambitious laser and ink-jet technology R&D effort, created new mass-production capabilities, and established a network of relationships with suppliers, third-party manufacturers, and channel partners. In addition to these physical investments and external alliances, HP made the human investment necessary to ensure the success of this new venture; Hackborn and his staff hired thousands of new employees, most notably talented engineers and managers with skills outside HP's existing capabilities. For example, the company needed engineers and scientists to run thousands of ink tests and create a reusable, inexpensive, and durable design for the masses, as well as marketing experts who could develop successful strategy and tactics to launch a new product into the retail channel.

Within ten years of its launch, HP's printer division had sold twenty million printers. Today the company is the undisputed world leader in general-purpose personal, small business, departmental, and work unit printing products—odds are you have a Hewlett Packard LaserJet or inkjet printer either in your home or at your office. With at least 50 percent market share in LaserJet and inkjet printers, the printer division regularly accounts for 40 to 50 percent of HP's overall profits. Peripheral sales drive over 50 percent of the printer group's revenue. Additionally, the printer business has helped transform the company into a high-volume manufacturing leader and has paved the way for a new lineup of profitable end-consumer products such as color printers, cameras, desktop and handheld computers, and compact disk recorders. Hackborn, who served briefly as the chairman of HP's board of directors, is now retired, but his legend lives on at the company.

Leadership Lessons

Hackborn was in a unique position to identify firsthand both emerging technology and market vulnerability, and he put the two together to identify value for both HP and a large group of potential new customers. That he had the latitude to develop such a maverick idea and present it to the CEO was a testament to the decentralized environment at HP, where employees felt comfortable creating and acting on new ideas. Tempo played a key role in both planning and execution: by the time incumbents had mustered a response to HP's infiltration of their market, they were stopped short by superior products, patents, and a sizable installed base of customers. Finally, the nonlinear results that Hackborn achieved would not have been realized without Young's full commitment.

ANALYSIS ACROSS EXAMPLES

The commonalities between these two examples offer three key insights into reconnaissance pull. First, both Schmidt and Young displayed a remarkable willingness to listen, be flexible, and provide necessary support, and their subordinates responded by delivering nonlinear results. Second, reconnaissance created a virtuous cycle: the collection and communication of timely and accurate information enhanced decision-making ability, which in turn facilitated decision-making speed and judgment. Once Schmidt and Hackborn "penetrated the gap," they maintained a rapid tempo as a result of their better information and faster decision making: by the time the Japanese had reacted to the Fourth Marine Division landing, the Second Marine Division was already ashore, and by the time competitors responded to HP's first ThInkJet, Hackborn was rolling out the lower-cost and higher-quality DeskJet 500 series and, shortly thereafter, color printers. Third, reconnaissance enabled Schmidt and Hackborn to reshape the rules of their respective competitive encounters. Schmidt attacked from a direction that the Japanese were not prepared to defend. Hackborn capitalized on a new technology to create an offering that incumbents could match only by undermining their existing market positions.

RECONNAISSANCE PULL . . . THE MARINE CORPS WAY

Marine Corps doctrine establishes reconnaissance pull as "the preferred method [of reconnaissance] during offensive operations (it takes advantage of the Marine Air-Ground Task Force's inherent flexibility and reconnaissance capabilities)."[5] Given this doctrinal preference, the Marine Corps has devoted considerable resources to developing and refining a wide range of capabilities related to reconnaissance pull. Moreover, it has made the human investment necessary to ensure the efficient flow of information from reconnaissance elements to key decision makers, and it has embraced flexibility as a key part of its culture. We believe the Marines' practices to be directly applicable to the business environment.

A Full Bag of Tricks

According to General Al Gray, former commandant of the Marine Corps and champion of modern-day Marine Corps maneuver warfare doctrine, reconnaissance pull should be called "integrated intelligence pull" to better reflect the "the influence of the full bag of your intelligence resources."[6] And the Marines, believing that a diverse set of capabilities enhances the effectiveness of reconnaissance pull, certainly employ a "full bag":

- *Recon*—Highly skilled special operators responsible for conducting reconnaissance and surveillance missions forward of frontline infantry units and sometimes far behind enemy lines.

- *Scout Snipers*—Expert marksmen that, in addition to their primary mission, observe extended battlefield areas and collect intelligence.

- *Radio Battalion*—Specialized communications units that intercept radio signals, locate enemy transmission sites electronically, and jam enemy communications.

- *Intelligence Battalion*—Secretive counterintelligence and interrogator-translator teams that gather information by questioning enemy prisoners of war and interacting with local informants.

- *Light Armored Reconnaissance*—Swift, eight-wheeled light armored vehicle (LAV) units that conduct reconnaissance, surveillance, and screening missions and provide firepower (as necessary) forward of the main fighting force or on its extreme flanks.

- *Air Assets*—Unmanned aerial vehicles (UAVs), F/A-18 Hornets, and EA-6B Prowlers. UAVs enable remote-controlled enemy surveillance and target acquisition, F/A-18s provide all-weather imagery collection, and EA-6Bs locate, intercept, and jam enemy signals from the air.

Integrating the information collected by this diverse set of capabilities are several specialized information systems. Most notable and modern is the Joint Maritime Command Information System (JMCIS), a distributed information system designed to provide a common collection point for real-time decision support.

Human Investment

While the role of the intelligence officer is by no means a novel concept, the Marine ground intelligence officers, who undergo both infantry and intelligence training, are dedicated full time to thinking like the enemy and determining potential enemy courses of action. Commanding recon and scout sniper platoons early in their careers, they enjoy direct reporting relationships to senior field commanders and serve as information conduits that enable real-time reaction to emerging opportunities.

"Semper Gumby" and "Improvise, Adapt, Overcome"

From day one, flexibility is reinforced in Marines' psyches. Drill instructors at boot camp and Officer Candidates' School intentionally and constantly change plans in an effort to accustom aspiring Marines to perpetual flux. Active duty in the Fleet Marine Force is a never-ending series of surprises, both intentional and unintentional. In light of the drill instructors' well-intended harassment and the trials and tribulations of active duty, some junior Marine somewhere coined the phrase *Semper Gumby*, a play on the motto *Semper Fidelis* that means "always flexible."

Another common maxim in the Marine Corps is "Improvise, Adapt, Overcome." Long before Hollywood popularized it, Marines used the phrase to reflect their preference for being a fluid, loosely reined force that could spontaneously react to rapidly changing situations, rather than a rigid outfit that moved in a specific direction with a precise plan.

APPLICATION IN BUSINESS

Reconnaissance pull is a natural bottom-up approach to seeking out and capitalizing on new opportunities. Harnessing the ingenuity and talent of those closest to the action, it arms the field commander or business manager, who is constantly faced with difficult decisions amid uncertainty, complexity, and constant change, with better and more timely information, thereby facilitating the evaluation of alternatives and enhancing tempo. It has the potential to deliver breakthrough results for you, just as it has for HP and the Marines.

First and foremost, develop and designate a wide range of reconnaissance functions in your organization. As we began to discuss in Chapter 4, these functions are often present in your sales or marketing force, but they may also reside with engineers, traders, researchers, analysts, product managers, or call center personnel—anyone who is removed from headquarters and close to the market. Give your people the latitude and support they need to develop reconnaissance capabilities, find opportunities, and bring new ideas to the attention of senior management. Complement this bottom-up nature of reconnaissance pull with top-down strategic guidance that orients your people to key market characteristics and guides efforts; with proper guidance, new ideas may not be so far-fetched. This top-down function should also serve to review and filter the information from the front line and commit resources as appropriate to the most deserving, strategically viable opportunities.

Employ distributed information systems that complement the decentralized nature of reconnaissance pull and are usable by all facets of your organization. This practice will enable the sharing of information between the front line and headquarters while avoiding the common pitfall of disconnected organizational entities. Invest time in training system users in the technology and provide them the bigger picture so that they may leverage the full potential of the system.

Like the Marines, ensure that a direct and unfettered conduit between senior leadership and your "reconnaissance force" exists. If you haven't already done so, consider designating a talented junior manager as your "ground intelligence officer." At first this position could be a secondary or ancillary duty; then, as its scope widens, it could evolve into a "stepping-stone" position through which other up-and-comers could rotate.

Also, create incentives for workers who find new opportunities or develop new ideas—Marines recognize initiative in the form of accelerated promotion and medals, while HP monetarily rewards any employee who develops a technology that leads to a new patent.

Finally, start breeding flexibility in your organization. This prescription is easier said than done—especially without drill instructors. But as a leader you are in the position to devise more flexible and fluid plans and create simulated situations in training that require rapid reaction on the part of your people to changing events.

CHAPTER 12

AN INTEGRATED ATTACK

Examples from Business

"We will deliver the right product to the right customer at the right time and at the right price."

—RICHARD FAIRBANK AND NIGEL MORRIS,
FOUNDERS, CAPITAL ONE[1]

In Chapter 2, we featured the Israelis' resounding victory in the 1967 War to illustrate how the maneuver warfare philosophy has been employed in full force to *achieve a maximum impact with a minimum expenditure of resources* in combat. In Chapters 1 and 3, we defined maneuver warfare and broke it down into seven guiding principles. In Chapters 4 through 10 we analyzed each principle in detail and provided numerous supporting examples from warfare and business. And in Chapter 11 we showed how the principles could be employed together in a subset.

In Chapter 12 we come full circle—to the employment of all seven guiding principles as an integrated whole in business. Two examples distinguish themselves among the many we have reviewed in our research efforts. Prominent New York arbitrageur and former U.S. Marine Corps captain Guy Wyser-Pratte has employed all seven principles as an active investor in underperforming companies to deliver, year-in and year-out, annual returns far in excess of the S&P 500. And Capital One Financial's emergence in the 1990s as a leading credit card issuer exemplifies how a corporation can apply all seven principles in an integrated manner to achieve explosive growth *and* superior profit margins.

WYSER-PRATTE & CO.

As we take a seat in his spartan, no-nonsense Wall Street office, which is reminiscent of a Marine Corps command post, and offer an introductory explanation of the seven guiding principles of maneuver warfare, Guy Wyser-Pratte responds matter-of-factly, "Oh, sure, we use them all the time. Let me tell you about Rheinmetall, COMSAT, Taittinger . . ."

Wyser-Pratte invests the several hundred million dollars his firm has under management in poorly managed, underperforming companies and battles fiercely to influence their corporate strategies—for the benefit of shareholders. Critics call him a "corporate raider," a term that typically carries a negative connotation. But Wyser-Pratte sees himself as correcting corporate governance malfunctions—misalignments between the interests of shareholders and those of management—which have significantly depressed companies' share prices relative to their potential unobstructed value. Two respected sources concur. *Barron's* magazine has praised him for a "solid record of adding value as a result of confronting management about poor governance."[2] Echoes the *Washington Post*, "[his] track record shows . . . [he has] been involved in several successful efforts to shake up the management of genuinely ailing companies, often in concert with respected shareholder activists."[3]

To close the "value gaps" created by corporate governance malfunctions, Wyser-Pratte purchases and holds, generally for one- to three-year periods, large blocks of companies' shares and employs a variety of tools to persuade or pressure management teams and their boards of directors to enact lasting change. The tools he employs include good ideas, letters to management and boards, public solicitations of shareholder votes by proxy,[4] special shareholder meetings, coalitions with other influential shareholders, lawsuits, changes in board of directors representation, the media, and a willingness to fight from within. Resulting reforms may come in the form of overhauls in corporate strategy, share buybacks, spin-offs/divestitures of noncore businesses, companywide restructurings/reorganizations, or an outright sale of the company.

Wyser-Pratte has long been a force to be reckoned with in the United States. In recent years he has expanded his theater of operations to continental Europe, where many closely held businesses have been slow to respond to technological advances, globalization, a unified currency, the relaxation of restrictive corporate governance measures, and an increasingly demanding investor base. In France he has begun to break the unholy alliance between the government bureaucracy and wealthy, established families. In Germany he is challenging a labyrinth of government agencies and laws that choke and inhibit the efficient functioning of equity capital markets.

No matter the "clime and place," Wyser-Pratte's pursuit of corporate governance malfunctions clearly illustrates the application of the maneuver warfare philosophy in the business arena. In the numerous investments he has made since he adopted his proactive investing approach in 1991, we see *all* of the principles that we have been articulating in the previous chapters.

Targeting Critical Vulnerabilities. After accumulating a sizable stake in Rheinmetall AG, a publicly traded German automotive, electronics, and defense conglomerate, Wyser-Pratte launched a public campaign in 2001 to enhance shareholder value. This campaign aimed to separate the company into three divisions and implement measures to improve poor profitability. The primary impediment to the realization of this plan was the Rochling family, which controlled 67 percent of Rheinmetall's voting rights. To convince the family of the merits of his ways, Wyser-Pratte targeted its critical vulnerability—a fear of media exposure.

When the family, divided as to whether it should cooperate with or resist Wyser-Pratte's plan, signaled its fear of discussing in the public forum allegations of mismanagement of Rheinmetall's defense business, Wyser-Pratte pounced. He made a series of announcements that culminated in an article titled "Conglomerate Forced to Sharpen Up Its Act," which was featured in the *Financial Times* on October 26, 2001.

The media exposure caused the Rochling family a good deal of embarrassment. Rheinmetall yielded to this pressure and reorganized into three divisions, sold noncore assets, and entered into strategic alliances that increased its presence in international markets. Moreover, before Wyser-Pratte agreed to sell his stake—at a 115 percent increase from his initial purchase—the Rochling family pledged to take further measures to enhance shareholder value, among them a program that tied management compensation to business unit performance.

Boldness. Wyser-Pratte's high-risk, high-reward investment approach defies traditional theories of portfolio diversification. To establish credibility in the eyes of a management team or board of directors, he must first act boldly and accumulate a sizable stake in the target company, normally 5 to 8 percent of total shares outstanding. Then, to attack corporate governance failures and enhance value for shareholders, he must undertake costly measures that may or may not be successful in effecting change. Finally, to realize an attractive return, he must find a way to liquidate his large holdings without flooding the market with the company's shares and driving the share price down. While the risks associated with this bold approach are substantial, they nevertheless merit the rewards, as we saw with Rheinmetall and as we will see later with other investments.

Surprise. Stealth precedes every corporate governance initiative Wyser-Pratte launches. He accumulates his shares in target companies through anonymous agents so as not to signal his intentions prematurely. Such notification eventually occurs in the form of public disclosure of ownership, as required by country-specific securities laws. In 1996 the share price of French investment company SIPAREX rose approximately 25 percent following a public announcement by Wyser-Pratte that his and another firm had acquired 10 percent of SIPAREX's outstanding shares. Had Wyser-Pratte tipped his hand to the market, most likely he would have eroded the majority of his returns. As it was, he ultimately sold his stake in SIPAREX at a share price approximately 35 percent higher than it was when he made his announcement public.

Wyser-Pratte's use of the element of surprise is not limited to stealth. He has also employed deception, as we will see in the case of French company Taittinger SA, and he has cleverly used the media to "create sunshine where there were shadows,"[5] thereby influencing the reasoning and behavior of his rivals, as we saw in the case of Rheinmetall.

Focus. As previously mentioned, acquiring a 5 percent or greater stake in a company's total shares outstanding entails a sizable commitment of financial resources from the outset. In several instances, most notably French avionics manufacturer Intertechnique SA, Wyser-Pratte has over time increased his ownership of shares outstanding and associated voting rights to exert greater influence on management teams and boards. In the case of Intertechnique, Wyser-Pratte increased his holdings from 5 percent of capital outstanding to a whopping 18 percent over a ten-month period. His intent was to convince the Dassault family and company management, who jointly controlled the majority of voting shares, to consider a sale of the undervalued company. Ultimately, French bidder Zodiac SA bought the company at a 46 percent premium to Wyser-Pratte's initial purchase.[6]

Decentralized Decision Making. With just four investment professionals and nine support personnel, Wyser-Pratte does not have a large enough staff to canvass the United States and Europe in search of investment opportunities. Instead he relies heavily on an informal network of in-country agents—businesspeople, investment bankers, and consultants who are familiar with his unique approach and who are attuned to local markets, culture, and politics. Wyser-Pratte provides these individuals with clear commander's intent with respect to investment criteria, gives them considerable latitude to exercise their judgment, and then trusts them to bring the right opportunities to him. Both Rheinmetall and Intertechnique are direct results of this process.

Tempo. During a 1997–98 campaign to turn around COMSAT, a laggard U.S. telecommunications provider and former government agency, Wyser-Pratte's rapid reaction to an unexpected event and radical redirection of strategy narrowly averted disaster and ensured success. Had he hesitated, COMSAT's board would have been able to mount an effective response. Instead his quick decision making enabled him to keep the upper hand.

COMSAT's exclusive access to the twenty-four-satellite Intelsat network afforded it a commanding advantage as a provider of communications services into and out of the United States. But the board's authorization of an ill-advised attempt to diversify into entertainment via acquisitions—a basketball team, a hockey team, a movie studio, and a hotel movie service—weighed heavily on COMSAT's share price. Sensing opportunity, Wyser-Pratte joined forces in early 1997 with investment firm Providence Capital to oust COMSAT's board of directors. Only after he accumulated a large stake in COMSAT and initiated a costly proxy fight to oust its board did Wyser-Pratte learn that Providence Capital was a faulty ally that had been involved in the bankruptcy of a Russian satellite maker just one year earlier. The taint associated with this involvement threatened to undermine the legitimacy of Wyser-Pratte's claim to be acting for the benefit of shareholders.

Upon receipt of this news, Wyser-Pratte immediately decided to abandon his relationship with Providence and continue his efforts to enhance shareholder value from *within* COMSAT. Seamlessly transitioning to the role of insider, he secured a seat on COMSAT's board of directors and assumed a more harmonious stance. Concurrent with Wyser-Pratte's appointment, COMSAT completed the spin-off of its noncore entertainment assets.

As a newly appointed board member, Wyser-Pratte moved quickly to form a special committee to review COMSAT's strategic plans and evaluate proposals from potential acquirers. He also began working with management to instill a more commercially focused mind-set in the company. As time progressed, owing to his relationships with influential U.S. government officials, Wyser-Pratte's role on COMSAT's board expanded—to that of key congressional liaison. He played an instrumental role in ensuring the enactment of two pieces of legislation that deregulated the company and enabled its ultimate sale to Lockheed Martin for $2.7 billion.

Combined Arms. In 1997, Wyser-Pratte launched a three-year campaign to unlock the potential value of Taittinger SA, one of the most celebrated of French family-controlled companies. His use of combined arms systematically eliminated all means of resistance available to the Taittinger family, whose disproportionately high voting rights had historically insulated the company from the demands of public shareholders. Indeed, owing to the family's disregard for the bottom line, from 1991 to 1996 the company's share price halved, while during the same period the Paris Bourse SBF 250 index more than doubled. Wyser-Pratte realized that Taittinger's assets—a famous champagne business, opulent hotels, and prestigious brands such as Baccarat crystal and Annick Goutal—were considerably undervalued; accordingly, he began amassing shares and launched a combined arms assault shortly thereafter.

The first "arm" was direct pressure on the Taittinger family from within the shareholder base: by forming coalitions with other minority shareholders, Wyser-Pratte accumulated sufficient voting power to prevent Taittinger from issuing additional shares and diluting its shareholder base in 2000. The second arm was the media: a series of announcements by Wyser-Pratte drew considerable public attention to shareholders' dissatisfaction and cast a negative light on the Taittinger family. The third arm was a reliance on outside financial advisers whose objective analyses validated Wyser-Pratte's claims of undervaluation.

To deliver a final blow, Wyser-Pratte employed a fourth arm: deception. Under the auspices of raising more capital to purchase an even larger stake in Taittinger, Wyser-Pratte organized a private road show, during which he met with leading hotel and real estate operators across Europe. His actual intent was not to raise additional capital but rather to ferret out a buyer for his stake in Taittinger. Two buyers emerged, one of whom was wealthy Belgian industrialist Albert Freres. Freres purchased Wyser-Pratte's stake at the end of 2000—at a share price approximately 145 percent higher than the original purchase price in 1997—and continued the quest to unlock the potential value of Taittinger's assets.

Rheinmetall, SIPAREX, Intertechnique, COMSAT, and Taittinger are but a handful of many investments, forty-eight in all, that Wyser-Pratte has completed since 1991. During this twelve-year period he has achieved an impressive 30 percent annualized rate of return on capital employed.

Leadership Lessons

As a "mere" minority shareholder, Wyser-Pratte has managed to exert considerable influence on numerous companies, move equity markets, and create lasting value for shareholders. At the heart of this ability to influence is a unique approach, born of his experience as a U.S. Marine, that exemplifies the application of maneuver warfare in the business environment.

Decentralized decision making pulls Wyser-Pratte to key opportunities. When a corporate governance failure is verified, he quickly weighs the risks and rewards associated with acting boldly and makes the investment decision. Immediately thereafter, he begins to focus his resources—under the cover of stealth so as to conceal his intentions—to establish a "beachhead" (incidentally, if, at this point, you find yourself asking why the authors have not articulated this series of actions as reconnaissance pull plus boldness, then you have learned something from this book). Once he makes public his corporate governance initiative, Wyser-Pratte masterfully uses the media to influence the behavior of his rivals and shape the rules of the game. As events unfold, he uses combined arms to eliminate systematically a rival's available responses, and, ultimately, he deals the decisive blow by targeting the rival's critical vulnerability.

While this kind of commitment to maneuver would not be surprising in a corporate raider with the morality, ethics, and resource endowment of a pirate, what is striking is that Wyser-Pratte has maintained his integrity throughout. He captures value for his firm and his investors, to be sure, but he succeeds because he has widespread shareholder backing, present only because of the value he delivers to all investors in his target companies.

CAPITAL ONE FINANCIAL

A division of Signet Bank until its initial public offering and subsequent spin-off in 1995, Capital One employed the seven guiding principles as an integrated whole to leapfrog rival credit card issuers in the 1990s and subsequently grow into a dominant global credit company.

The founders of Capital One, Richard Fairbank and Nigel Morris, while working as management consultants in the mid-1980s, observed that banks were not exploiting modern technology to identify profitable customers and deliver a customized product. They realized that not all customers were alike: a strong *customer profitability gradient*, or huge difference in the profitability of best, worst, and average customers, existed.

Credit card issuers earn money primarily from interest charges on the balances that customers carry on their cards and through a variety of fees (e.g., late fees). An issuer's best customers, "love 'ems"—those who carried a high balance and paid it off slowly over time—were as much as a hundred times more profitable than average customers. Worst customers, or "kill yous," who paid their charges off every month, held no balance, and thus paid no interest or fees, represented a loss. Accordingly, Fairbank and Morris decided to build a business to serve the love 'ems and carefully avoid the kill yous.

Whereas national credit card issuers at the time were following a strategy based on *scale*—spreading fixed expenses over the largest possible customer base—Capital One employed an information-based strategy based on *skill*. The systematic gathering and analysis of detailed customer information created opportunities for detailed customer segmentation, targeted marketing, and differential pricing campaigns. By employing sophisticated data-mining techniques and simple screening mechanisms, Capital One identified the most profitable customers and determined which combination of price and characteristics would be most desirable to each individual. Hypotheses were developed to predict how to attract and retain profitable customers, and live tests were developed and launched to assess these hypotheses. This hypothesis-driven "test and learn" approach formed the basis of the company's information-based strategy and, ultimately, Capital One's success.

Targeting Critical Vulnerabilities. The critical vulnerability of incumbent credit card issuers such as Citibank, AT&T, and other major players was their inability to recognize the source of their profits. Oblivious to the differences between love 'ems and kill yous, incumbent issuers charged the same card rate to all customers; this one-size-fits-all rate meant that profitable love 'ems were cross-subsidizing unprofitable kill yous.

Capital One created a major dilemma for Citibank, AT&T, and others by opportunistically picking off their best customers. If the incumbents ignored Capital One's attack, they would lose their profitable accounts. If they wanted to mount an effective response, they would have to replicate Capital One's information-based strategy or lower the rates for the best accounts. Lowering rates charged to the best accounts would erode profits by reducing the cross-subsidy for the worst accounts, and state usury laws inhibited raising the rates charged to the worst accounts to offset this action. Replicating Capital One's strategy would require a major investment in information technology. Reluctant to respond, the incumbents opted to do nothing.

Boldness. Having identified this opening, Capital One weighed the risks of its unproven concept—high start-up costs with a small customer base and a considerable lag time between market testing and payback (if any at all)—against the potential benefits of redefining the credit card market. Despite the rejection of Capital One's idea by more than twenty of America's largest banks, Signet, a small regional bank in Virginia, finally saw the merits of Fairbank's and Morris's idea. Signet afforded them the opportunity to make the massive investments in information technology and people that their new approach required. The company's initial difficulties highlighted the boldness of the move: from the start of operations in 1988 until 1991, Capital One accumulated steep losses.

Boldness was thus central to Capital One's initial success, and it continues to be a central tenet of the company's culture today. To encourage risk taking and individual initiative throughout the organization, CEO Rich Fairbank hands out Capital One's version of the toilet seat award mentioned in Chapter 5 to the employee who has come up with the most promising idea but the least effective results.

Surprise. To carve out its place in the industry, Capital One relied heavily on stealth to surprise its competitors. It used a difficult-to-detect direct-mail campaign to poach customers from unwitting banks. Unlike the large majority of its competition, it developed its data systems in-house, shrouded from the prying eyes of outside vendors. It was and continues to be extremely disciplined in its dealings with the media in an effort to prevent critical company information from being divulged in the public forum. It has avoided markets, even those with strong customer profitability gradients such as retail insurance, where regulation required full disclosure of pricing strategy to protect its sophisticated pricing models from competitors. And it has limited the scope of consultants' projects to prevent reengineering of its pricing models and best practices.

Focus. Capital One brought overwhelming resources to bear on a small yet highly profitable segment of the market: cardholders who carried a high recurring balance, presented a relatively low risk of default, and were inclined to pay high finance charges. The company made massive investments in building databases, learning account management, and recruiting top performers; Capital One claims to pay as much as double for talented managers. As the company has sought growth opportunities and expanded into new businesses such as automobile lending, small business lending, medical lending, and credit recovery, it continues this practice of focusing its best people, best systems, and utmost attention from senior management on high-value opportunities.

Decentralized Decision Making. Capital One has always relied heavily on the judgment of talented problem solvers who, at the point of decision, conduct market tests, interpret trial data, and identify profitable market opportunities.

As evidenced by the more than forty-five thousand market tests conducted in 2002, all Capital One employees have the freedom to formulate hypotheses, undertake sometimes-costly efforts to prove them, and immediately present promising results directly to their supervisors. A successful test can result in a new product, and the employee who identifies it may receive more than praise: he or she may be awarded the opportunity to manage the new product.

To ensure a greater likelihood of success for its decentralized approach, Capital One meticulously screens its employees in the recruiting phase and then conducts comprehensive training and mentoring throughout their employment. During the recruiting phase stringent personality and analytical tests and a lengthy case-based interview process ensure all new hires have the integrity, intelligence, and leadership skills necessary to perform in Capital One's highly decentralized, quantitative, and somewhat free-wheeling culture. Though Capital One has some of the highest relative recruiting costs in corporate America, the exhaustive screening efforts outweigh the potential downfalls of errant decentralized actions. Further, Capital One employees go through extensive ongoing job-related training—in areas such as risk management, legal compliance, and ethics—throughout their careers.

Tempo. Refining its offerings so frequently that competitors found themselves in a constant state of reaction—often to one of its earlier moves—Capital One also maintained a rapid tempo. When AT&T's Universal Card finally responded with a differential pricing technique of its own, Capital One had three hundred differently priced account offerings to AT&T's twenty. When AT&T matched Capital One's three hundred, Capital One had more than four thousand. Indeed, even as the rest of the industry showed signs of slowing down in 1998, "the company introduced successful new products at a blistering pace . . . Of the more than six thousand credit-card deals it offer[ed in 1999], half didn't exist six months [previously]."[7]

And when competitors finally responded to its information-based strategy with similar offerings intended to poach its customers, Capital One had already staffed highly trained employees as retention specialists. These specialists were afforded the authority to negotiate with individual customers to preserve relationships with Capital One—albeit at lower but still profitable rates.

Time and time again, competitors' responses to Capital One's moves were "too little, too late." But as these responses have become increasingly sophisticated, Capital One has had to innovate new methods to stay one step ahead. Recognizing that its products' life cycles "melt like ice cream"[8] when market conditions change or new competitors replicate its strategy, Capital One quickly exits markets, such as dial-around long distance and cell phone capacity reselling, when it deems that they have become structurally untenable. To make these timely exits, it relies heavily on the judgment of its people and even goes so far as to evaluate managers on the timeliness of their decisions to enter and exit a product's life cycle.

Combined Arms. Whereas most credit card issuers were configured into divisions of independently functioning "silos" that rarely interacted with one another, had misaligned incentives, and thus acted with different goals in mind, Capital One combined marketing, information technology, and credit risk management into a single unified function. Marketing associates and data analysts were formed into integrated "marketing and analysis" teams within each business unit with a singular objective of maximizing their respective business's profitability. The aim of this combined arms approach was to exploit information technology to accomplish marketing's goal of maximizing revenues *and* credit risk management's goal of minimizing exposure to potential defaults. Within each team programmers tapped the powerful databases and built sophisticated data models, and business analysts in turn used the data to segment customers and create credit policies down to the individual customer level. And the team members worked hand-in-hand to constantly test and learn and refine the millions of customer profiles.

The findings from these vast, continual analyses provided Capital One with invaluable and unique insights into the behavior of credit card holders and guided the company's successful efforts to profitably grow its information-based business. Capital One was able to extend credit judiciously to love 'ems while carefully screening out the kill yous. Moreover, statistically derived screening mechanisms watched for signs of deteriorating customer quality, and differential pricing captured greater revenue per card by estimating with greater certainty individual customers' willingness to pay.

With data information technology, marketing, and credit risk management housed separately in different silos, competitors could not match Capital One's growth without increasing their exposure to potential defaults. Nor could they match Capital One's low-risk profile without sacrificing growth.

Capital One's exhibition of all seven principles has produced dramatic results. In the seven consecutive years since going public, revenue has grown at a nearly 40 percent compounded annual rate, earnings have grown at more than a 20 percent rate, and return on equity has remained above 20 percent.[9] Given that very few companies in the S&P 500 achieve this triple-double in a single year, this track record is remarkable.

Today, even in an economic downturn, Capital One continues to thrive. Owing to a customer base that has reached nearly forty-eight million internationally—a 900 percent increase since the IPO—its data processing operations enjoy considerable economies of scale, making it a low-cost producer. At the same time, its revenues per customer continue to rank near the top of the industry, while its bad-loan charge-offs remain relatively low. Its marketing slogan "What's in your wallet?!" has overtaken both American Express's "Don't leave home without it" and MasterCard's "Priceless . . . for everything else there's MasterCard" in recognition among credit card holders across the United States. And it has even become the single largest customer of the U.S. Postal Service. Beyond these successes in its core competency, Capital One has successfully extended its hypothesis-driven test-and-learn approach to numerous new markets and established operations in six countries outside the United States.[10]

Leadership Lessons

More impressive than Capital One's exhibition of all seven principles is the way in which the principles complemented and reinforced one another. Both the boldness and the focus of its initial attack reinforced the company's use of surprise to stealthily pick off competitors' customers: while the audacity and long odds of Capital One's offensive meant that competitors dismissed the threat at first, the attack's narrowness and precision made it less immediately noticeable. Decentralized decision making reinforced Capital One's efforts to maintain a rapid tempo: because frontline employees could quickly refine or add product offerings and even change the terms or rates on a card, without having to wait for approval from superiors far removed from the action, competitors were constantly forced to play catch-up. And decentralized decision making, targeting critical vulnerabilities, tempo, and focus enabled reconnaissance pull: most of Capital One's new product innovations and new market entries were the result of frontline employees' identification of critical vulnerabilities and management's immediate willingness to commit the resources necessary for exploitation.

REPLICATION IN BUSINESS

The examples of Wyser-Pratte & Co., a small firm that has moved markets, and Capital One, a large company that has redefined a market thus illustrate the ultimate aim of the application of the *Marine Corps Way* in the business environment. While these master practitioners' command of the seven principles may seem intuitive and therefore daunting, you can replicate their successes—through careful study and deliberate, systematic effort.

Use the seven guiding principles as a mental checklist to guide your thought process, decisions, and actions. Ask yourself regularly, if not religiously:

- What are my competitors' Achilles' heels, and where are customers' needs most underserved?

- What risks am I willing to take to capitalize on these opportunities, and what are the potential rewards?

- How can I legally exploit and/or control information to shape encounters with competitors before those encounters even begin?

- Where and when am I willing to commit the maximum amount of my organization's finite resources to achieve a decisive outcome?

- How many of my people have the guidance and latitude they need to make decisions at their respective levels? What am I doing to arm them with information and supervise them?

- How can I accelerate my own decision-making speed and my organization's overall pace of operations so as to force competitors into a constant state of reaction to my moves?

- How can I creatively combine my organization's complementary capabilities to increase their collective effectiveness and eliminate all of my competitors' potential responses?

As you begin to internalize each of the principles, look beyond the individual questions posed—to the logical order in which they appear. In so doing, you will move from the use of each principle on a one-off basis toward a fully integrated application. And remember that you are not the only member of your organization that needs to internalize this mind-set; as a leader it is your duty to ensure that your people understand and can implement the principles.

CHAPTER 13

LEADERSHIP
The Backbone
of Maneuver Warfare

"More than anything else, Marines have fought and . . . won because of a commitment—to a leader and to a small band of brotherhood where the ties that bind are mutual respect and confidence, shared privation, shared hazard, shared triumph, a willingness to obey, and determination to follow."

—LT. GEN. VICTOR KRULAK, USMC (RET.)[1]

Our stated intent at the beginning of this book was to convince you that maneuver warfare has the potential to deliver breakthrough results in business as well as in armed conflict. We hope the examples and prescriptions presented support this assertion. But we would not consider our mission accomplished without a concluding discussion of the backbone of maneuver warfare—*leadership*. Leadership fosters the intangibles that make maneuver warfare work.

Maneuver warfare is, by nature, decentralized, risk seeking, fast paced, and collaborative. Its successful implementation, therefore, requires the utmost *trust*, *integrity*, *initiative*, and *unselfishness* at all levels of an organization.

Trust. Seniors must trust that juniors will provide them with valuable insights and execute plans capably, in accordance with the organization's overall objectives. Juniors must trust that the directions they receive are well intended, competent, and legitimate. And peers must be able to trust each other's contributions when working together toward a common goal.

Integrity. A junior who is entrusted with making risk-reward trade-offs must have the integrity always to consider the good of the greater organization and always to admit mistakes when wrong. In other words, the junior must be willing to do the right thing in the absence of constant supervision. A senior who expects to engender the respect of juniors must exhibit the highest integrity. Similarly, the senior must be willing to do the right thing in the absence of supervision—as if there were no one to sanction his or her behavior.

Initiative. Identifying an opportunity, weighing the associated risks and rewards, and pursuing its exploitation in a timely manner requires a willingness to decide and act on the spot, without explicit instructions. Such initiative cannot be imposed from the top down; detailed orders can never be a substitute for initiative.

Unselfishness. Working together toward a common objective sometimes requires the subordination of one's own interests to the interests of the greater organization. For juniors, unselfishness may entail executing a senior's order as if it were their own, even if they dissented during the decision-making process. For seniors, unselfishness may entail accepting blame when the organization stumbles or passing credit on to juniors when the organization succeeds. For peers, unselfishness may entail helping a buddy out, even if the payoff is neither immediate nor certain.

Unfortunately, these intangibles do not always occur naturally; they must be inspired and reinforced continually. Owing to an unparalleled emphasis on leadership, the Marine Corps has mastered the two-step art of inspiring and reinforcing these intangibles, and we believe that its leadership philosophy can serve as a useful guide to the aspiring practitioner of maneuver warfare. While a comprehensive treatment of this complex matter warrants its own book, we have, for the purposes of this discussion, distilled this leadership philosophy into three pillars: *leadership by example, taking care of those in your charge,* and *leadership development.*

In this chapter we will first provide an in-depth treatment of each of these three pillars. We will then profile two successful companies, FedEx and Southwest Airlines, whose respective leadership philosophies resemble that of the Marines Corps. And we will conclude by suggesting ways you can adopt and encourage in your organization leadership practices that will ensure the success of a maneuver warfare–based approach.

LEADERSHIP . . . THE MARINE CORPS WAY

Setting the example for others to follow is the point of departure for Marine leadership. All Marines consider themselves leaders and therefore hold themselves to the highest standards of professional and ethical behavior. At the same time, they display a deeply genuine concern for their fellow Marines. Indeed, taking care of your Marines receives a priority second only to accomplishing the mission. And even as the former is subordinated to the latter, the time-honored saying "Take care of your Marines, and they will take care of the mission" illustrates that the Marines perceive the two concepts as interrelated. Finally, leadership development is a comprehensive and never-ending process in the Corps. Marine officers and noncommissioned officers (NCOs) are constantly reminded that the development of their subordinates is a direct reflection of their abilities as leaders.

Leadership by Example

The Marine Corps's approach to leadership rests on the simple premise that motivating Marines to achieve a desired result requires that their leaders first exert the effort and make the sacrifice they are asking of their Marines. This premise, that leadership can be achieved by setting an example for others to follow, is integral to maneuver warfare because it inspires and reinforces integrity and trust.

A willingness to share hardship and perform above and beyond the call of duty—no matter how miserable or inconsequential the task—ripples throughout the entire unit, inspires higher levels of performance at all levels, and creates an undeniable credibility for the leader. If the leader expects his Marines to maintain neat and orderly personal appearances, the leader's appearance must be impeccable. If the leader expects his Marines to be able to march twenty miles with a heavy rucksack, the leader must be at the front of the marching formation, smiling the whole way. If a leader expects his Marines to maintain a vigilant defensive posture through the night under a cold rain, the leader had better be out in the rain at all hours checking on the Marines in their fighting holes, not behind the lines under the shelter of a warm, dry tent. If the leader expects his Marines to maintain their composure during a difficult situation, the leader must display a cool, soothing outward appearance. These actions, and numerous others in a similar vein, require a tremendous amount of self-discipline on the part of the leader. And Marine leaders embrace this requirement because they view the leadership of other Marines as a privilege—not a right—that must be earned every day.

Leadership by example thus derives its overall effectiveness from actions, not words. As it pertains to maneuver warfare, a leader's sound moral character and willingness to share hardship elicit trust from the Marines in his charge. Moreover, the leader can push his unit to uphold the highest standards of integrity, so long as his own personal integrity is beyond reproach.

Taking Care of Those in Your Charge

While probably not the first trait that comes to mind when thinking about an outfit whose members call themselves "Devil Dogs," compassion is, nonetheless, the crucial second pillar in the Marine Corps's leadership philosophy. Marine leaders prioritize the accomplishment of the mission first, the welfare of their Marines second, and their own personal needs third. This willingness to place the welfare of those in their charge before their own needs inspires and reinforces not only the higher levels of performance necessary to accomplish the mission but also unselfishness, initiative, and trust.

Enhanced unit performance is an obvious motivator for this altruistic behavior, but Marine leaders take care of their Marines, first and foremost, because it is the right thing to do. When a leader assumes the helm of a given unit, he wastes little time in getting to know each and every Marine—names, hometowns, family members, personal interests—in an effort to gain intimate familiarity with the individual psychologies that constitute the unit. When meals are served, the lowest-ranking enlisted Marines eat first, and the highest-ranking officers eat last, so that each level of leaders ensures that Marines more junior are fed first. When Marines stand guard duty on weekends or holidays, their leaders often sacrifice their own personal time to check in and see how they are doing. When their Marines experience personal or administrative problems, leaders work relentlessly to achieve resolution. When leaders discover that an individual Marine is struggling, they make time in their busy schedules to help that Marine improve his performance and provide counseling in private as necessary.

Similarly, when an individual Marine makes a successful achievement, his leaders publicly recognize that achievement, in the form of praise in front of his peers, formal mention in front of the entire unit, or even a medal. When Marines are considered for promotion, their leaders champion their candidacies.

When communicating downward, leaders share information in a timely manner, provide honest and frank assessments of situations, and explain the context into which the unit's actions fit in an effort to uphold the seventh of the eleven Marine Corps leadership principles: "Keep your Marines informed."[2] Similarly, when Marines offer observations, insights, or recommendations, leaders listen attentively. Finally, in perhaps the ultimate demonstration of caring, one of the most sacred and honored traditions of the Marine Corps is that leaders never leave fallen comrades behind on the battlefield.

With the notable exception of the last, the preponderance of the aforementioned examples occurs in peacetime. Obviously a leader's commitment to taking care of his Marines continues in combat, but a baseline must be established before the battle begins. Moreover, these gestures require from the leader not only a tremendous amount of self-discipline, similar to that required in the case of leadership by example, but also *sincerity*, which differentiates a genuine concern for others' well-being from a superficial display.

Unselfishness is the first direct result of leaders' ongoing, disciplined, and sincere commitment to the welfare of their Marines: when Marines see their leaders placing the group's needs before their own, they feel compelled to do the same for those in their charge and for their peers. Initiative is the second: a leader's willingness to take care of his Marines prompts those Marines to take actions proactively that keep the leader "out of trouble" and handle matters at their respective levels with greater attention to detail. Trust is the third: a leader's ability to convince his Marines—through actions, not words—that he truly cares for them fosters fierce loyalty and unwavering willingness to follow.

Leadership Development

The Marines themselves best describe the third pillar of Marine Corps leadership philosophy: "Because people are our most precious asset, how we recruit them, train them, instill in them our core values, and equip them will forever be our institutional focus."[3] Indeed, this never-ending commitment to recruiting, training, and mentoring develops, at all levels, confident, aggressive leaders whose initiative and integrity drive the implementation of the maneuver warfare–based approach.

With respect to recruiting, the Marines hire for character, not skills. Slogans such as "Maybe you can be one of us . . . the Few, the Proud, the Marines" and "We didn't promise you a rose garden" are deliberately designed to attract can-do, challenge-seeking, take-charge personality types. Members of this self-selected applicant pool that meet the Marine Corps's stringent acceptance criteria—academics, physical fitness, community standing, leadership potential, and a selection officer's all-important subjective evaluation—then proceed to boot camp or Officer Candidates' School (OCS). Enlisted recruits endure thirteen weeks of boot camp to see if they have the mettle required to earn the title "U.S. Marine." Officer candidates are screened rigorously for leadership potential and sound moral character over an intense ten-week period at OCS before earning the title "Officer of Marines." While time-consuming and costly, this thorough process of self-selection, objective and subjective review, and earned entrance into the organization ensures that new members possess the traits and determination that the Marine Corps covets.

Formal leadership training begins with an initial "overinvestment" in instilling core values of *honor, courage,* and *commitment* and leadership traits (see Appendix, "Chapter 13," for a list and full explanation of both) and continues throughout a Marine's career. During their first ten to thirteen weeks, aspiring Marines spend seventeen-hour days immersed in an isolated environment under the tutelage of the fiercest and most professional of role models, drill instructors (DIs), who are selected from the Marine Corps's top quartile of NCOs. Rising before their recruits and candidates and retiring after, demonstrating an unwavering intensity, and maintaining a flawless appearance and an even more flawless composure, DIs personify Marine Corps leadership and, as described in the 1999 *Harvard Business Review* article, "Firing Up the Front Line," lead their young hopefuls in "physically and emotionally stressful exercises designed to encourage mutual accountability. If a recruit fails to complete a 15-mile hike, his comrades must carry his rifle and 60-pound rucksack for the rest of the hike. If someone errs during a close-order-drill movement, the entire unit must repeat the movement until it is flawless."[4] Upon completion of boot camp, enlisted Marines, who learn to follow before they learn to lead, proceed to infantry training and occupational specialty schools. Newly commissioned officers proceed from OCS to The Basic School, where, over a six-month period, they lead their peers in numerous hands-on practical learning opportunities, such as field exercises, participate frequently in small-group discussions about leadership, and receive extensive individualized leadership coaching from senior officers, who, like DIs, represent the Marine Corps's top performers.

Beyond this initial "overinvestment," officers and NCOs attend full-time schools every few years and receive formal instruction intended to reinforce core values and leadership traits and prepare leaders for increased levels of responsibility. These career-level schools may last a few weeks, as in the case of the corporals' course or sergeants' course, or an entire year, as in the case of the Marine Corps War College for senior officers. To staff these schools, the Marine Corps once again pulls top performers off the front lines to serve as instructors.

In addition to the formal mechanisms of recruiting and training, the Marine Corps relies heavily on informal mentoring to develop its leaders. As immortalized by the words of the late Major General John A. Lejeune, Thirteenth Commandant of the Marine Corps, senior Marines consider mentoring their juniors one of their greatest responsibilities as leaders: "The relationship between officers and enlisted men should in no sense be that of superior and inferior nor that of master and servant, but rather that of teacher and scholar."[5] Feedback is clear, constructive, candid, and regular. Guidance is specific, thoughtful, individually tailored, and intended to help the junior Marine grow both personally and professionally.

While such interaction serves as an effective means of imparting wisdom, mentoring in the Marine Corps is actually a two-way street. In active-duty units the Marines create "leadership partnerships"[6] between officers and NCOs. Under such arrangements, NCOs mentor upward by providing invaluable advice based on years of practical experience and a fundamental understanding of the perspective of the enlisted Marines in the unit. Borrowing from "Firing Up the Front Line" a second time: "The experience and maturity of the [NCO] complement the tactical education and fresh ideas of the [officer]. The two learn from each other and jointly solve tactical challenges and problems about people. . . . Each leader has more time to attend to the training and professional growth of the [unit's] . . . members than if he were the sole officer in charge."[7]

The Marines' *recruit, train, mentor* approach to leadership development implies a major investment in personnel. Nevertheless, the Marine Corps believes that the return on this investment—a greater incidence of initiative and integrity among its members—more than justifies the costs, especially given the possibility that lives will hang in the balance. A rigorous recruiting process attracts and selects those individuals who exhibit a natural predisposition to desired traits and weeds out the complacent, hesitant, timid, and ethically shaky. An extensive initial and ongoing training program led by top performers transmits the Marine Corps's values and leadership traits to its members in the most effective manner. And a top-down, bottom-up approach to mentorship provides timely feedback and thoughtful advice. The end result of this three-step process is a greater likelihood that, when left to their own judgment in an uncertain situation, Marines take charge, make the right decisions for the right reasons, and act in accordance with the organization's overall objectives.

COMPANIES THAT GET IT

As we thought about companies whose success can be attributed to superior leadership that resembles that of the Marine Corps, FedEx and Southwest Airlines immediately came to mind. FedEx Chairman, CEO, and founder, Fred Smith, is a former Marine, and the lessons he learned during two tours in Vietnam, first as a platoon and company commander in the infantry and later as an aerial observer, have directly influenced the leadership philosophy that he has instilled in his company. Southwest Airlines cannot claim a former Marine as its CEO, but it can claim the next best thing: to have participated with the Marines in a two-day joint leadership development workshop that reinvigorated the company's celebrated culture of caring, fun, and "outrageous customer service."[8]

FedEx

Fred Smith trusts approximately two hundred thousand FedEx employees and contractors around the world to put forth the extra effort necessary to ensure that his company can deliver on its promise of "absolutely, positively the broadest array of transportation, e-commerce and supply chain solutions in the world."[9]

In building and leading FedEx, Smith has relied heavily on the lessons he learned in the Marine Corps. And he has even gone so far as to articulate, adapt, and institutionalize those lessons through the *Manager's Guide*, which has been a mainstay for all FedEx managers since he penned it in the early days of the company's existence.

FedEx considers each and every contact with the customer "the moment of truth"[10] and therefore calls on its managers to set an example that encourages frontline employees to project the highest standards of professionalism and put forth the extra effort necessary to deliver 100 percent satisfaction to extremely demanding customers. To these ends, FedEx managers maintain the highest standards of personal appearance and exhibit a positive, composed external demeanor at all times. They admit to mistakes and apologize when wrong. And they make themselves both available and visible during peak periods of activity, such as night shifts and holidays. Finally, FedEx managers are expected to "earn the trust of their employees by doing what's right"[11] and are reminded that "their jobs exist primarily to help their employees exceed customer expectations."[12]

At the core of FedEx's corporate philosophy of *People—Service—Profit* is the belief that if the company takes care of its people, they will take care of the customer, and profits will naturally follow. Says Smith, "Federal Express, from its inception, has put its people first both because it is right to do so and because it is good business as well."[13] Of the many ways in which FedEx takes care of its people, three stand out as particularly noteworthy: *People Help*, *Encouraging the Heart*, and *Survey-Feedback-Action*.

People Help is a company-funded program that provides FedEx employees with support and counseling services should they encounter serious personal challenges, such as substance abuse, marital discord, financial distress, or work-related issues. Encouraging the Heart is a tiered system of positive reinforcement built on the tenets of the Marine Corps, whereby the company recognizes and rewards the superior efforts of employees. Recognition ranges from "atta-boy" stickers reading "Bravo Zulu"—a term borrowed from the U.S. Naval Service—to Five Star Awards, which are accompanied by stock options and formal mention in company meetings and publications, to Golden Falcon awards for heroic acts, such as performing CPR, saving someone from a burning building, or stopping a robbery. And since 1979, FedEx has employed the Survey-Feedback-Action program to ensure that it "listens" to all of its employees by each year soliciting their ideas as to how to improve the corporation's work environment.

Finally, borrowing heavily from Smith's experiences in the Marine Corps, FedEx employs a structured process that can best be described as *screen, train, coach* to develop its leaders, most of whom are promoted from within the organization. The ASPIRE[14] program, FedEx's equivalent of OCS, screens potential leaders and places considerable emphasis on company values and principles. Candidates either volunteer or are selected by frontline managers and then attend an ASPIRE workshop. After the workshop candidates must successfully complete three tests: a standardized employment test, a managerial personality profile, and a peer evaluation. Needless to say, attrition is high.

Graduates of ASPIRE proceed to level 1 of the FedEx *Leadership* Institute, the company's equivalent of The Basic School, where they receive extensive training in those practices that FedEx considers central to leading—note the deliberate distinction from managing—high-performing businesses. Graduates of level 1 return to the Leadership Institute later in their careers for levels 2 and 3, and FedEx also offers other ongoing continuation education courses outside of the Leadership Institute.

Once screened and trained, managers at FedEx spend a good deal of their time coaching. Not only must they motivate those employees who have no desire to become managers to maintain superior levels of performance, but they must also groom future managers. Frontline-level managers must select and mentor ASPIRE candidates, and each middle and senior management position in the company must have two identified successors. According to the *Manager's Guide*, "An infallible measure of success for any managerial assignment is its legacy."[15]

Owing to his efforts to articulate, adapt, and institutionalize what he learned in the Marine Corps, Smith has not only built a winning organization at FedEx but also secured his own legacy as a leader among chief executives in corporate America.

Southwest Airlines

In December 1998, twenty midlevel and senior managers from Southwest Airlines "reported for duty" at the Marine Corps base in Quantico, Virginia. Their mission: to exchange ideas with twenty Marine counterparts on the topics of instilling and reinforcing organizational values, inspiring higher levels of frontline performance, and developing leadership. The groundbreaking workshop accomplished two major objectives for Southwest: validation of current leadership practices and the stimulation of new companywide initiatives.

The workshop validated many of the company's existing leadership practices. Former CEO Herb Kelleher had already made a regular habit of joining his frontline employees on holidays to help load bags or attend to customers. Company leaders had long maintained a close-knit, supportive, and familylike work environment and placed considerable emphasis on celebrating and rewarding the successes of employees. And Southwest had already established its own recruit, train, mentor approach to leadership development. Zany messages such as "Work in a place where Elvis has been spotted . . . send your résumés attention Elvis" (caption below a photo of Kelleher in an Elvis costume) and a rigorous review process ensured new applicants' attitudes fit with Southwest's unique culture. A department known as the University for People had been established to house most of the company's formal training and leadership development programs. And Southwest had already established a mechanism, the Quest Program, to encourage inexperienced frontline supervisors to create leadership partnerships with older, more experienced employees.

The workshop also spawned four companywide initiatives. Company leaders began to place greater emphasis on encouraging employees to hold one another accountable for upholding Southwest's standards of excellence. "More than anything, the workshop made us realize that we hadn't been focusing on what parts of our organization were truly important," said Donna Conover, workshop participant and now executive vice president of customer service.[16] First, concerned that it was falling short on instilling company core values in new hires, Southwest overhauled and renamed its orientation program. The new and improved "FLY" program—for *Freedom, Love,* and *You*—assigned considerable importance to caring as a means to promote mutual trust among all employees and loyalty to the organization as a whole. Second, Southwest shifted the emphasis of its leadership training efforts from empowerment to decision making. According to Conover, "Empowerment is about giving people options; leadership is about making decisions. We wanted our people to be more than frontline employees. We wanted them to be frontline *decision makers.*"[17] Third, to emulate the Marines' practice of carrying a core values card, inscribed with "honor, courage, and commitment," Southwest included on all company identification cards the motto "Spirit." And fourth, impressed with the Marine Corps hymn, Southwest had a company song written.

The impact of the workshop can be seen clearly in the company's words. Said one workshop participant during a teleconference in 2002: " 'If people don't see leaders modeling the behavior, they're not going to believe it,' " and " 'The bottom line takes care of itself when you take care of your people.' "[18]

And in the difficult years following the workshop, Southwest's actions and accomplishments have done justice to its strong leadership tradition, "warrior spirit,"[19] and interaction with the Marines. In the wake of the September 11, 2001, terrorist attacks, which plunged the airline industry into perhaps its worst-ever market downturn, Southwest management went to great lengths to keep concerned employees informed of the company's operational plans and provide reassurances that there would be no layoffs. Amid a wave of bankruptcies or near bankruptcies among its competitors, Southwest has managed to remain profitable—without layoffs—by avoiding infighting and pulling together as an organization.

APPLICATION IN BUSINESS

Leadership . . . the Marine Corps Way is a demanding philosophy. Leadership by example requires that leaders share hardship with their people, make a regular habit of exerting effort that is above and beyond the call of duty, and hold themselves to the highest professional and moral standards, particularly when no one is watching. Taking care of those in your charge requires that leaders place the needs of their people before their own. And the recruit, train, mentor approach to leadership requires that leaders make a time-consuming, costly investment in their most precious asset—people—sometimes at the expense of day-to-day operations.

Nevertheless, as evidenced by repeated references earlier in the chapter to "willingness," "self-discipline," "actions not words," and "ongoing commitment," the Marines embrace these requirements as necessary to inspire and reinforce the intangibles that ultimately ensure the success of the maneuver organization. As an aspiring practitioner of maneuver warfare in business, you would be well advised to do the same.

Leadership by Example

Instead of thinking that "rank has its privileges," consider your rank as a privilege that must be earned every day. Be your own toughest critic. Constantly remind yourself that your people are looking to your actions to set an example. Inspire superior levels of performance by exhibiting superior effort, and when you ask your people to perform certain tasks, be sure you would be willing to perform the same tasks yourself.

Taking Care of Those in Your Charge

Instead of thinking that your people exist to support you, constantly ask yourself what you can do to support your people and what you can do to make their personal and professional lives better. Get to know your people and what makes them tick. Keep them informed and listen to their input. Praise successes in public and counsel shortcomings in private. When your organization succeeds, pass the credit on to your people; when it stumbles, accept personal responsibility and shelter your people from blame. Take care of your people, and they will take care of your customers. Finally, always remember the words of retired Marine brigadier general Thomas Draude, a three-time combat veteran and now Senior Vice President at USAA, a major insurance company, "Caring cannot be delegated. . . . It is not an HR requirement. . . . You can't fake it."[20]

Leadership Development

Instead of dismissing leadership development as a costly distraction from day-to-day operations, consider each and every member of your organization a leader and potential successor to your job and invest in his development accordingly. Hire for character, not skills, and challenge applicants to earn their way into your organization. Overinvest in initial training; your commitment will pay disproportionately large dividends later. Do not merely pay lip service to values and leadership traits; make them a primary consideration from day one and reinforce them over time. Use your most talented and experienced managers as instructors and role models. Train your people to take charge in uncertain situations and instill in them the courage and resourcefulness necessary to adapt to changing conditions and capitalize on emerging opportunities. Mentor your people and be mentored by your people. Observe, respond to, and coach failure: sit down with your juniors one-on-one and give them candid, constructive, and timely feedback on how to improve individual performance instead of shying away from such difficult, sometimes awkward, encounters. Form leadership partnerships and listen to more experienced juniors, whose insights will lead you to self-improvement. Push your managers to mentor their people and establish mentorship as an important performance evaluation criterion.

Each of these efforts will contribute to the cohesion of your organization, with all the benefits stressed in the preceding dozen chapters. Without cohesion, whether the senior team develops the right strategy, attempts to focus on critical vulnerabilities, or correctly makes bold risk-reward trade-offs matters little. Furthermore, without cohesion, tactical implementation is impossible: decentralized command degenerates into chaos, commander's intent is either incomprehensible or ignored, tempo is replaced by randomness, focus is lost, and combined arms disappears in a race for individual gain and self-interest.

FINAL THOUGHTS

A valid question, as we come to the close of the book, might be "If maneuver warfare is so overwhelmingly effective, why aren't more people employing it?" Our response: because it is difficult. Maneuver warfare requires considerable self-confidence, sound moral character, a healthy appetite for calculated risk, and a high degree of commitment on the part of the leader. Maneuver warfare may also require a radical cultural overhaul that most organizations are not willing to undertake; in particular, it requires more trust in subordinates than most seniors are willing to grant and more trust from subordinates than most seniors are willing to earn.

But given the likelihood that there may very well be someone out there aiming to use maneuver warfare against you, the potential benefits of adopting the *Marine Corps Way* may far outweigh the costs. You do not have to be a master tactician, nor do you have to be a CEO to implement maneuver warfare in your organization; you just need to be prepared to make a full commitment.

With study and practice you can internalize the seven guiding principles, just as hundreds of newly minted Marine second lieutenants—"butter bars"—do each year at The Basic School. Moreover, whether you are the CEO, a division head, a department manager, or even the leader of a small team, it is your prerogative to lead your little piece of the world as you see fit. In the short term you will need to commit to sweeping and possibly painful organizational change. Over the longer term you will need to ensure that your mastery of the seven guiding principles and accompanying core values and leadership traits evolves ahead of rivals'—lest you risk an unexpected and humiliating defeat at the hands of a rival who uses maneuver warfare against you. The rewards, though, will more than repay your efforts.

We hope we have now accomplished our mission. We thank you for your time and interest and welcome any thoughts, feedback, or personal accounts of the actual implementation of maneuver warfare in your organization. To this end, please visit us at www.themarinecorpsway.com.

APPENDIX

SUMMARY OF KEY PRESCRIPTIONS

CHAPTER 1

Maneuver Warfare Defined

"A state of mind bent on shattering the enemy morally and physically by paralyzing and confounding him, by avoiding his strength, by quickly and aggressively exploiting his vulnerabilities, and by striking him in a way that will hurt him most."

Factors That Mediate Competitive Encounters

The four human and environmental factors that shape military conflict are also inherent aspects of business.

Friction: The force that "makes the simple difficult and the difficult seemingly impossible"

Uncertainty: The "fog of war"

Fluidity: The continuous cycle of cause and effect "replete with fleeting opportunities and unforeseen events"

Disorder: The state toward which competitive situations deteriorate as time progresses

CHAPTER 3

The Elements of Maneuver Warfare

The concepts of maneuver warfare, while valuable individually, are most powerful when applied in an integrated fashion.

Targeting Critical Vulnerabilities: Analyze and probe rivals with the aim of identifying and rapidly exploiting those weaknesses that will most effectively undermine their competitive position.

Boldness: Take calculated risks that have the potential to achieve major, market-shifting results.

Surprise: Use stealth, ambiguity, and deception to degrade the quality of information available to competitors and impair their ability to deploy resources efficiently.

Focus: Bring overwhelming resources to bear at critical points and times to capitalize on key market opportunities.

Decentralized Decision Making: Push decision-making authority to those who are closest to the point of decision and who possess superior local information. Align these individual decisions by communicating "commander's intent"—or final result desired—throughout the organization.

Tempo: Identify opportunities, make decisions, and implement plans faster than competitors do to seize the initiative and force them into a constant state of reaction.

Combined Arms: Look for ways to combine complementary resources in a manner that increases their collective effectiveness and places competitors on the horns of a dilemma.

CHAPTER 4

Building and Improving the Capacity to Target Critical Vulnerabilities

- Targeting critical vulnerabilities is a top-down, bottom-up process.

- Gaps in opponents' defenses often lead to critical vulnerabilities.

- Remember the powerful psychological impact of exploiting a competitor's Achilles' heel.

- Top down identification:

  - *Lead from the front:* position yourself as close to the point of decision as possible without crowding your people.

- Bottom-up identification: Rely on your people to lead you to critical vulnerabilities

  - *Lead by walking around:* regularly ask your people to identify critical vulnerabilities in their respective spheres of influence. Compile and synthesize this information. Recognize and reward their efforts.

- Top-down identification:

  - Formulate your own hypotheses about where the market is going at your level and anticipate critical vulnerabilities *before* they appear.

  - Reconnaissance, intelligence, and war gaming have their equivalents in business; they are known as market study, environmental scan, and scenario analysis.

- Top-down exploitation:

  - When you identify critical vulnerabilities within your sphere of influence, relentlessly push your people to exploit them as rapidly as possible.

- Bottom-up exploitation:

  - When the critical vulnerability identified exceeds your sphere of influence, gather the information necessary to make a convincing case, formulate a plan of action, and challenge your superiors to act.

- Minimize the lag time between identification and exploitation.

  - Critical vulnerabilities are fleeting opportunities.

- Continually scrutinize your own organization to identify its critical vulnerabilities and prevent rivals from targeting them.

CHAPTER 5

Fostering Boldness in Your Organization

- Analyze everything in terms of risk-reward trade-offs.

  - Calculated risk taking steers bold actions away from desperate recklessness.

- (Probability of Success×Potential payout)−(Probability of failure×Potential cost of failure)=Expected outcome

  - Other key decision-making parameters include time to completion, magnitude of upside vs. that of downside, cost of exit, and ability to exit.

  - Leverage your experience *and* the expertise of your people to refine the inputs.

  - Proactively take steps to mitigate the risk associated with the risk-reward trade-offs that you face.

- Do not be afraid to defy consensus if your analysis and instincts support a divergent viewpoint.

- Train employees to make decisions and to act decisively no matter how incomplete their information.

  - *80 Percent Rule:* any decision made with more than 80 percent of the necessary information is hesitation.

- Foster an *obligation to dissent* among those in your charge, especially during the decision-making process.

- Reward initiative—both successful and unsuccessful.

  - Do you hand out toilet seat awards?

- Correct mistakes that stem from bold zeal; punish indecision, timidity, or lapses in judgment/integrity.

- And when all else fails, remember that *it is better to beg for forgiveness than ask for permission.* Nevertheless, be cognizant of how your actions fit into the larger context.

CHAPTER 6

How to Use Stealth, Ambiguity, and Deception to Achieve Surprise

- Conceal your intentions or coordinate your timing so that your first moves do not announce or block your later efforts.

- Announce a list of plausible courses of action and make a selection among them only after your opponent attempts to prepare for all of them; in this manner you create options for yourself while he is confused.

- Use all channels available to you when deliberately conveying selected information to influence the behavior of your rivals.

  - Perhaps the most effective channel is the media.

- Remember that a disciplined follow-through must accompany every well-intended use of information to shape the rules of the competitive encounter.

- Foster a heightened sense of security throughout the firm to protect critical corporate information from snooping competitors.

  - Ensure that employees remain tight-lipped about competitively sensitive information—a never-ending responsibility.

- Be wary of posting "too much" information on channels like the Internet that are easily accessible by your competitors.

- Be extremely disciplined when releasing information to the media.

- Plan operations to convey selected information and indicators to rivals to influence their perceptions, emotions, motives, objective reasoning, and, ultimately, their behavior.

- Create your own "IO cell" to create ambiguity or deception for rivals, thereby impairing their decision-making ability.

- Does surprise have its own section in your OpOrd?

CHAPTER 7

Bringing Overwhelming Resources to Bear on the Customer's Needs

- Use information to understand and anticipate customers more effectively than your rivals can.

- Shuffle personnel to the most critical areas of your business.

- Designate a main effort and be prepared to redesignate it if market conditions warrant such a shift.

- Understand that focusing resources in one area requires economy of force elsewhere and proactively take steps to mitigate the accompanying risk.

- Communicate your intentions to your people and build flexibility into your plan to commit resources.

CHAPTER 8

Decentralizing Decision Making

- Specify *what* needs to be done, leave the *how* to your people, and always remember to explain "the why."

- No one can exceed expectations that he or she does not understand.

- Trust your people to crimp detonators with their teeth.

- But demand honesty and open communication in return.

- *Leadership Reaction Course:* train people to make decisions and lead under simulated conditions of uncertainty. Evaluate them and provide immediate feedback.

- *Teach-ins:* convey your philosophy to your people from the outset so they can understand how you think; eventually they will be able to anticipate your thoughts.

- Align individual decisions by communicating commander's intent—final result desired—throughout the organization.

    - Provide commander's intent "two levels up."

    - Remember that commander's intent is a two-way street; it requires the willing participation of both leader and follower.

- The *S* in BAMCIS stands for *supervise.*

    - Be ever vigilant and hold people accountable for their actions.

    - Inspect what you expect.

- Reinforce the right behavior among your people.

    - Provide them with real-time feedback.

    - Correct mistakes on the spot.

    - Punish timidity, indecision, and lapses in integrity in a forceful manner.

- Develop systems that share information both vertically and horizontally throughout the organization to increase the information available to and thus the decision-making capacity of those in your charge.

    - Be creative in leveraging the capabilities of existing ERP (enterprise resource planning) systems.

- Always remember that you are ultimately responsible for everything your team does or fails to do.

  - You can delegate authority, but you can never delegate responsibility.

CHAPTER 9

Achieving a Rapid Tempo and Accelerating from There

- *OODA:* Observe, Orient, Decide, and Act

  - Identify opportunities, make decisions, and implement plans faster than competitors do to seize the initiative and force them into a constant state of reaction.

- Constantly challenge yourself and those in your charge to make sound decisions as rapidly as possible.

  - Be your own harshest critic.

- Position decision-making authority as close to the action as possible.

  - Lead from the front or delegate.

  - Decentralized decision-making breeds tempo.

- *⅓-⅔ Rule:* reserve a third of the time remaining before a deadline for yourself and two-thirds for those in your charge who will be executing the task at hand. Give them time to plan and coordinate at their respective levels.

- *Obligation to Dissent, Part 2:* Always uphold the obligation to dissent, but only *until* the decision is made. Once it is made, execute it as if it were your own.

- Consider competitive encounters multiperiod, multiarena engagements.

- Train decision-making speed.

  - Make the investment necessary to prepare your people to make sound and timely decisions under pressure.

- *R2P2:* make the commitment necessary to create an effective rapid response planning process in your organization.

  - Use SOPs to free your people to focus their attention on situation-specific matters.

- Use technology to accelerate a process, not extend the time available before a deadline.

- Employ network operations and systems security measures to help maintain rapid tempo—prevent your high-tempo organization from grounding to a halt.

CHAPTER 10

Combined Arms

- Use information technology to add value to resources that you enjoy and a competitor lacks.

- Provide an initial common training—shared foundation.

- Cross-train and move employees regularly to create mutual trust and implicit understanding throughout the organization.

  - Don't let employees stagnate in one job by leaving them there for too long.

- Bring critical functions in-house and assemble custom-tailored teams to capitalize on emerging market opportunities.

- The complexity associated with combining different resources requires an even more comprehensive and even more integrated use of information.

  - Air, artillery, and direct fire in a SEAD mission

  - Marketing, sales, production, and distribution in a new product launch

- Align incentives to promote cooperation across divisions.

- Practice, practice, practice.

- And when you are done practicing, throw a happy hour.

- Ensure communications systems offer flexibility and reliability needed to meet the task at hand.

CHAPTER 11

Reconnaissance Pull

A real-time response to weakness, whereby an individual identifies an opportunity, directs the organization toward it, and then immediately leads the organization in its exploitation, reconnaissance pull encompasses:

- Decentralized Decision Making

  - Entrust talented frontline employees and junior managers with the necessary authority to decide when and where to pursue breakout opportunities.

- Targeting Critical Vulnerabilities

  - Individuals on the front lines are ideally positioned to identify and rapidly exploit market openings or rivals' critical vulnerabilities.

- Tempo

  - A timely response to the identification of an opportunity requires rapid decision making on the part of the leader.

- Focus

  - The leader must be willing to commit maximum available resources to the exploitation of identified opportunities.

- Develop and designate a wide range of reconnaissance capabilities in your organization.

- Employ distributed information systems to complement and enable pervasive information sharing.

- Ensure a direct conduit exists between senior leadership and the reconnaissance force.

- Consider making a human investment in the form of the appointment of a talented up-and-comer as your "ground intel officer."

- Recognize and reward individuals who discover new opportunities or develop new ideas.

- Build flexibility into your organization.

CHAPTER 13

Marine Corps Core Values

Honor: Integrity, responsibility, and accountability

Courage: Do the right thing in the right way for the right reason

Commitment: Devotion to the Corps and to my fellow Marines

Marine Corps Leadership Principles

Know yourself and seek self-improvement.

Be technically and tactically proficient.

Develop a sense of responsibility among your subordinates.

Make sound and timely decisions.

Set the example.

Know your Marines and look out for their welfare.

Keep your Marines informed.

Seek responsibility and accept responsibility for your actions.

Ensure tasks are understood, supervised, and accomplished.

Train your Marines as a team.

Employ your command in accordance with its capabilities.

Marine Corps Leadership Traits

Justice: Giving reward and punishment according to the merits of the case in question. The ability to administer a system of rewards and punishments impartially and consistently

Judgment: The ability to weigh facts and possible solutions on which to base sound decisions

Dependability: The certainty of proper performance of duty

Initiative: Taking action in the absence of orders

Decisiveness: Being able to make decisions promptly and to announce them in a clear, forceful manner

Tact: The ability to deal with others without creating offense

Integrity: Uprightness of character and soundness of moral principles; includes the qualities of truthfulness and honesty

Enthusiasm: The display of sincere interest and exuberance in the performance of duty

Bearing: Creating a favorable impression in carriage, appearance, and personal conduct at all times

Unselfishness: Avoidance of providing for one's own comfort and personal advancement at the expense of others

Courage: The mental quality that recognizes fear of danger or criticism but enables a man to proceed in the face of it with calmness and firmness

Knowledge: Understanding of a science or an art. The range of one's information, including professional knowledge and an understanding of your Marines

Loyalty: The quality of faithfulness to country, the Corps, the unit, one's seniors, subordinates, and peers

Endurance: The mental and physical stamina measured by the ability to withstand pain, fatigue, stress, and hardship

NOTES

INTRODUCTION

1. Phone conversation with Fred Smith, May 12, 2003.

CHAPTER 1

1. United States Marine Corps, *Warfighting*, MCDP 1, 21.
2. Ibid, 73.
3. Ibid, 5.
4. Ibid, 7.
5. Ibid, 9.
6. Ibid, 10–11.

CHAPTER 2

1. Harell, Yehuda, *Follow Me: the Story of Moshe Dayan*, 140.
2. Ibid.
3. The Six Day War, www.geocities.com/acid_talking_2u/Wars/ six_day_war_idf.html.
4. Oren, Michael B., *Six Days of War: June 1967 and the Making of the Modern Middle East*, 173.
5. Ibid, 176
6. Ibid, 178.
7. Higgins, Peter E., "Historical Applications of Maneuver Warfare in the 20th Century," Marine Corps Command and Staff College, 1990.

CHAPTER 3

1. Slim, Sir William, *Defeat into Victory*, 550–51.
2. *Warfighting*, 47.
3. Collins, James, and Porras, Jerry, *Built to Last*, 91–93.
4. *Warfighting*, 41.
5. Based on Juniper 10-K filings: research and development expenses 1999–2002.
6. *Warfighting*, 94.

CHAPTER 4

1. Hamilton, Edith, *Mythology*, 278.
2. *Warfighting*, 35.
3. Pascual, Aixa, "Lowe's Is Sprucing Up Its House," *BusinessWeek Online*, June 3, 2002.
4. Ibid.
5. Wack, Pierre, "Scenarios: Uncharted Waters Ahead," *Harvard Business Review*, September/October 1985, 72.
6. Foote, Shelby, *The Civil War—A Narrative: Red River to Appomattox*, 535.
7. This quote, and other versions of it, is widely used by the Marines but most often credited to George S. Patton.

CHAPTER 5

1. Cohen, Morris, *The Wisdom of Generals*.
2. Perret, Geoffrey, *Old Soldiers Never Die*, 547.
3. Ibid, 546.
4. Miller, Nathan, *The U.S. Navy: A History*, 253.
5. Morris, Betsy, "He's Smart. He's Not Nice. He's Saving Big Blue," *Fortune*, April 14, 1997, 68.
6. Johnson, Curt, and McLaughlin, Mark, *Battles of the Civil War: From Bull Run to Petersburg: Four Hard Years of Strategy and Bloodshed*, 92.
7. Davis, Burke, *Gray Fox*, 246.
8. Kadlec, Daniel, "The Fall of the Mighty Buffett, Soros, Robertson. They're out of synch with stocks and you can learn from their errors," *Time*, May 15, 2000.

9. Jay, John, "Time for Buffett to Break Up Berkshire Hathaway," *Sunday Times* of London, January 9, 2000.

10. Budworth, David, "How to Be a Successful Investor," *Sunday Times* of London, November 17, 2002.

11. Serwer, Andy, "The Oracle of Everything," *Fortune*, November 11, 2002, cover.

12. Buffett led a consortium of investors that invested in Level 3's convertible bonds, which pay a 9 percent coupon and can be converted into equity at a premium to Level 3's share price at the time of investment. Given the relatively high coupon and low share price at the time the deal was struck, this investment was very attractive. Buffett's initial investment was $100 million; Longleaf Partners invested $300 million, and Legg Mason contributed the remaining $100 million.

13. Level 3's all-time high share price was $130.19 on March 10, 2000.

14. As of May 23, 2003.

15. Serwer, 74.

CHAPTER 6

1. Imboden, John D., B Gen, CSA, "Stonewall Jackson in the Shenandoah."

2. United States Marine Corps, *Information Operations*, MCWP 3–40, 49.

3. *Warfighting*, 44.

4. Ibid.

5. Ibid, 39.

6. Houston, Sam, Official Battle Report of the Battle of San Jacinto.

7. Latin America and U.S. Relations website, Dr. Antonio de la Cova, Rose Hulman University.

8. Chura, Hillary, "Code Red Soft Drink Sales Explode," *Advertising Age* (AdAge.com), August 27, 2001.

9. Interview with Bart Casabona, spokesperson for Pepsi North America, May 20, 2003.

10. Theodore, Sarah, "Code Red's Stealth Attack," *Beverage Industry*, January 2003, 28.

11. Interview with Bart Casabona, May 20, 2003.

12. Ibid.

13. U.S. Navy War College, *The United States Navy in "Desert Shield" / "Desert Storm,"* May 1991.

14. Prabhu, Jaideep, and Stewart, David W. "Signaling Strategies in Competitive Interaction: Building Reputations and Hiding the Truth," *Journal of Marketing and Research*, February 1, 2001, 62.

15. Ricciuti, Mike, "Microsoft Weaves a .Net over Win XP," *ZDWire*, October 18, 2001.

16. Bayus, Barry L.; Jain, Sanjay; and Rao, Ambar G., "Truth or Consequences: An Analysis of Vaporware and New Product Announcements," *Journal of Marketing and Research*, revised March 2000.

17. "Centennial Journal: 100 Years in Business—Merrill Lynch CMAs Draw Interest, 1977," *Wall Street Journal*, November 3, 1989.

18. Marine Corps White Paper 3-40.4, Information Operations, December 10, 2001, 5.

CHAPTER 7

1. United States Marine Corps, *Dictionary of Military and Naval Quotations*, 63.

2. *Warfighting*, 41.

3. Leckie, Robert, *Delivered from Evil, The Saga of World War II*, 150.

4. Ibid, 160.

5. Taylor, Alex, "Here Come Japan's New Luxury Cars," *Fortune*, August 14, 1989, 62.

6. Barnett, Steve, U.S.-based cultural anthropologist, personal conversation, 2002.

7. Historical performance in J. D. Power and Associates surveys, 1999–2003.

8. Green, Jeff, "Toyota Expects Luxury Sales Surge as Boomer's Pay Peaks," *Bloomberg*, April 15, 2003.

9. In an era of wind- and sail-powered vessels, the forces upwind had an advantage in forcing combat at the time and place of their choice.

10. Nelson's original signal was to have been "England confides that every man will do his duty," but *confides* was not in the telegraphic vocabulary. Nelson thus agreed to substitute *expects*, which changed

the meaning of the message and caused confusion among British
sailors, who felt strongly that they would always do their duty and
should not have to be asked.

11. www.andalucia.com/history/trafalgar.htm.
12. As of May 28, 2003.
13. Binkley, Christina, "Lucky Numbers," *Wall Street Journal*, May 4,
    2000, A1.
14. Levinson, Meredith, "Jackpot!," *CIO Magazine*, February 1, 2001,
    and Ashbrook Nickell, Joe, "Welcome to Harrah's," *Business 2.0*,
    April 2002, 48.
15. Ibid.
16. Based on 10-K annual reports from Harrah's, MGM-Mirage, Park
    Place, and Mandalay Bay.

CHAPTER 8

1. www.generalpatton.com.
2. *Warfighting*, 78.
3. Province, Charles M., "The Third Army in WWII," The Patton
   Society Research Library, 1994.
4. www.geocities.com/Pentagon/Quarters/5433/breakout.html.
5. Now acquired by Merrill Lynch.
6. Conversation with Anthony Abrahams, head of trading at Smith
   Newcourt.
7. Miller, John G., *The Bridge at Dong Ha*.
8. Druckerman, Pamela, "How to Project Power Around the World,"
   Wall Street Journal, November 13, 2000, A23.
9. Markels, Alex, "Team Approach: A Power Producer Is Intent on
   Giving Power to Its People," *Wall Street Journal*, July 3, 1995, A1.
10. Woellert, Lorraine, "Not Acting at All Like a Utility," *BusinessWeek*,
    December 13, 1999, 94.
11. Druckerman, A23.

CHAPTER 9

1. www.execunet.com.
2. Dunlap, Charlotte, "The Builders," *Computer Reseller News*,
   November 15, 1999, 133.

3. www.cisco.com.

4. Segil, Larraine, "Alliances: Preemptive Alliances: The Object of Some Partnerships Is to Thwart a Competitor," *Industry Week,* August 21, 2000, 27.

5. Stewart, Thomas A., "Making Decisions in Real Time," *Fortune,* June 2000, 332.

6. Foote, Shelby, *The Civil War—A Narrative: Fort Sumter to Perryville,* 453.

7. Imboden, John D., B Gen, CSA, "Stonewall Jackson in the Shenandoah."

8. U.S. National Park Service, "Study of Civil War Sites in the Shenandoah Valley," September 1992.

9. Johnson, Curt, and McLaughlin, Mark. *Battles of the Civil War: From Bull Run to Petersburg: Four Hard Years of Strategy and Bloodshed,* 65.

10. McClellan, George B. "Report of Major General George B. McClellan, U.S. Army, Commanding the Army of the Potomac, of operations August 14–November 9, 1862."

11. Not quite the ⅓-⅔ rule, but even the Marines aren't perfect.

12. United States Marine Corps, *Marine Corps Planning Process,* MCWP 5-1 with Change 1, J-16 2001.

CHAPTER 10

1. Lehmann, Gary C., Lt Col, USMC. "Transforming Marine Corps Leadership," *Marine Corps Gazette,* April 1, 2002.

2. *Warfighting,* 75.

3. Liddell-Hart, B. H., *Strategy,* 2nd ed.

4. October 25 happened to be a popular holiday named for St. Crispin, the patron saint of shoemakers, who lived in the third century A.D.

5. Historians' troop-strength estimates range widely. English strength is estimated to have been six thousand to thirteen thousand, while French strength is estimated to have been twenty thousand to fifty thousand. However, most historians agree that the English were outnumbered by a four-to-one margin.

6. The Great Battles, Agincourt 1415 (www.geocities.com/beckster05).

7. Battle of Agincourt (www.aginc.net/battle/ops.html).

8. Vasilash, Gary S., "The Lexus GX-470: You Want Me To Drive This Where?" *Automotive Design and Production*, December 2002.

9. Stertz, Bradley, "Trying to Crack the Luxury Car Market," *Wall Street Journal*, August 7, 1999.

10. Sachtleben, James L., "Artillery Raids in Southwestern Kuwait," *Field Artillery Journal*, October 1991, 26.

11. Ibid, 29.

12. Pricing from NetJets 2003 brochure.

13. Bettridge, Jack, "Inside NetJets' Control Room: How They Manage the World's Sixth Largest Airline," *Cigar Aficionado Magazine*, July/August 2002.

14. Moskal, Brian S., "Up, Up and Away," *Aviation Magazine*, June 17, 1995, 17.

15. www.netjets.com, April 2003.

16. For the purposes of simplicity, we have limited the scope of our discussion to the SEAD mission, but Marines also involve in their combined arms attacks electronic warfare assets and combat engineers to eliminate further the enemy's potential responses. Electronic warfare assets jam enemy communications and radar, and combat engineers restrict the enemy's movement with mines and other obstacles.

CHAPTER 11

1. www.cyberquotations.com.

2. United States Marine Corps, *History of the U.S. Marine Corps Operations in World War II: Central Pacific Drive, Volume III*, FMFRP 12-34-III, 1966.

3. Pitta, Julie, "It Had to Be Done and We Did It (HP's Management Strategy Keeps HP Profitable)," *Forbes*, April 26, 1993, 148.

4. "Hewlett Packard Marks Sale of 20 Millionth Printer," *BusinessWire*, November 9, 1993.

5. United States Marine Corps, *Marine Corps Operations*, MCDP 1-0, 2001, 10-11.

6. Scharfen, John C., *Tactics and Theory of Maneuver Warfare (Tactical Fundamentals—MCI 7401)*, 30.

CHAPTER 12

1. www.capitalone.com.
2. Smalhout, James, "Doing Well by Doing Good: There's Some Evidence Good Corporate Governance Can Pay Off for Investors," *Barron's*, January 27, 2003, 35.
3. Knight, Jerry, "At COMSAT, It May Be Back to Redrawing the Board," *Washington Post*, May 19, 1997, F29.
4. Proxy: Individual shareholders give written authorization that enables selected representatives to vote on their behalf.
5. Wyser-Pratte, Guy, personal interview, March 18, 2003.
6. This price represented a 20 percent premium to his last purchase.
7. Byrnes, Nanette, "The BW 50: The Best Performers," *BusinessWeek*, March 29, 1999, cover story.
8. Overholser, George, senior vice president, new business development, Capital One, personal conversation, November 10, 2002.
9. Barton, Scott, Capital One, personal conversation, 2002.
10. Overholser, George, personal conversation, November 10, 2002.

CHAPTER 13

1. Krulak, Victor, Lt Gen, *First to Fight: an Inside View of the U.S. Marine Corps*, 160–61.
2. See the Appendix for a full list.
3. *www.usmc.mil*, 2003.
4. Katzenbach, Jon, and Santamaria, Jason, "Firing Up the Front Line," *Harvard Business Review*, May/June 1999, 110.
5. United States Marine Corps, *Marine Corps Manual*, Edition 1921.
6. Katzenbach and Santamaria, 113.
7. Ibid.
8. Southwest company slogan.
9. FedEx company slogan.
10. Smith, Frederick W., et al., *Manager's Guide—USA: The FedEx Express Guide to Leadership*, February 2002, 52.
11. Ibid, 73.
12. Ibid, 188.
13. Ibid, 1.

14. *Assessing Skills, Performance, and Interest Required for Entry* into management.
15. Smith, 116.
16. Phone conversation with Donna Conover, June 17, 2003.
17. Ibid.
18. Devlin, Dory, "Culture Helps Airline Stay Aloft," *The Star-Ledger*, November 4, 2002.
19. Company slogan. Also appears in Freiberg, Kevin and Jackie, *Nuts: Southwest Airlines' Crazy Recipe for Business and Personal Success*, 1996, 27.
20. Draude, Thomas, B Gen (USMC, Ret.), Zweig Speaker Series Presentation, the Wharton School, 2001.

SOURCES

BOOKS

Alexander, Bevin. *Robert E. Lee's Civil War.* Holbrook, Mass.: Adams Media Corporation, 1998.

Ambrose, Stephen E. *Citizen Soldier: The U.S. Army From the Normandy Beaches to the Bulge to the Surrender of Germany.* New York: Simon & Schuster, 1997.

Ambrose, Stephen E. *The Victors, Eisenhower and His Boys: The Men of World War II.* New York: Simon & Schuster, 1998.

Bethune, Gordon, with Huler, Scott. *From Worst to First.* New York: John Wiley & Sons, 1998.

Blumenson, Martin, and Patton, George S. *The Patton Papers (1940–1945).* New York: DeCapo Press, 1996.

Bullock, Alan. *Hitler: A Study in Tyranny.* New York: Konecky & Konecky, 1962.

Carroll, Paul. *Big Blues: The Unmaking of IBM.* New York: Crown Publishers, Inc., 1993.

Chanoff, David, and Sharon, Ariel. *Warrior: An Autobiography.* New York: Touchstone Books, 2001.

Cohen, Morris. *The Wisdom of Generals.* New York: Prentice Hall Press, 2001.

Collins, James C., and Porras, Jerry I. *Built to Last: Successful Habits of Visionary Companies.* New York: HarperCollins Publishers, 1994.

Coram, Robert. *Boyd, The Fighter Pilot Who Changed the Art of War.* Boston: Little, Brown & Co., 2002.

Crumley, B. L. *The Marine Corps.* San Diego: Thunder Bay Press, 2002.

Davis, Burke. *Gray Fox: Robert E. Lee and the Civil War.* New York: Wings Books, 1956.

D'Este, Carlo. *Patton: A Genius for War.* New York: HarperCollins, 1995.

Dodd, Annabelle. *The Essential Guide to Telecommunications* (2nd ed.). New York: Prentice Hall, Inc., 2000.

Dupuy, Trevor N. *The Military Life of Genghis, Khan of Khans.* New York: Franklin Watts Inc., 1969.

Foote, Shelby. *The Civil War—A Narrative: Fort Sumter to Perryville.* New York: Vintage Books, 1986.

Foote, Shelby. *The Civil War—A Narrative: Fredericksburg to Meridian.* New York: Vintage Books, 1986.

Foote, Shelby. *The Civil War—A Narrative: Red River to Appomattox.* New York: Vintage Books, 1986.

Fraser, David. *Knight's Cross, A Life of Field Marshall Erwin Rommel.* London: HarperCollins Publishers, 1993.

Guderian, Heinz. *Achtung-Panzer! The Development of Tank Warfare.* London: Cassel & Co., (tr. Christopher Duffy), 1992. (Original German publication in 1937.)

Hamilton, Edith. *Mythology.* New York: Little, Brown and Company, 1942.

Harell, Yehuda. *Follow Me: the Story of Moshe Dayan.* Jerusalem: Yessod Press, 1970.

Hirshson, Stanley. *General Patton: A Soldier's Life.* New York: Harper-Collins Publishers, 2002.

Hooker, Richard, Jr. *Maneuver Warfare—an Anthology.* New York: Presidio Press, 1993.

Johnson, Curt, and McLaughlin, Mark. *Battles of the Civil War: From Bull Run to Petersburg: Four Hard Years of Strategy and Bloodshed.* New York: Crown Publishing, 1977.

Krulak, Victor, Lt Gen. *First to Fight: an Inside View of the U.S. Marine Corps.* Annapolis: Naval Institute Press, 1984.

Leckie, Robert. *Delivered from Evil, The Saga of World War II.* New York: Harper and Row Publishers, Inc., 1987.

Liddell-Hart, B. H. *Strategy* (2nd ed.). London: Faber & Faber, 1954, 1967.

Lind, William S. *Maneuver Warfare Handbook.* Boulder, Colorado: Westview Press, Inc., 1985.

May, Ernest. *Strange Victory: Hitler's Conquest of France.* New York: Hill and Wang Publishers, 2001.

Miller, John G. *The Bridge at Dong Ha.* Annapolis: Naval Institute Press, reprinted in 1996.

Miller, Nathan. *War at Sea: A Naval History of World War II.* New York: Scribner, 1995.

Miller, Nathan. *The U.S. Navy: A History.* New York: American Heritage, 1977.

Millett, Allan R. *Semper Fidelis: The History of the United States Marine Corps.* New York: Free Press, 1991.

Montor, Karel E. *Ethics for the Junior Officer* (A Gift From the USNA Class of 1964 to the USNA Class of 1995). Annapolis: Naval Institute Press, 1994.

Montor, Karel E., et al. *Naval Leadership, Voices of Experience.* Annapolis: Naval Institute Press, 1987.

Nordin, Richard; Builder, Carl H.; and Bankes, Steven C. *Command Concepts: A Theory Derived from the Practice of Command and Control.* Arlington, Virginia: Rand Corporation, 1999.

Oren, Michael B. *Six Days of War: June 1967 and the Making of the Modern Middle East.* New York: Oxford University Press, Inc., 2002.

Patton, General George S., Jr. *War As I Knew It.* New York: Houghton Mifflin, 1979.

Perret, Geoffrey. *Old Soldiers Never Die.* New York: Random House, 1996.

Province, Charles M. *Patton's Third Army.* New York: Hippocrene Press, 1994.

Robertson, James I., Jr. *Stonewall Jackson: The Man, the Soldier, the Legend.* New York: MacMillan Publishing Company, 1997.

Rommel, Erwin. *Attacks.* Provo, Utah: Athena Press Inc., 1979.

Roush, Chris. *Inside Home Depot.* New York: McGraw-Hill, 1999.

Scharfen, John C. *Tactics and Theory of Maneuver Warfare (Tactical Fundamentals—MCI 7401).* Washington, D.C.: Marine Corps Institute.

Schneier, Bruce. *Secrets & Lies: Digital Security in a Networked World.* New York: John Wiley & Sons, Inc., 2000.

Schwartz, P. *The Art of the Long View,* Doubleday, 1991.

Selby, John M. *Stonewall Jackson as Military Commander.* Princeton, NJ: Van Nostrand, 1968.

Slim, Sir William. *Defeat into Victory.* London: Cassell & Company, Ltd., 1956.

Strothman, J. E. *The Ancient History of System/360. American Inventions: A Chronicle of Achievements That Changed the World.* New York: Barnes & Noble Books, 1995, 152–58.

Tzu, Sun. *The Art of War.* New York: Delacorte Press, reprinted 1983.

Waugh, John C. *The Class of 1846.* New York: Warner Books Inc., 1994.

ARTICLES

Ashbrook Nickell, Joe. "Welcome to Harrah's," *Business 2.0*, April 2002.

Banks, Howard. "The Flying Buffett," *Forbes*, September 21, 1998.

Bayus, Barry L.; Jain, Sanjay; and Rao, Ambar G. "Truth or Consequences: An Analysis of Vaporware and New Product Announcements," *Journal of Marketing and Research*, revised March 2000.

Becker, David O. "Gary Loveman, the Man Who Brought the Customer Service Revolution to Gaming, Explains How He Helped Double Harrah's Revenues and Earnings," *The McKinsey Quarterly*, 2003, Number 2.

Benson, Mitchell. "AES's Bakke Becomes Latest CEO in Power Industry to Step Down," *Wall Street Journal*, June 19, 2002.

Berman, Phyllis. "Throwing Away the Book," *Forbes*, November 2, 1998.

Bettridge, Jack. "Inside NetJets' Control Room: How They Manage the World's Sixth Largest Airline," *Cigar Aficionado Magazine*, July/August 2002.

Binkley, Christina. "Lucky Numbers," *Wall Street Journal*, May 4, 2000.

Bowen, Kent H., and Clark, Kim B. "Make Projects the School for Leaders," *Harvard Business Review*, September/October 1994.

Brooker, Katrina. "Why Companies Hate Risk Arbitrageurs. They Call Them the Swarm," *Fortune*, August 3, 1998.

Budworth, David. "How to Be a Successful Investor," *Sunday Times of London*, November 17, 2002.

Burrows, Peter. "Why Fiorina Convinced an Icon to Become Chairman," *BusinessWeek Online*, August 2, 1999.

Byrnes, Nanette. "The BW 50: The Best Performers," *BusinessWeek*, March 29, 1999.

"Centennial Journal: 100 Years in Business—Merrill Lynch CMAs Draw Interest, 1977," *Wall Street Journal*, November 3, 1989.

Chura, Hillary. "Code Red Soft Drink Sales Explode," *Advertising Age*, August 27, 2001.

Chura, Hillary; Friedman, Wayne; MacArthur, Kate; and Thomaselli, Rich. "Coke v. Pepsi: Return to War," *Advertising Age*, November 25, 2002.

Clemons, Eric K. "Using Scenario Analysis to Manage the Strategic Risks of Reengineering," *Sloan Management Review*, Vol. 3, No. 4, Summer 1995.

Clemons, Eric K., and Thatcher, Matt E. "Capital One: Exploiting an Information-Based Strategy," *Proceedings, 31st Hawaii International Conference on System Sciences*, January 1998.

Clemons, Eric K.; Croson, David C.; and Weber, Bruce W. "Market Dominance as a Precursor of a Firm's Failure: Emerging Technologies and the Competitive Advantage of New Entrants," *Journal of Management Information Systems*, Vol. 13, No. 2, Fall 1996.

Clemons, Eric K., and Row, Michael C. "Information Technology at Rosenbluth Travel: Competitive Advantage in a Rapidly Growing Global Service Company," *Journal of Management Information Systems*, Vol. 8, No. 2, 1991.

Clemons, Eric K., and Row, Michael C. "The Merrill Lynch Cash Management Account Financial Service: A Case Study in Strategic Information Systems," *Proceedings, 21st Hawaii International Conference on System Sciences*, January 1988.

Clemons, Eric K., and Hann, Il-Horn. "Rosenbluth International: Strategic Managing of Technology-Driven Discontinuous Change at a Successful Global Enterprise," *Journal of Management Information Systems*, Fall 1999.

Clemons, Eric, and Santamaria, Jason. "Maneuver Warfare: Can Modern Military Strategy Lead You to Victory?" *Harvard Business Review*, April 2002.

"Conglomerate Forced to Sharpen Up Its Act," *Financial Times*, October 26, 2001.

Cook, William. "A Drag Race for Blue Bloods," *U.S. News and World Report*, December 19, 1998.

Corcoran, Elizabeth. "COMSAT, Dissidents Reach Deal," *Washington Post*, June 6, 1997.

Daum, Juergen. "How Scenario Planning Can Significantly Reduce Strategic Risks and Boost Value in the Innovation Chain," *The New Economy Analyst Report*, September 8, 2001.

Deutschman, Alan. "How H-P Continues to Grow and Grow," *Fortune*, May 2, 1994.

Devlin, Dory. "Culture Helps Airline Stay Aloft: Southwest Airlines," Newark *Star Ledger*, November 4, 2002.

Druckerman, Pamela. "How to Project Power Around the World," *Wall Street Journal*, November 13, 2000.

Dumaine, Brian. "How I Delivered the Goods," *Fortune Small Business*, October 2002.

Dunlap, Charlotte. "The Builders," *Computer Reseller News*, November 15, 1999.

Eisenhardt, Kathleen M., and Brown, Shona L. "Patching: Restitching Business Portfolios in Dynamic Markets," *Harvard Business Review*, May/June 1999.

Fein, Adam J. "Scenario Planning for Managers," *Modern Distribution Management*, 2003.

Fishman, Charles. "Face Time with Fred Smith," *Fast Company*, June 1, 2001.

Gaither, Chris. "Hewlett Sees Compaq Merger as Fuel for Its Printer Division," *New York Times*, December 24, 2001.

Goldblatt, Henry. "Go West!" *Fortune*, November 22, 1999.

Goulding, Vincent, Jr. "From Chancellorsville to Kosovo, Forgetting the Art of War," *Parameters, U.S. Army War College Quarterly*, Summer 2000.

Green, Jeff. "Toyota Expects Luxury Sales Surge as Boomer's Pay Peaks," *Bloomberg*, April 15, 2003.

Hamme, Christopher. "The Miracle of Agincourt," *British Heritage Magazine*, February 2001.

Hein, Kenneth. "Cracking the Code for Pepsi," *Brandweek*, October 14, 2002.

Heskett, Ben, and Wong, Wylie. "Juniper Finds Its Own in Networking Niche," *CNET News*, August 16, 1999.

Higgins, Peter E. "Historical Applications of Maneuver Warfare in the 20th Century," Marine Corps Command and Staff College, 1990.

Holstein, William J. "The Joust for Big Pipes," *U.S. News and World Report*, April 5, 1999.

House, Jonathan M. (Captain, USA). "Toward Combined Arms Warfare: A Survey of 20th-Century Tactics, Doctrine, and Organization," U.S. Army Command and General Staff College, August 1984.

Hughes, Charlie (Major, USMC). "Air Strategy in the 1967 Arab/Israeli War," Marine Corps Command and Staff College, 1997.

Jay, John. "Time for Buffett to Break Up Berkshire Hathaway," *Sunday Times of London*, January 9, 2000.

Jouret, Guido. "Cisco Acquisition and Integration Model," Cisco Systems, 1999.

Kadlec, Daniel. "The Fall of the Mighty Buffett, Soros, Robertson," *Time*, May 15, 2000.

Kamm, Thomas. "Free to Paint a Hotel Pink," *Wall Street Journal Europe*, November 11, 1998.

Katzenbach, Jon R., and Santamaria, Jason A. "Firing Up the Front Line," *Harvard Business Review*, May/June 1999.

Knight, Jerry. "At COMSAT, It May Be Back to Redrawing the Board," *Washington Post*, May 19, 1997.

Konrad, Rachel. "Lucent's Hits and Misses," *CNET News*, May 29, 2001.

Kreider Yoder, Stephen. "H-P Official, Hackborn, Plans His Retirement," *Wall Street Journal*, November 22, 1993.

Kreider Yoder, Stephen. "Shoving Back: How H-P Used Tactics of the Japanese to Beat Them at Their Game—It Hogged Patents, Cut Costs and Pared Prices to Grab Market in Inkjet Printers—Tested on Tortillas and Socks," *Wall Street Journal*, September 8, 1994.

Lehmann, Gary C. (Lt Col, USMC). "Transforming Marine Corps Leadership," *Marine Corps Gazette*, April 1, 2002.

Levinson, Meredith. "Jackpot!," *CIO Magazine*, February 1, 2001.

Lewis, Diane E. "Q&A: FedEx CEO Frederick W. Smith, on Challenges Facing Executives," *Boston Globe*, November 10, 2002.

London, Simon. "IT and Horsepower Are a Winning Formula," *Financial Times*, October 10, 2002.

Lund, Scott. "Maneuver Warfare in Business," OPIM 899, The Wharton School, December 4, 2002.

McElligott, Tim. "IM Somebody," *Telephony Online*, April 2, 2001.

McKay, Betsy. "Pepsi's Code Red May Score with Subtlety," *Wall Street Journal*, September 28, 2001.

Markels, Alex. "Team Approach: A Power Producer Is Intent on Giving Power to Its People," *Wall Street Journal*, July 3, 1995.

Martin, Jennifer. "Fractional Fascination: Partial Ownership of Jets Lets Smaller Players Enjoy Prestige and Privilege," *Crain's Chicago Business*, January 13, 2003.

Martin, Richard. "The Oracles of Oil," *Business 2.0*, January 2003.

Matlack, Carol. "The Raiders Are Coming! The Raiders Are Coming!" *BusinessWeek*, April 24, 2000.

Mazzetti, Mark. "The D Is for Deception," *U.S. News and World Report*, August 26, 2002.

Melzer, Bruce. "The Uncertainty Principle," *CIO Insight*, June 1, 2001.

Mills, Mike. "A Signal of Change at COMSAT," *Washington Post*, August 18, 1997.

"Module 1: Tactics. SB01 Principles of War," Civil War Living History Institute, 2003.

Morris, Betsy. "He's Smart. He's Not Nice. He's Saving Big Blue," *Fortune*, April 14, 1997.

Moskal, Brian S. "Up, Up, and Away: A Unique Program of Fractional Jet Ownership Polishes the Image of the Time-Share Concept," *Industry Week*, June 19, 1995.

"NetJets to Offer Wealthy Chance to Soar Higher," *St. Petersburg Times*, March 7, 2003.

O'Reilly, Brian. "The Mechanic Who Fixed Continental," *Fortune*, December 20, 1999.

Pascual, Aixa M. "Lowes Is Sprucing Up Its House: By Appealing to Women It Aims to Hammer Home Depot," *BusinessWeek Online*, June 3, 2002.

Pitta, Julie. "It Had to Be Done and We Did It (HP's Management Strategy Keeps HP Profitable)," *Forbes*, April 26, 1993.

Pogash, Carol. "From Harvard Yard to Vegas Strip: Trading Ivy for Neon, Former B-School Professor Gary Loveman Is Teaching Harrah's Some Wired New Ways," *Forbes ASAP*, October 7, 2002.

Pollack, Andrew. "Hewlett's Consummate Strategist," *The New York Times*, March 10, 1992.

Prabhu, Jaideep, and Stewart, David W. "Signaling Strategies in Competitive Interaction: Building Reputations and Hiding the Truth," *Journal of Marketing and Research*, February 1, 2001.

Prince, Greg W. "Dew Catches Code," *Beverage World*, May 15, 2001.

Province, Charles M. "The Third Army in WWII," The Patton Society Research Library, 1994.

"The Quickest War," *Time Europe*, June 16, 1967.

Ray, Gary N. "Microsoft Blows Smoke, Just Like the Old IBM," *Computerworld*, August 17, 1992.

Ricciuti, Mike. "Microsoft Weaves a .Net over Win XP," *ZDWire*, October 18, 2001.

Rodman, David. "The Role of the Israel Air Force in the Operational Doctrine of the Israel Defense Forces: Continuity and Change," *Air and Space Power Chronicles*, June 29, 2000.

Roundtable Discussion. "All in a Day's Work," *Harvard Business Review*, December 2001.

Sachtleben, James L., Lt Col. "Artillery Raids in Southwestern Kuwait," *Field Artillery Journal*, October 1991.

Sager, Ira. "How IBM Became a Growth Company Again," *BusinessWeek*, December 9, 1996.

Segil, Larraine. "Alliances: Preemptive Alliances: The Object of Some Partnerships Is to Thwart a Competitor," *Industry Week*, August 21, 2000.

Serwer, Andy. "The Oracle of Everything," *Fortune*, November 11, 2002.

Smalhout, James. "Doing Well by Doing Good: There's Some Evidence Good Corporate Governance Can Pay Off for Investors," *Barron's*, January 27, 2003.

Smith, Rebecca. "AES Sees Charges of $2.7 Billion for 4th Quarter," *Wall Street Journal*, January 28, 2003.

Spinney, Franklin. "Genghis John," Proceedings of the U.S. Naval Institute, July 1997.

Stertz, Bradley. "Trying to Crack the Luxury Car Market," *Wall Street Journal*, August 7, 1999.

Stewart, Thomas A. "Making Decisions in Real Time," *Fortune*, June 2000.

Taylor, Alex. "Here Come Japan's New Luxury Cars," *Fortune*, August 14, 1989.

Tedeschi, Bob. "What Do Diet Services Have in Common with Pornography and Financial Data? They May Be a Viable Net Business," *The New York Times*, April 30, 2001.

Theodore, Sarah. "Code Red's Stealth Attack," *Beverage Industry*, January 2003.

Tkacik, Maureen, and McKay, Betsy. "Code Red: PepsiCo's Guerrilla Conquest," *Wall Street Journal*, August 17, 2001.

Varner, William C. "Six Days in June," The Friends of Israel, *date unknown.*

Vasilash, Gary S. "The Lexus GX-470: You Want Me To Drive This Where?" *Automotive Design and Production*, December 2002. (http://www.autofieldguide.com/columns/gary/12020ncar2.html)

Wack, Pierre. "Scenarios: Uncharted Waters Ahead," *Harvard Business Review*, Vol. 63, No. 5 (1985).

Wack, Pierre. "Scenarios: Shooting the Rapids," *Harvard Business Review*, Vol. 63, No. 6 (1985).

"Wake Up and Smell the Napalm," *Forbes*, 1999.

Woellert, Lorraine. "Not Acting at All Like a Utility," *BusinessWeek*, December 13, 1999.

Zagorin, Adam. "NetJets: Rent-a-jet Cachet," *Time*, September 13, 1999.

PUBLIC INFORMATION: OFFICIAL REPORTS, COMPANY REPORTS, AND PRESS RELEASES

Beverage Digest, Volume 42. No 6. February 24, 2003. *Special Issue: Top 10 U.S. Carbonated Soft Drink Companies and Brands for 2002.*

Collingwood, Vice Admiral Cuthbert, Commencement of the Battle of Trafalgar, 21 October 1805. Dispatch to William Marsden Esq., Admiralty, London.

"Do The Dew: Mountain Code Red Launched Nationally with Smooth Rush of Cherry." PepsiCo Press Release, May 1, 2001.

"Hewlett-Packard Marks Sale of 20 Millionth Printer," *BusinessWire*, November 9, 1993.

Houston, Sam. Official Battle Report of the Battle of San Jacinto, to D. G. Burnett, President of the Republic of Texas, April 25, 1836.

"HP Board Member Dick Hackborn Issues Letter to Shareowners, HP Employees," *BusinessWire*, March 11, 2002.

"HP Continues Market Share Growth in U.S. Printer Market," *BusinessWire*, February 24, 2003.

Imboden, John D., B Gen, CSA, "Stonewall Jackson in the Shenandoah." Report following the Shenandoah Valley Campaign of 1862.

McClellan, George B. "Report of Major General George B. McClellan, U.S. Army, Commanding the Army of the Potomac, of operations August 14–November 9, 1862."

U.S. National Park Service, "Study of Civil War Sites in the Shenandoah Valley," September 1992.

Wyser-Pratte & Co. Confidential Private Offering Materials. 2002.

Wyser-Pratte & Co. Corporate Governance Summaries. 2002.

To gain historical financial information for all public companies mentioned we used publicly available annual reports (10-Ks).

PERSONAL INTERVIEWS

Anthony Abrahams, head of trading at Smith Newcourt, in 1986, 1987, and 1988.

Steve Barnett, U.S.-based cultural anthropologist and consultant to Lexus. 2002.

Bart Casabona, Pepsi North America spokesperson, May 20, 2003.

Donna Conover, executive vice president, Southwest Airlines, June 17, 2003.

Bill Covaleski, president of Victory Beer, 2002.

George Overholser, senior vice president, new business development, Capital One, November 10, 2002.

Fred Smith, founder and CEO, FedEx Corporation, May 12 and May 29, 2003.

Guy Wyser-Pratte, March 18 and April 17, 2003.

MILITARY PUBLICATIONS

Boyd, John. *Patterns of Conflict*, Pentagon presentation, 1986.

United States Marine Corps, *Campaigning*, FMFM 1-1, 1990.

United States Marine Corps, *A Chronology of the United States Marine Corps, 1935–1946*. Washington D.C.: History and Museums Division, Headquarters, U.S. Marine Corps, 1965.

United States Marine Corps, *Command and Control*, MCDP 6, 1996.

United States Marine Corps, *Dictionary of Military and Naval Quotations*, Annapolis, Maryland: U.S. Naval Institute, 1966.

United States Marine Corps, *History of the U.S. Marine Corps Operations in World War II: Central Pacific Drive, Volume III*, FMFRP 12-34-III, 1966.

United States Marine Corps, *Information Management*, MCWP 3-40.2.

United States Marine Corps, *Information Operations*, MCWP 3-40.

United States Marine Corps, *Intelligence Operations*, MCDP 2-1, 1998.

United States Marine Corps, *Leading Marines*, FMFM 1-0, 1995.

United States Marine Corps, *Marine Corps Manual*, Edition 1921.

United States Marine Corps, *Marine Corps Operations*, MCDP 1-0, 2001.

United States Marine Corps, *Marine Corps Planning Process*, MCWP 5-1 with Change 1, 2001.

United States Marine Corps, *Warfighting*, FMFM 1, 1989.

United States Marine Corps, *Warfighting*, MCDP 1, 1997.

Unites States Navy War College, *The United States Navy in "Desert Shield" / "Desert Storm,"* May 1991.

United States Department of Defense Joint Doctrine for Information Operations, October 9, 1998, Joint Pub 3-13.

WEBSITES

American Civil War (www.americancivilwar.com).

The American Civil War, the Struggle to Preserve the Union (www.swcivil war.com).

Balagan: Six Day War (www.balagan.org.uk).

The Battle of Agincourt, Agincourt Computing (www.aginc.net/battle/ops.html).

Battle of Trafalgar, Andalucia.com (www.andalucia.com/history/trafalgar.htm).

The Battle of Trafalgar, About.com (militaryhistory.about.com/library/weekly/aa101600a.htm).

The Battle of Traflagar, BBC (www.bbc.co.uk/history/timelines/britain/geo_battle_trafalgar.shtml).

Beer Advocate (www.beeradvocate.com).

Cisco Company Website (www.cisco.com).

Engines of Our Ingenuity: The IBM 360 Computer, by John H. Lienhard (www.uh.edu/engines/epi1703.htm).

The Fourth Marine Division Association (www.fightingfourth.com).

The Great Battles, Agincourt 1415 (www.geocities.com/beckster05).

The Haganah, Al-Queda, Ariel Sharon and the 1956 Suez War (www.leins dorf.com/1956war.htm).

Israeli Defense Forces, The Six Day War (www.idf.il/english/history/six day3.stm).

Knowledge At Wharton (knowledge.wharton.upenn.edu/articles.cfm?catid=13&articleid=697).

Latin America and U.S. Relations, Dr. Antonio de la Cova, Rose Hulman University (www.rose-hulman.edu/~delacova/gl322.html).

Machar (www.machar.org/peacelast.html).

The Napoleonic Guide (www.napoleonguide.com/battle_trafalgar.htm).

Patton Uncovered (www.pattonuncovered.com).

Public Broadcasting Service, Korean War (www.pbs.org).

NetJets Company Website (www.netjets.com).

Ratebeer (www.ratebeer.com).

Tanks of World War II, by Chris Shimp (www.sandiego.edu/~cshimp/strength1940.htm).

Wikipedia: Six Day War (http://www.wikipedia.com/wiki/Six-Day_War).

World War Two Database, Breakout Internet Site (www.worldwar2database.com/breakout).

United States Marine Corps, History Website (www.usmc.mil/history.nsf).

United States Marine Corps, Main Website (www.usmc.mil).

United States Military Academy, History Website (www.dean.usna.edu/history)

Victory Beer Website (www.victorybeer.com/).

INDEX